ROYAL HISTORICAL SOCIETY

STUDIES IN HISTORY 66

FACTIONAL POLITICS AND
THE ENGLISH REFORMATION
1520–1540

FACTIONAL POLITICS
AND THE
ENGLISH REFORMATION
1520–1540

Joseph S. Block

THE ROYAL HISTORICAL SOCIETY
THE BOYDELL PRESS

First published 1993

A Royal Historical Society publication
Published by The Boydell Press
an imprint of Boydell & Brewer Ltd
PO Box 9 Woodbridge Suffolk IP12 3DF UK
and of Boydell & Brewer Inc.
PO Box 41026 Rochester NY 14604 USA

ISBN 0 86193 223 4

ISSN 0269–2244

British Library Cataloguing-in-Publication Data
Block, Joseph S.
  Factional Politics and the English Reformation, 1520–40. –
(Royal Historical Society Studies in History,
ISSN 0269–2244;No.66)
I. Title II. Series
942.05
ISBN 0–86193–223–4

Library of Congress Cataloging-in-Publication Data
Block, Joseph S., 1942–
  Factional politics and the English reformation, 1520–1540 / Joseph
S. Block.
     p.   cm. – (Royal Historical Society studies in history, ISSN
0269–2244 ; no. 66)
  Includes bibliographical references (p.   ) and index.
  ISBN 0–86193–4 (acid-free paper)
  1. Great Britain – Politics and government – 1509–1547.
2. Christianity and politics – History – 16th century. 3. England –
Church history – 16th century. 4. Reformation – England. I. Title.
II. Series.
DA332.B53 1993
941.05'2 – dc20   92–42871

The paper used in this publication meets the minimum requirements
of American National Standard for Information Sciences –
Permanence of Paper for Printed Library Materials, ANSI Z39.48–1984

Printed in Great Britain by
St Edmundsbury Press Ltd, Bury St Edmunds, Suffolk

FOR NANCY

Contents

The Society records its gratitude to the following whose generosity made possible the initiation of this series: The British Academy; The Pilgrim Trust; The Twenty-Seven Foundation; The United States Embassy's Bicentennial funds the Wolfson Trust; several private donors.

Preface

This book is based on two early and continuing premises. The first is that ideas matter. I firmly believe that we are capable of leading principled lives, and thus that it would be both arrogant and erroneous to deny such a possibility in the lives of those men and women who involuntarily fall under our scrutiny. This is not to disclaim or to subordinate the historical role played by impersonal social and economic forces, but rather to recognise that these forces are merely the starting point for the variety of options available within the human experience. My second premise is that narrative is the most effective way for me at least to relate history across the gap in time from the Henrician world to the present. I am well aware that there is no way to separate subjective historians from their material. Nevertheless, I am most in accord with a methodology which attempts to allow the voices of the period to be heard unfiltered whenever possible and which uses analysis in the service of the evidence rather than the other way round. The term 'vulgar empiricist' which I first heard amiably ascribed by Muriel McClendon is one I comfortably endorse.

I have been looking forward to the publication of this book not least because it affords me the opportunity to thank those who have contributed so much to my professional undertakings. In the realm of this particular book it has been Sir Geoffrey Elton to whom I have looked for help in developing the work from its earliest incarnation to its present form. Not only did he provide invaluable advice in the preparation and revision of the typescript, he also generously offered support and advice in helping it achieve publication. My debt can only be acknowledged.

Research on this book took place in a number of libraries and record repositories. I would like to thank especially the helpful staffs at the UCLA University Research Library, the Huntington Library, the Public Record Office, the British Library, and the Institute of Historical Research. I wish also to thank Christine Linehan, the executive editor of the Royal Historical Society Studies in History series for her patient assistance. Diana Martin and Diahann Harris have my thanks for countless hours devoted to typing, wordprocessing, and printing various drafts of the typescript.

I have had the extreme good fortune to have spent many years in the supportive company of scholars in Southern California. My UCLA graduate school colleagues included the late Andrew Appleby, Gary Bell, Charles Carlton, Joe Kinner, Roy Ritchie, Mary Robertson, Royston Stephens, Bob Woods, and Michael Zell. In 1984 I became a charter member of the British History Seminar at the Huntington Library in San Marino, California. I have presented several papers at meetings of the seminar, and I wish to thank its members for their valuable criticism and their constant support. I am particularly grateful to Retha Warnicke whose friendship and ideas I much value. I have also benefited from the dedicated scholarship which characterises the annual meetings of the Pacific Coast Conference on British Studies.

Two people have been most significant for me, not merely for their contributions direct and indirect to this present work, but for so much more besides. By her example Professor Reba Soffer opened for me a meaningful and engaging universe of teaching and scholarship. Her tangible backing allowed me to begin the process of converting undergraduate enthusiasm into a career as an historian. To Professor A. J. Slavin I owe my greatest intellectual and professional debts. He directed my graduate work and found teaching jobs for me when there were none to be found; he has continued active in his encouragement and endorsement of my current work. More importantly, as a mentor and as a true friend, Joe helped me to build and will always be a welcomed player on my field of dreams.

My deepest acknowledgements for a lifetime of love and shared experience are reserved for my family – for Nancy to whom this work is dedicated and for our daughters, Rebecca and Allison, who have always showed me where to find happiness. They make it all worthwhile.

Joseph S. Block
April 1991

Abbreviations

Alum. Cant.	*Alumni Cantabrigienses*, ed. J. Venn and J. A. Venn, 4 vols, Cambridge 1922–7
Ath. Cant.	*Athenae Cantabrigienses*, ed. C. H. Cooper and T. Cooper, 3 vols, Cambridge 1858–1913
Ath. Oxon.	*Athenae Oxonienses*, ed. J. Foster, 4 vols, Oxford 1891–2
BL	British Library
CSP Span.	*Calendar of State Papers. Spanish*, ed. G. A. Bergenroth et al., 13 vols, 2 supplements, London 1862–1912
Cranmer's Letters	*Miscellaneous Writings and Letters of Thomas Cranmer*, ed. John Cox, Cambridge 1846
DNB	*Dictionary of National Biography*, ed. L. Stephen and S. Lee, 22 vols, London 1908–9
Elton, *Reform and Reformation*	G. R. Elton, *Reform and Reformation: England 1509–1558*, London, 1977
Elton, *Studies*	G. R. Elton, *Studies in Tudor and Stuart Politics and Government*, 3 vols, Cambridge 1974–83
Friedmann, *Anne Boleyn*	Paul Friedmann, *Anne Boleyn: a chapter of English history, 1527–1536*, 2 vols, London 1884
LP	*Letters and Papers, Foreign and Domestic, of the Reign of Henry VIII*, ed. J. S. Brewer, J. Gairdner and R. H. Brodie, 21 vols, London 1862–1932
PROB 11	Prerogative Court of Canterbury, Registered Copy Wills in the Public Record Office
Stat. Realm	*Statutes of the Realm*, ed. A. Luders et al., 11 vols, London 1810–28
SP	State Papers in the Public Record Office
STC	*A Short-Title Catalogue of Books Printed in England and Ireland and of English Books Printed Abroad*, ed. A. W. Pollard and G. R. Redgrave, London 1969
VE	*Valor Ecclesiasticus*, ed. J. Caley and J. Hunter, 6 vols, London 1810–24

References to MS without a location refer to the Public Record Office. I have modernised the spelling of all quotations.

1

Introduction: Faction and Reform

During the years from 1520 to 1540, English politics and reformed religion flowed together in the same channel. Before 1520 England knew neither the religion of Martin Luther nor competition between factions strongly tinged with overtones of religious commitment. The two decades which are the subject of this study saw both Revolution and Reformation introduced to England. The Royal Supremacy, devised to meet Henry VIII's domestic needs, ended Roman jurisdiction and vested in the crown responsibility for the governance and spiritual direction of the English Church. Important laws issued from parliament which defined the Supremacy and demanded uncompromising obedience to the new ecclesiastical order. Money followed sovereignty along the path which led from pope to king. Taxes and fees that had helped to enrich the papacy began to augment royal revenues. The land and fabric of the monastic establishment promised to provide a permanent patrimony for Tudor kings and new sources of wealth for those in royal favour. Religious orders disappeared from the English landscape: the lives of thousands of former monks and nuns were transformed, as were the livelihoods of those who had served and been supported by the cloistered communities.

Spiritual reformation rode in the shadow of political revolution, bringing continental Protestantism from small centres of advocacy to the very heart of English religious life. Blending with native religious dissent and deep-seated anticlericalism, reformed religion created a powerful ideological force which threatened to erode long-held political loyalties and challenged traditional patterns of religious commitment and expression. In response to new structures and opportunities Henrician politics became more intense. Wealth and power still furnished ample rewards to stimulate political ambition, but increasingly ideology in the form of competing visions of the English Church and commonwealth commanded the allegiance of Tudor politicians.

Historians who would understand the politics of reform confront a dual problem. There must be sensitivity to the details of particular events in their own terms. Modern analytical preferences should not intrude. At the same time, however, it is necessary to recognise the structures of society and government, the framework which defined and limited the field in which the contest and resolution of politics took place. This is a crucial task, because the passage of time has masked the points of contact. From our own experience we must choose carefully the interpretative windows which will allow us to see revealed the inner workings of Henrician politics during the early stages of the English Reformation.

For almost four decades historians have employed faction as the clearest window through which to view the dynamic elements of Tudor politics. The

1

term has the advantage of meaning the same thing in the sixteenth and twentieth centuries; the single party state furnishes common ground between the Tudor world and our own. A comprehensive view of faction, then, recognises faction as a group of individuals linked together by mutual political interests, 'a personal following employed in opposition to another personal following'.[1] The political challenge for competing factions was to win the king's approbation. England had no political parties vying for the right to govern. The battle, therefore, was waged to win the king's ear, an organ so potent that it could elevate to power the sons of Ipswich butchers or Putney clothworkers; yet so slippery that it could end the hopes and lives of those who lost their grip, even for a moment.

A broad approach to the question of the 'mutual political interests' comprising faction encompasses at least three major elements – affinity, the exercise of patronage, and ideology. English Reformation politics rose on the triad of personal connection, a desire for wealth and status, and a commitment to a particular religious ideology. Any or all of these interests might operate to promote factional identification and cohesion.

Unfortunately, the use of the term faction as an analytical lens has a history of its own. I say unfortunately, because it has not been the custom of Tudor scholars to view ideology and political faction in the same frame. Rather, they have seen in the form and substance of faction corporate means to personal ends. In such interpretations it has been assumed that self-interest, exclusively expressed in terms of money and power, constitutes an element of human nature, self-evident. 'Men', wrote Sir Geoffrey Elton, in 1951, 'followed whatever star was in the ascendant and were careful of nothing but themselves. It was no time for party manoeuvres: winner took all, and to be on his side was, therefore, exceptionally important.'[2] This statement was written almost four decades ago and has been modified by its author. But others, less judiciously, have continued to hammer the same theme.

The still widely-held definition of Tudor faction has been set down by Eric Ives who has used Anne Boleyn's fall and execution to comment on the factional structures of Tudor politics. His restrictive model argues that Tudor faction comprised 'a group of people which seeks objectives that are seen primarily in personal terms – either positive (gaining or keeping privileges, grants, jobs, office for members or their associates), or negative (denying such things to rivals)'.[3] Ives does recognise that there are links between ideology and faction. He notes that factions in power were responsible for policy; policy might attract ideological adherents to faction. Ideology, thus, might be both a cause and consequence of factional allegiance. As Ives is careful to point out,

[1] Simon Adams, 'Faction, clientage, and party: English politics, 1550–1603', *History Today*, xxxii (1982), 34. This is a companion piece to David Starkey, 'From feud to faction: English politics c. 1450–1550', ibid. 16–22. Both articles are worthy of attention.
[2] G. R. Elton, 'Thomas Cromwell's decline and fall', in Elton, *Studies*, i. 192.
[3] E. W. Ives, *Faction in Tudor England*, London 1979, 1.

however, ideology and concern for policy always remained secondary considerations. Personal advantage never yielded to ideological pressure.[4]

Ives and other champions of this view, who base their interpretation of
faction on restricted *a priori* assumptions about human nature, deny the possibility of principled political action. They exhibit in their rejection of an ideological component in politics the deep distrust of ideas and ideals,
characteristic of much of the work of historians in the latter half of the twentieth century. Materialists all, we recognise greed when we see it, and we expect
to find evidence of greed wherever we look. 'Follow the money' has become the
sole epistemological guideline for scholars nurtured on government scandals
and teaching in an atmosphere which values nothing above the bottom line.
Modern implications aside, this one-sided approach to political questions offers
little to our effort to understand English Reformation politics. Unless we expand our analytical vision to encompass religious commitment as a motivating
force, we distort beyond acceptable limits our ability to lay bare the dynamics of
the Henrician political world. From 1520 to 1540 religion acted as a major
catalytic agent, moving towards the forefront of public consciousness, where it
endured as a permanent feature of Tudor politics. Reformers backed by Anne
Boleyn and Thomas Cromwell had their conservative counterparts. Often
fierce confrontations discovered inspiration in ideology and expression in
faction.

This study, then, takes a different path on the question of political motivation, keeping close to the evidence which shows conclusively that religious
commitment mattered to people in all strata of society, and, at times, outweighed all other considerations. The importance of money, status, and power
as motive forces for political involvement should not preclude an investigation
of faction which acknowledges that human beings are more complex than the
mere sum of their material parts.

It is no simple task to distinguish conviction, often intertwined with self-
interest, but the ideological content of English Reformation politics fluently
comes forth if we allow those involved to tell their own stories. My sense of the
importance of religious divisions in the political world of the 1530s has been
informed by the priorities of the participants. Their awareness of the connection between politics and ideology moulds the interpretative framework of this
study which argues that politics and religion operated together as the building
blocks of the early Tudor state. Initially under the banner of Anne Boleyn, then
guided and supported by Thomas Cromwell, a reform faction emerged, determined to use the authority and resources of the Henrician state to advance
Protestant religious interests in England.

That an ideologically based factional structure carried the edifice of Henrician politics is not an entirely new idea. My own early research delineated a
distinct relationship between ideology and faction.[5] And David Starkey has
made much of the factional nature of court politics, particularly within the

---

[4] Idem. 'Faction at the court of Henry VIII: the fall of Anne Boleyn', *History*, lvii (1972), 177.
[5] Joseph Block, 'Church and Commonwealth: ecclesiastical patronage during Thomas
Cromwell's ministry, 1535–1540', unpublished PhD diss., UCLA 1973; idem. 'Thomas
Cromwell's patronage of preaching', *The Sixteenth Century Journal*, viii (1977), 37–50.

circle of politicians closest to the king.[6] Starkey, perhaps, makes too much of the issue of proximity in his analysis of the nature of politics. He assumes that because members of the privy chamber attended the king's personal needs, they enjoyed disproportionate political influence. His argument does not differentiate between domestic and political expertise. More importantly, Starkey's assumption that the king was a passive recipient of his servants' advice no longer occupies a central historiographical position, and rightly so. Whatever the framework of politics, however, faction furnished the active elements, and Starkey, I think, has correctly observed two major themes worth noting; the first is that principle could be involved in the formation of faction, and the second that the combination of faction and ideology has its starting point in Anne Boleyn:

> Once again it all goes back to Anne Boleyn. Not only had she triggered faction; she introduced ideology as well. Anne was a convinced evangelical and a determined patroness of the 'new' in religion. She was not of course the first. But she was the first in high places to be so blatant in her preference. The effect was to polarize the court. Those who supported her tended to support 'reform' as well; while most of those who opposed her were stalwart defenders of the 'old' faith.[7]

Starkey does not do much to give substance to his insight concerning Anne Boleyn's involvement in factional politics, but he does bring into question earlier accounts which neglect completely a consideration of Anne, either as a political figure in her own right, or as an active agent in control of her own destiny. She has been characterised as a catalyst, provoking momentous events, but not herself prominent on the historical stage as anything more than an object of desire, bursting into flame for a brief moment before being consumed and cast aside. A. F. Pollard, for example, regarded Henry's love for Anne as the king's 'great folly', the one 'overmastering passion in his life'. The king's love in this typical portrayal becomes the historical force, and Anne in any terms becomes indecipherable. Early biographical studies of Anne Boleyn have concentrated on her physical appearance, moral character, and personal behaviour to the absolute exclusion of any public political role. Anne's place in history, concludes the still persistent consensus, 'is due solely to the circumstances that she appealed to the less refined part of Henry's nature; she was pre-eminent neither in beauty nor in intellect, and her virtue was not of a character to command or deserve the respect of her own or subsequent ages'.[8]

The moralising attitudes which permeate studies of Anne's life and career provide a storehouse of similar material, but there is a serious thread of misinterpretation inherent in an approach to a major historical figure such as Anne which denies her the possibility of a serious political role on the basis of gender. Not only are modern values offended; more importantly, contemporary values are ignored, and we have been offered an inadequate picture of the principles

---

6 See for example David Starkey, 'Court and government', in Christopher Coleman and David Starkey (eds), *Revolution Reassessed*, Oxford 1986, 29–58.

7 Idem. *The Reign of Henry VIII*, London 1985, 29–30.

8 A. F. Pollard, *Henry VIII*, New York 1966, 149–54.

by which the Tudor political world operated. It does not require a feminist perspective to build a case for Anne's participation in Henrician political life. A generation after the executioner's sword ended Anne's brief career, her daughter ascended the throne. No one would deny Elizabeth's femininity, and the romantic dance of Elizabethan court life is well documented. But anyone writing about Elizabethan politics also recognises that the queen occupied the central place, not merely as a figurehead, but as the person who mattered. Tudor courtiers, as well as foreign princes, looked to the queen to exercise the generative political functions. No sexist attitude blurred their understanding of the mechanisms by which policy developed or by which patronage could be obtained. Some men might have lamented what John Knox called 'the monstrous regiment of women', but the need for practical political realism triumphed, at least among successful suitors for royal favour. There is no reason or evidence to lead us to assume that the political pragmatism of the earlier generation was any less pronounced.

Anne's more recent biographers have all worked to bring her out of the shadows, to restore to her, at least, the charge of her own life, but they have had great difficulty in placing her on the religious spectrum of the late 1520s. Few, it seems, want to classify Anne or to recognise that she came to court committed to the advancement of reform, but to ignore Anne's spiritual allegiance creates problems both with language and evidence. We are somewhat at the mercy of an imprecise religious vocabulary, and here again, the issue of current versus contemporary usage can be both confusing and deceptive. There are apparently no absolute conventions regarding the use of 'reformer', 'Protestant', or 'evangelical'; each has its advocates and its problems. The Reformation, it should be observed, in the 1520s and 1530s supplied few if any definitive tests of orthodoxy or distinct identifying labels. The word 'Protestant' first came forth from the Diet of Speyer in 1529, when certain German principalities and municipal corporations protested against the decree against religious innovations, particularly in the performance of the mass. Later it came to be used to distinguish those Churches that broke from the Roman communion. Other forms of religious expression received more careful definition. For example, Sacramentarianism, the denial of the real presence in the sacrament of the altar, and Anabaptism, the rejection of infant baptism, were categorised as heresies by all established Churches, although it is not always certain when a concern for religion or defence of social hierarchies operated as the principal motivation.

Modern scholars, faced with the task of identifying Anne Boleyn's religious beliefs have adopted a variety of approaches. Maria Dowling, along with Starkey, prefers to use 'the blanket term evangelical' rather than 'the anachronistic Protestant' in describing Anne and those who favoured doctrinal innovation. She correctly states that reformers referred to themselves as 'upholders of the gospel' rather than as Protestants.[9] I have for the most part followed Dowling's use of 'evangelical' to describe Anne's religious beliefs, but there are

---

[9] Maria Dowling, 'Anne Boleyn and reform', *Journal of Ecclesiastical History*, xxxv (1984), 30; idem. *Humanism in the Age of Henry VIII*, Beckenham, Kent 1986, note and acknowledgement page.

shortcomings in this application. Dowling tends to view the English Reformation in isolation, separating English 'evangelicals' from the matrix of continental Protestantism, particularly in the 1530s. The English experience of reform drew inspiration and designation from continental sources. English reformers did not reject the name 'Protestant'; the term was not in current usage. Dowling's own effective demonstration of Anne's deep personal and political involvement in the careers of men who became pillars of reform in England thus highlights a national segment of the history of the Protestant Reformation,[10] and one must be careful not to allow the use of 'evangelical', a word of convenience, to exclude Anne and those who identified themselves with reform in England from the broader movement unfolding across the Channel.

Ives's approach engenders greater confusion. On the one hand he closely follows Dowling, whose work he regards as a 'seminal exposition',[11] but then he states that 'Anne's particular affinity was with the Christian humanists of France'. Apart from the problems of trying to define French humanism,[12] Ives leaves hanging Anne's role as a patron of radical reformers who had no connection to French humanism, however defined, gathering inspiration, instead, from German Protestant sources. In his own words, Ives has noted that 'Indeed, of the ten elections to the episcopate between 1532 and Anne's death in 1536, seven were reformers who were her clients.'[13] To call these men humanists would bend the word beyond comprehension, and Anne's patronage influence went much deeper than her participation in the process of episcopal selection.[14]

Finally, Retha Warnicke has insisted adamantly that Anne did not incline toward Protestantism, an assertion made by later Protestant writers. She skirts problems of definition by challenging the major premise. Warnicke agrees with both Dowling and Ives that Anne favoured vernacular Scripture, a Protestant benchmark,[15] but she claims that many groups advocated an English Bible while remaining loyal to Catholic forms and usages. She places Anne within this group, and denies that she participated in a factional relationship with Cromwell. Moreover, she suggests that Anne's love of Scripture might have had a purely domestic motive, and that Anne's interest in religion might have been an attempt to make herself better able to converse with the king on theological topics.[16] Warnicke rejects out of hand the statements of Eustace Chapuys, the imperial ambassador and John Foxe, the Protestant martyrologist, that Anne was a Lutheran. She cites problems in accurately defining Lutheran-

---

[10] Ibid., passim

[11] E. W. Ives, *Anne Boleyn*, Oxford 1986, 303.

[12] Alistair Fox, 'Facts and fallacies: interpreting English Humanism', in Alistair Fox and John Guy (eds), *Reassessing the Henrician Age*, Oxford 1986, 9–33. Fox's argument places in doubt any analytical use of the term humanism. Without effective definition Ives's notion of Anne's attachment to French Humanism does little to advance our understanding of her religious orientation.

[13] Ives, *Anne Boleyn*, 303.

[14] See below, chs ii, iii.

[15] Retha M. Warnicke, *The Rise and Fall of Anne Boleyn: family politics at the court of Henry VIII*, Cambridge 1989, 109.

[16] Ibid. 110. This is an intriguing piece of speculation for which no evidence has been presented.

ism and believes that contemporaries used the term with great imprecision. Further, she argues that 'The major issue separating Catholics, even some known as reformers, from heretics was the concept of justification by faith', and that this doctrine is often impossible to separate from a host of traditional Catholic attitudes.[17]

Warnicke rightly recognises the difficulty of trying to place people on an indistinct doctrinal scale. Fortunately, we don't have to undertake this burden. Political orientation furnishes a definite line of demarcation between reformers and conservatives, those who saw themselves as belonging to one camp or the other. Both conservatives and reformers might agree on the importance of Scripture, even in English. Their opinions about the efficacy of faith and works in the process of salvation might become blurred. But only reformers believed that the state should be employed as the instrument to correct ecclesiastical abuses and to promote a radical rebirth of spiritual life. Since Anne placed herself among such men, it would be unwise to assume that she did not believe as they did.

Nevertheless, Warnicke would have us understand Anne as a well-read but fundamentally orthodox woman of her time, an aristocratic woman, who acted as queens were expected to act but neither practised nor encouraged reformed religion. She explains away Anne's contemporary reputation as a leading light of the reform faction by arguing that it was Cromwell, rather than Anne, who espoused reform and created alone the faction which carried the ideological baggage of Protestantism into English political life.[18] This seems a difficult position to maintain; the analysis, wrongly I think, dismisses the perception of those reformers who appealed to Anne for protection and advancement and received her patronage as evidence of her commitment to shared spiritual values.[19]

It should, therefore, be understood that I have tried to take the least restrictive approach to points of religious vocabulary. No specific theological weight should be added to my use of terminology. Before the Act of Supremacy I have employed 'reformer' or 'evangelical'. After 1534 I have added 'Protestant'. Nowhere do I argue the need to apply specific doctrinal labels to those who participated in the politics of reform. Commitment to faction did not require arduous examination on specific dogmatic points. We must also understand that the human participants in the factional struggle over England's spiritual orientation might have changed their minds and even acted inconsistently at different times and under varying circumstances. Nevertheless, a pattern of behaviour can be seen in the history of English Reformation politics. Faction did take on a decidedly ideological tone. Almost immediately after Cardinal Wolsey's fall, the reform faction with Anne Boleyn at its centre began to take

[17] Ibid. 108.
[18] Ibid. 152–62.
[19] A careful reading of Warnicke's book is essential. In areas such as Anne's religious values and her role as a leader of the reform faction, Warnicke and I agree on very little. We often use the same evidence but reach contradictory conclusions. A chapter and verse examination of each point of contention seems inappropriate. It is enough to note that my own interpretation of the evidence offers a fundamentally different explanation. See below, especially chs ii, iii.

shape. From 1529 to 1533 Anne and Cromwell both occupied visible leadership positions; the divorce and an attachment to reform supplied ideology and a focus for patronage. After 1533, Cromwell first eclipsed Anne, then replaced her as the dominant instigator of both policy and patronage for the reform faction. By the end of his life factional politics, driven by religious ideology had become firmly embedded in the Tudor political world, and no amount of wishful thinking could remove it.

My own recognition of the importance of this sequence of events on the lives of people far from the centre of national politics developed a number of years ago, during my first stay in England. One Sunday I had the opportunity to go to Ely to see the cathedral and its famous Lady Chapel. Assisted by the guidebook, I learned that the Lady Chapel was the last addition to the cathedral. Alan of Walsingham laid the first stone on Lady Day 1331, but the dedication did not take place until 1349; completion had been delayed by the collapse of the cathedral's central tower. Then, the story is told, a monk called John of Wisbech took over supervision of the chapel, helped by the discovery of a brazen pot full of old coins, found by a workman digging the foundation. The money allowed the chapel to be completed. Myths are made for us to breathe life into.

Today, the Lady Chapel at Ely retains the outlines of its medieval opulence and harmonious proportions. There is the immediate impression of space. John of Wisbech and the generation of Benedictine monks who carried out his design achieved the widest contemporary vault in England by creating a roof with a span of forty-six feet, only eighteen inches higher at its centre than at its sides – so delicate that a person cannot safely cross it. There are many tall windows, then filled with strongly coloured glass, which once were framed by brightly painted walls. The chapel, then, must have been dark inside, but flowing with colours which softened the lines of the stone canopies above forty stalls which contained small sculptures representing scenes from the life of the Virgin.

Beautiful still, the Lady Chapel now reflects the passions of anonymous reformers during the reign of Edward VI, executing the orders of Bishop Thomas Goodrich, who had been appointed by Cromwell to the diocese of Ely in 1534. Much has changed. The windows still appear noble and spacious, but the glass is clear. The walls are stark white; light pervades the room and highlights the statues, still secure in their elaborately carved niches – but each figure has been neatly decapitated by a careful iconoclast, responding to the call to put an end to the practice of worshipping images. This dramatic visual tableau must have been the first comprehensible sign for many in Ely of the national religious transformation produced by the ongoing interaction of factional politics and reform – an interaction with a history of its own.

2

The Boleyn Faction

The origins of the Boleyn faction are to be found in family connection. Thomas Boleyn's marriage to Elizabeth Howard, shortly before 1500, united two ambitious Norfolk families and supplied the core of faction. The marriage itself occasioned small notice. The Howards had not yet regained national pre-eminence. Thomas Howard, then earl of Surrey, made solid but unspectacular matches for his younger daughters.[1] In accepting the suit of Thomas Boleyn, the earl joined his eldest to the most promising son of a fast-rising family which emerged from obscurity in the mid-fifteenth century.[2]

Geoffrey had Boleyn brought the family name to public attention in 1457 through his election as Lord Mayor of London, an honour enriched by the dignity of a knighthood. With wealth obtained from his mercantile career and lands in Norfolk, Geoffrey attracted and wed the daughter and heiress of Thomas, lord Hoo and Hastings. He fathered at least four children who reached adulthood; his daughters also married well, and Geoffrey left to his son, William, a good inheritance with solid prospects. At the coronation of Richard III, William attended as one of the eighteen knights of the Order of the Bath. Firmly established and freed from the need to continue in his father's business enterprises, Sir William bought large estates in Norfolk, Essex, and Kent, preferring the life of a wealthy country gentleman with some influence at court. He married Margaret Butler, second daughter of the earl of Ormond, an heiress in her own right. Their sons gained considerable prestige and influence. James inherited a portion of the family's Norfolk estates when William died in 1505. He remained an active force in East Anglian local politics. Edward married a daughter of Sir John Tempest, Anne, a favourite attendant of Queen Catherine. William, a priest, became a successful clerical pluralist. Thomas, born in 1477, went to court to seek his fortune.

Tradition portrays Thomas Boleyn as little more than a pimp for his daughters, placing first Mary, then Anne, in the path of his lust-driven monarch and reaping a golden harvest from his grateful royal client. Even the unlikely tale of the highly prejudiced Catholic partisan, Nicholas Sander, that Henry had meddled with Lady Elizabeth Boleyn has been given credence as a reason for her husband's visibility at court.[3] Reflection, however, and a closer look at the evidence illuminate Thomas Boleyn's career in a more comprehensible if less salacious light. Certainly he lost nothing from Henry's attachment

---

[1] Thomas Bryan; Sir Henry Wyatt; Sir Griffith ap Rice.
[2] Several biographies of Anne furnish information about the origins of the Boleyn family. Among these are Friedmann, *Anne Boleyn*, i; Philip Sergeant, *The Life of Anne Boleyn*, New York 1924; Ives, *Anne Boleyn*; Warnicke, *Rise and Fall*.
[3] See Sergeant, *Life of Anne Boleyn*, 14–15.

to his daughters, but Thomas Boleyn had carved his niche in royal service long before the thought of trading on his daughters' charms could have crossed his mind.

In fact Thomas Boleyn's rise to courtier status preceded the birth of Anne in 1507.[4] He first appears on the historical record in 1497, as a soldier, fighting at his father's side against the Cornish rebels.[5] Rewarded for his loyalty by Henry VII, Boleyn is described as 'Yeoman of the crown' in the Patent Roll for 1507. By the first year of the new reign he enjoyed the status accorded a man of property. The Pardon Roll for 1509 mentions Thomas Boleyn, esquire, son and heir of William, of Blickling, Norfolk; Hever, Kent; New Inn without Temple Bar; and Hoo, Bedfordshire.[6] Blickling had come to the Boleyns by 1450 and served as their country seat,[7] but Thomas Boleyn and Elizabeth, his wife, chose to live at Hever in Kent. Originally purchased by Sir Geoffrey Boleyn in 1458, Hever Castle by all accounts furnished an environment of security and domestic comfort.[8] Thomas had received it with his other properties as a bequest from his father. Specifically, his Hever inheritance brought the house, the yield of the home farm, £50 a year, and the honour of a knighthood.[9] By itself, his legacy would have allowed him to lead a simple but easy gentry lifestyle. Sir Thomas, however, had grander goals, and his lofty ambitions could be satisfied only at court. He attended Henry VII's funeral, with the title of squire for the body,[10] and he remained in London to participate in Henry VIII's coronation. On 22 June 1509, Boleyn served among twenty-six 'honourable persons' at a celebration dinner for the king at the Tower of London. The next day brought his induction into the Order of the Bath.[11]

Sir Thomas Boleyn built his career on talents for financial administration and diplomacy. He started in July 1509 with the office of Keeper of the Exchange at Calais and of the Foreign Exchange in England.[12] In 1512 he went on his first embassy with Dr John Young to meet the emperor. Joined later by Sir Edward Poynings and Sir Richard Wingfield, they remained in the Low Countries for about a year, negotiating at Brussels and Mechlin for the formation of a Holy League against the French. In residence with the emperor elect, Maximilian, Boleyn had the opportunity to discuss international politics with papal

---

4 The century-long controversy about the date of Anne's birth, and whether she was the elder or the younger sister of Mary Boleyn has been convincingly resolved by Retha M. Warnicke, 'Anne Boleyn's childhood and adolescence', *Historical Journal*, xxviii (1985), 939–52. She argues that Anne was the elder sister, born in 1507. Cf. Hugh Paget, 'The youth of Anne Boleyn', *Bulletin of the Institute of Historical Research*, liv (1981), 162–70; Ives, *Anne Boleyn*, 17–21.
5 *DNB* ii. 783.
6 *LP* i. 483 (1).
7 W. L. E. Parsons, 'Some notes on the Boleyn family', *Norfolk and Norwich Archaeological Society*, xxv (1935), 395.
8 *DNB* ii. 783.
9 Friedmann, *Anne Boleyn*, i. 39.
10 *LP* i. 20.
11 Ibid. 81.
12 Ibid. 123 (grant 92).

representatives, Margaret of Savoy and the king of Aragon.[13] His daughters, Anne and Mary, respectively, were five and three years of age.

Service to the crown produced additional wealth and status. With several of his Howard kinsmen in November 1509 he obtained from the king the lease of all the possessions of Sir John Grey, viscount Lisle, during the minority of his daughter, Elizabeth.[14] In February 1511 the king granted him for life, in reversion, the keepership of the park of Beskwode, Nottinghamshire.[15] In July he acquired the grant in tail male of the reversion of several manors forfeited by Francis, viscount Lovell and others escheated from the estate of John de Veer, earl of Oxford.[16] Another grant in July brought a life interest in the lordship of three manors and a park in Kent,[17] and in November Boleyn became sheriff of Kent.[18] The following year quickened the flow of rewards. With Sir Henry Wyatt, his brother-in-law, he received the office of constable and keeper of the castle of Norwich in February 1512.[19] Three months later, he and John Sharp, groom of the chamber, procured the lands, wardship, and marriage of John Hastynges.[20] Early autumn of the same year witnessed the grant to Sir Thomas of several manors in Essex and Hertfordshire,[21] along with the manor of Wykmer, Norfolk.[22] Boleyn's Norfolk holdings further increased in May 1514 with the grant for life of the manors or lordships of Saham Tony, Nekton, Panworth Hall, and Cressingham Parva, with the hundreds of Waylond and Grymmeshow, at an annual rent of £71 6s 8d.[23]

Clearly, Boleyn's access to royal patronage reflected his increasing responsibilities, particularly in the realm of diplomacy. Henry used Sir Thomas at various times to handle sensitive negotiations touching England's foreign policy. Boleyn with other diplomats met the emperor in 1521 at Courtraye and Oudenarde, and at Valladolid in 1522. He served as ambassador to France from mid-June 1519 to March 1520.[24] As Boleyn thus moved toward the centre of Henrician political life through his diplomatic and administrative service, his recognition at court increased, and he established a conspicuous presence at ceremonials. Sir Thomas participated in the royal christening on 21 February 1516, carrying the canopy which shielded Princess Mary.[25] At state dinners he held the post of queen's carver, receiving £10 in May 1517 for executing his

---

13 Gary Bell, A *Handlist of British Diplomatic Representatives, 1509–1688*, London 1990, passim. I am grateful to Professor Bell for sharing with me pre-publication material he compiled about Boleyn's diplomatic career. See also *LP* i. 1525 (g. 39); ibid. 1750. Boleyn received a substantial *per diem* allowance of 20s: *DNB* ii. 783.
14 *LP* i. 257 (g. 40).
15 Ibid. 709 (g. 19).
16 Ibid. 833 (g. 14).
17 Ibid. (g. 40).
18 Ibid. 969 (g. 23).
19 Ibid. 1083 (g. 26).
20 Ibid. 1221 (g. 27).
21 Ibid. 1415 (g. 3).
22 Ibid. (g. 4).
23 Ibid. 2964 (g. 63).
24 Again, I am much indebted to Professor Bell for this information.
25 *LP* ii. 1573.

official duties.[26] His country status also mirrored his rise in court circles. Throughout the early years of the reign, his name regularly appears on a number of commission appointments in Kent and Norfolk.

Founded on merit, Sir Thomas's career undoubtedly accelerated during the years of his daughter Mary's affair with Henry. Since 1521 the wife of William Carey, a gentleman of Henry's chamber, Mary soon afterwards became the king's mistress. Their liaison, which lasted until 1526, coincided with a rapid upward surge in her father's position at court, but there is no direct evidence of a causal connection. Boleyn's preferments were well earned. Early in 1522 he obtained the patent for the office of treasurer of the household. On 29 April he became steward of Tunbridge, receiver of Bramsted, and keeper of the manor of Penshurst in Kent.[27] In 1524 he acquired the keepership of Thundersley, Essex,[28] the stewardship of Swaffham, Norfolk,[29] and the collation and disposal of the next presentation to a prebend in the collegiate chapel of St Stephen's, Westminster.[30] Several years later, Boleyn claimed that he had begun his married life with only £50 a year.[31] By February 1524, he was assessed for the subsidy at £1,100 in lands, wages, and fees.[32] The next year saw his elevation to the nobility as Viscount Rochford to participate with sufficient rank in Henry Fitzroy's elevation to the earldom of Nottinghamshire and the dukedoms of Richmond and Somerset.[33]

George Boleyn also came to notice in these years, and the grants to this very young and inexperienced youth must have resulted from the valuable if diverse services rendered by his father and sister. George received the manor of Grymston, Norfolk in 1524,[34] and in the same year was admitted to the king's privy chamber.[35] He married Mistress Jane Parker, granddaughter of Henry, lord Morley and Monteagle,[36] and Henry granted him an additional £20 a year to support himself and his wife at court.[37]

Mary Boleyn's influence with the king had withered by 1527; their affair ended, but by then Henry's attraction to her sister Anne had moved beyond rumour. Murmurs of an impending divorce grew ever stronger, and Anne enjoyed the king's constant attention. In the autumn of 1528, Henry installed Anne in royal estate at Greenwich, Catherine's favourite residence. The Boleyn family could not have been much better placed. Thomas Boleyn, viscount Rochford, occupied a position in the company of officials who managed royal business. His son George added Boleyn presence to the privy chamber. Edward Boleyn, Thomas's brother, also resided at court. The second duke

---

26 *DNB* ii. 783.
27 Friedmann, *Anne Boleyn*, i. 43.
28 *LP* iv/1. 297 (undated grant).
29 Ibid. 1298 (undated grant).
30 Ibid. 895 (g. 25).
31 *SP* 1/105/5–6 (*LP* xi. 17).
32 *LP* iv/1. 136.
33 Ibid. 1431 (8).
34 Ibid. 546 (g. 2).
35 Sergeant, *Life of Anne Boleyn*, 55.
36 Ibid.
37 *LP* iv/1. 1939.

of Norfolk, Thomas Howard, Rochford's father-in-law, had died in 1524, but his son, Thomas, earl of Surrey, who succeeded to the title, was prominent in the Boleyn faction.

Born in 1473, Surrey had already established a reputation as a man of considerable power and status. Married in turn to Anne, a daughter of Edward IV, and Elizabeth, a daughter of the late duke of Buckingham, military competence gave substance to the position he enjoyed as a birthright. From the earliest years of the reign, Howard, numbered among the king's closest friends, received substantial rewards from royal grants of lands and offices. In 1509 Henry appointed him earl marshal to participate in the coronation; a year later the patent was extended for life with £20 per annum. Three years later he succeeded his brother Edward as lord admiral. He served for twelve years before surrendering the patent to Henry Fitzroy.[38] Surrey already held the post of lord treasurer from Henry VII, during pleasure with an annual income of £365. Henry VIII renewed the grant at his accession and again in 1514. In 1522 Howard passed the office to his son with royal approval.[39] Also in 1514, at his creation as earl of Surrey, he received a life interest in lands valued at £366 6s 8d.[40] Finally, in 1520 Henry appointed Surrey as lord lieutenant of Ireland, the first English deputy to serve in this office during the reign.[41]

Norfolk, together with Charles Brandon, duke of Suffolk[42] and the Boleyn family were the hub around which turned aristocratic opposition to Cardinal Thomas Wolsey, who ruled supreme among Henrician royal ministers. Norfolk had long been critical of Wolsey. In 1522 his client, the poet John Skelton, savagely attacked the displacement of traditional aristocratic governance by an obvious social inferior. The dukes shared the belief that the cardinal had usurped their rightful place as the king's 'natural councillors', and they saw in Anne Boleyn a useful weapon with which to rid themselves of Wolsey.[43] The divorce issue furnished their opportunity, and the newly formed Boleyn faction entered the political arena.

Wolsey had no principled objections to a royal divorce, although he would have preferred to have selected the king's next wife himself. Marriage, of course, to the right foreign princess could create no end of diplomatic advantages. Moreover, Catherine's circle of supporters, who had become entrenched

---

[38] Helen Miller, *Henry VIII and the English Nobility*, Oxford 1986, 167–8. See also Warnicke, *Rise and Fall*, 10–11, and R. Virgoe, 'The recovery of the Howards in East Anglia, 1485–1529', in E. W. Ives, R. J. Knecht, and J. J. Scarisbrick (eds), *Wealth and Power in Tudor England*, London 1978, 1–20.

[39] Miller, *Henry VIII*, 170.

[40] Ibid. 211–12.

[41] Ibid. 186. This proved to be a less than rewarding office. As late as 1537 the then duke feared that he was out of royal favour and about to be sent into Irish grief and obscurity.

[42] On Charles Brandon see S. J. Gunn, *Charles Brandon, duke of Suffolk, c. 1484–1545*, Oxford 1988. For the relationship between Howard and Brandon see Diarmaid MacCulloch, *Suffolk and the Tudors: politics and religion in an English county, 1500–1600*, Oxford 1986, 57ff. Brandon's career from the standpoint of his role in and rewards from Henrician government is examined by Miller, *Henry VIII*, passim.

[43] J. J. Scarisbrick, *Henry VIII*, London 1968, 228–32.

at court, would lose their places, enhancing Wolsey's power with the king.[44] But Henry's infatuation with Anne Boleyn offered the cardinal nothing but trouble. Marriage to Anne would cancel any international benefits; Wolsey would not have the pliable French princess he might have hoped for. Rather, a woman who owed him nothing would come to court, trailing in her wake a gang of hungry men eager to see him dragged down. The King's Great Matter and persistent discontent with Wolsey's arrogant domination of Henrician politics sufficed to stimulate old dreams and new ambitions in those bold enough to seize the moment. A faction had crystallised; family had provided its initial focus under the titular leadership of Norfolk and the magnate support of Suffolk and Rochford. But significantly, Anne too wore the mantle of a leader in the emergent faction, generating her own political energy, a force that would increase in the years ahead.

From the moment that Anne entered public life through her relationship with Henry VIII she functioned and was recognised as a leading member of the faction which grew to prominence around her rising fortunes. Almost immediately, she took an active interest in the development of policy for the divorce, opening channels of communication with trusted friends and family members. John Barlow, rector of the Boleyn home parish of Hever, Kent,[45] a family chaplain, carried letters between the king and William Knight in Rome in November 1527[46] and remained engaged in diplomatic service. He was, during this time, a member of Anne's household, described as her servant, and his employment in connection with the divorce gave Anne a valuable source for information.[47] Sir Francis Bryan, Anne's cousin, also undertook a number of ambassadorial missions on behalf of the divorce project.[48] He too could be depended upon to supply accurate reports to the Boleyns about the intricate moves made and contemplated to free Henry from Catherine. Most significantly, Anne herself can be seen at this time making constant demands on Henry for greater urgency in the struggle to bring their cause to a successful conclusion.

Particularly in 1527 and throughout the early months of 1528, Henry and Anne spent much time apart. A small measure of discretion, perhaps, wedded to a greater measure of fear of illness kept the lovers at a distance. Sweating sickness ravaged parts of the countryside in the late spring of 1528, reaching the Boleyns in June. Anne and her father recovered, but others of the household died, including William Carey, Anne's brother-in-law, who succumbed on 22 June. In the circumstances, Henry and Anne resorted to correspondence to keep alive their romance. Anne's letters to the king have not survived, but those from Henry to Anne have, and they offer evidence of Anne's early knowledge of the steps being taken in the matter of the divorce.

---

[44] Wolsey's battle with the privy chamber is discussed in several places by David R. Starkey. See, for example, 'Court and government', 33–4; 'From feud to faction', 16–22.

[45] A. B. Emden, A Biographical Register of the University of Oxford, 1501 to 1540, Oxford 1974, 26.

[46] LP iv/2, 3553.

[47] E. G. Rupp, Studies in the Making of the English Protestant Tradition, Cambridge 1966, 64.

[48] Geoffrey de C. Parmiter, The King's Great Matter, London 1967, 80–9.

Henry, in this famous series of love letters might have preferred to pour out the passion of his heart, but he soon found himself spurred to provide Anne with the latest news on the subject closest to her heart. Anne's curiosity was not misplaced. Henry was deeply involved in the intellectual effort that ultimately led to the solution to his marital impasse. Virginia Murphy has discovered manuscripts which show that from the summer of 1527 Henry played a significant part in the debates over the validity of his marriage to Catherine.[49] At least three tracts appeared in that year which argued the king's case. Murphy believes that Henry oversaw these works, and in fact, wrote a version of one of them. The king wrote to Anne in the summer of 1527, complaining of a headache brought on by four hours' work on a text in favour of the divorce, but he felt 'right well comforted in so much that my book maketh substantially for my matter'.[50] A new picture of the monarch thus reveals itself. Rather than a passive monarch who reluctantly took control of policy for the divorce only after Wolsey's fall and quickly surrendered that control to Cromwell, Henry, committed to Anne, and believing from the first that God had cursed his marriage to Catherine, vigorously worked to secure an annulment from the pope.[51]

Henry most often, it seems, relayed his plans and thoughts to Anne in person or through private messages carried by trusted agents. A letter written in February 1528 was brought by Stephen Gardiner, who with Edward Foxe was about to be sent abroad, 'with as many things to compass our matter'.[52] Anne presumably obtained a full account of the proposed mission before allowing Gardiner to depart, and this must have been Anne's regular practice, because Henry cautioned her to 'keep him not too long with you, but desire him, for your sake, to make more speed; for the sooner our matter come to pass'.[53] The summer brought more activity. The king and Cardinal Wolsey had initiated several missions to Rome intent on convincing the pope to allow the divorce case to be tried in England. After much travail the papacy issued a decretal commission authorising the trial and dispatched Cardinal Campeggio from Rome to join with Wolsey to hear the suit. In September 1528 Henry wrote to Anne to inform her of the news that Campeggio had reached Paris and would soon arrive at Calais. The trip, however, did not go well, and a month later, the king had to write to explain to Anne that a severe attack of gout, unfeigned, had delayed the legate, and that, 'when God shall send him health, he will with diligence recompence his demur'.[54]

Anne finally arrived at court to stay by the end of 1528 and could receive

---

[49] *The Divorce Tracts of Henry VIII*, ed. Edward Sturtz and Virginia Murphy, Angers 1988, pp. i–xxxvi.

[50] *The Letters of Henry VIII*, ed. M. St Clare Byrne, London 1936, 82 (*LP* iv/2. 4597).

[51] Murphy, *Divorce Tracts*, p. iii. Murphy's discoveries create the need for a new chronology of the divorce. The idea that 1529–32 were years without a policy will no longer serve. Nor, it seems, was Wolsey's domination of the king nearly as complete as suggested by either Elton or Scarisbrick. Recent texts skirt the issue: Starkey, *The Reign of Henry VIII*, divides the reign by personalities; J. A. Guy, *Tudor England*, Oxford 1988, compresses Wolsey's ascendancy and the break with Rome into two discreet chapters.

[52] *Letters of Henry VIII*, 61 (*LP* iv/2. 3990).

[53] Ibid.

[54] Ibid. 85 (*LP* iv/2. 4895). Campeggio arrived in London on 8 October 1528 with private

directly information about the progress of the divorce case. At the same time, she began to establish political relationships with those who counted at court, most notably with Cardinal Wolsey. Anne probably remained steadfast in her dislike for Wolsey, who years before had intervened to squash her adolescent romance with Henry Percy. Furthermore, opposition to Wolsey's rule was good politics. It offered an important rallying point for potential Boleyn adherents. But neither Anne nor the cardinal chose at this early stage to play the fool. As long as they both enjoyed royal favour, Anne and Wolsey treated each other with cordial respect.

At first Wolsey underestimated Anne's attraction for the king. He assumed that she had become Henry's mistress, and that the affair would last a few months. He believed that if indeed the king remained determined to seek to divorce Catherine, it would neither benefit the Boleyns nor diminish his position. He and Henry worked together in the initial stages. In May 1527 the cardinal called the king to a secret tribunal set up to examine the validity of Henry's marriage to Catherine. William Warham, archbishop of Canterbury, joined him in citing the king to answer a charge that he had lived unlawfully with the wife of his dead brother Arthur for eighteen years. Everything seemed to be moving smoothly toward a favourable verdict. Even after Catherine's refusal to co-operate and the sack of Rome by imperial troops blocked the collusive suit, Wolsey remained confident that he could meet the king's needs by persuading Clement to grant him the authority to adjudicate the case.[55] He had not reckoned on Clement's inability to accede to Henry's wishes.

In the meantime the cardinal extended helping hands toward Anne and her family. He mediated in a dispute between the Boleyns and the Butlers in February 1528 which eventually brought the Ormond title and estates to Rochford.[56] For a time the Boleyns reciprocated the friendly overtures. On 3 March 1528 Anne lightly remarked to Thomas Heneage, Wolsey's man with the king in Windsor, that she feared the cardinal had forgotten her, as she had received no token from a messenger lately arrived from London. Heneage had dined with Anne and relayed her wish 'to have some good meat from Wolsey such as carps, shrimps, or other. I beseech your Grace pardon me that I am so bold to write unto your Grace hereof; it is the conceit and mind of a woman'.[57] Wolsey provided the Boleyns with more substantial proof of his friendly intent. On 28 March 1528, from the foundation of his newly created Cardinal's College, Oxford, Wolsey granted Thomas Boleyn the site or mansion place of the manor of Tunbridge, with demesne lands and appurtenances, at a rent of £26 8s per annum.[58] And in September 1528, George Boleyn secured an annuity of fifty marks, payable by the chief butler of England, out of the issues of the prizes of wines, a grant facilitated by Wolsey.[59]

instructions from Pope Clement to avoid reaching a decision in the case: Elton, *Reform and Reformation*, 109.
[55] Scarisbrick, *Henry VIII*, 155.
[56] SP 1/46/265–9 (*LP* iv/2. 3728, 3937).
[57] SP 1/47/56–7 (*LP* iv/2. 4005).
[58] *LP* iv/2. 4106.
[59] Ibid. 4779.

Soon, however, the Boleyns began pursuing more serious and contentious issues with Wolsey. On 16 March 1528, at Anne's request, Heneage wrote to Wolsey in favour of Sir Thomas Cheyney, who had apparently offended the cardinal and had been put out of court. Anne asked Wolsey to be good and gracious lord to Cheyney, who, she said, 'is very sorry in his heart that he hath so displeased your grace, more sorry than if he had lost all the goods he hath'.[60] Anne's request left the cardinal unmoved. She intensified her efforts. According to DuBellay, the French ambassador, Anne caused Cheyney to be brought back to court and used very rude words of Wolsey. The political implications of this disagreement did not pass unnoticed.[61] The cardinal had met a will as strong as his own, and Anne was closer to the king.

Distance from the royal presence greatly reduced Wolsey's authority with the king. Responding to the pope's imprisonment by Charles V, the cardinal left for France on 22 July 1527 and did not return to England until late September, three crucial months during which, without Wolsey's advice or knowledge, Henry began to take responsibility for policy for the divorce into his own hands.[62] Even after his return, Wolsey found himself isolated. He knew now that the king intended to marry Anne Boleyn, and that she had the power to restrict his access to Henry.[63] While Wolsey carried on with business in London, the king hunted in the country, surrounding himself with the cardinal's enemies. Through agents such as Heneage and Sir William Fitzwilliam, Wolsey kept tabs on the king's activities, but Henry dined in his privy chamber with the dukes of Norfolk and Suffolk and with Lord Rochford.[64]

Conflicts over patronage measured the swing of influence toward Anne and the Boleyn faction. On 24 April 1528, the death of the abbess of Wilton brought Wolsey and the Boleyns into direct conflict over the election of the next incumbent.[65] Thomas Benet, Wolsey's chaplain, reported from the scene that the prioress and convent would soon be writing for the congé d'élire: 'It may like your grace to be advertised that the more part of the convent a great deal beareth their good will towards dame Isabel Jordan, prioress there which surely is ancient, wise, and very discreet.'[66] Benet cautioned, however, that 'there is also one Dame Eleanor Carey, sister to Master Carey of the court for whom there will be great labour made'.[67] Master Carey, of course, was William Carey, Anne's brother-in-law, who through Heneage had asked Wolsey to favour his

[60] SP 1/47/120 (LP iv/2. 4081); Ives, Anne Boleyn, 127.

[61] LP iv/3. 5210. Cheyney is listed as a gentleman of the privy chamber in April 1532: BL, Add. MS 9835, fo. 24 (LP v. 927).

[62] While Wolsey was in France, Henry made a direct appeal to the pope to resolve his marital problems. Through William Knight, his secretary, he asked Clement to seal a document that has been described as a licence to commit bigamy: Scarisbrick, Henry VIII, 158–62.

[63] Ibid. 162.

[64] SP 1/42/255–6 (LP iv/2. 3318).

[65] David Knowles, 'The matter of Wilton', Bulletin of the Institute of Historical Research, xxxi (1958), 92–6.

[66] SP 1/47/236 (LP iv/2. 4197).

[67] Ibid.

sister for the preferment. Carey died on 22 June 1528,[68] but Anne, with growing confidence in her powers, took up the suit. Henry, at first, supported Anne.
Then he discovered that Dame Eleanor's unchaste life precluded her advancement. He told Anne that Dame Eleanor had confessed to having had two
children by two sundry priests, and had since been kept by a servant of Lord
Broke. 'Wheref I would not, for all the gold in the world, clog your conscience
or mine to make her the ruler of a house, which is of so ungodly demeanour.'[69]
To placate Anne, Henry promised that Isabel Jordan, the cardinal's choice,
would also be denied the office, and he asked Wolsey to find a suitable third
candidate. But Wolsey ignored the king's command, proceeded to appoint
Jordan, and managed to escape with a surprisingly mild rebuke.

Wolsey's triumph in the matter of Wilton did little to arrest his slow slide
from the political heights. Unable or, as his enemies saw it, unwilling to deliver
the master stroke to secure the divorce, the cardinal could not reach an accommodation with those for whom Anne's cause meant everything. The King's
Matter pervaded all areas of business, and Wolsey, tightly confined, could not
break free. When Rochford wrote in August 1528 to obtain the living of
Sundridge, Kent for Master Barlow,[70] the cardinal sent his blessings for the
benefice of 'Tonbridge'. Days later, Anne herself intervened, caustically writing
to inform Wolsey that Tunbridge was in her father's gift and not vacant. She
hoped that the cardinal would rectify the error. Secure in her own stature and
influence, Anne took the occasion to press Wolsey sarcastically about the slow
pace of his activity in the divorce case, promising 'for all those that hath taken
pain in the king's matter it shall be my daily study to imagine all the ways I can
devise to do them service and pleasure'.[71] Wolsey could not have missed the
point. Time had all but run out for the cardinal.

Wolsey's predicament had clear antecedents. From 1527, under Henry's
direction and with his participation, arguments against the king's marriage to
Catherine moved through two fields. The first of these, narrow in scope,
concerned the original dispensation issued by Pope Julius II, which, it was
alleged, contained faults which invalidated both the dispensation and the
marriage.[72] The second, and more comprehensive, asserted that God's law,
revealed in scriptural texts from Leviticus, prohibited the marriage and that no
dispensation was possible. According to Murphy, the king favoured attacking
the legality of the marriage on these grounds.[73] She shows that, from mid-1527,
he consistently affirmed divine and natural law against the position of papal
legalism regarding the dispensation.[74] Wolsey, whose own legatine powers, had
papal origin, did not advance the divine law argument with its implied rejec-

---

[68] Soon after Carey's death, Anne was granted custody of his lands, during the minority of
Henry, his son and heir, with the wardship and marriage of the said Henry: *LP* v. 11.
[69] *Letters of Henry VIII*, 75.
[70] SP 1/50/1 (*LP* iv/3. 4647). *LP* argues that this was John Barlow; Rupp, *English Protestant
Tradition*, 71, that it was William.
[71] BL, Cotton Vespasian F iii, fo. 34 (*LP* iv/addenda. 197).
[72] Murphy, *Divorce Tracts*, pp. i–ii.
[73] Ibid. p. xvii. For contrary argument see Parmiter, *King's Great Matter*, 34, 125.
[74] Murphy, *Divorce Tracts*, p. xvii.

tion of papal authority. Rather, he based the king's case on the technical inadequacies of the original dispensation.[75] When this line failed with Cardinal Campeggio's adjournment of the king's suit at Blackfriars on 31 July 1529, Wolsey had nowhere to turn and no one to help.

Thus blocked on the divorce issue, Wolsey could do little more than watch as the Boleyn faction launched ever bolder forays against his once invulnerable position of political dominance. There is no need here to rehearse again the final act of Wolsey's fall.[76] Resentment, almost universal, but pragmatically muted, blared forth, creating antagonistic crescendos of political energy. Nobles hating the cardinal's arrogance which challenged their own, land-holders displeased by his opposition to wholesale enclosures, churchmen and others whose ancient rights and privileges had been trampled, taxpayers from all strata of society, at last had their opportunity, and they expressed themselves through loud support for the Boleyn faction.

Both DuBellay and Eustace Chapuys, who arrived in London in September 1529 in the role of imperial ambassador, recognised Wolsey's predicament and its principal cause. Early in 1529, DuBellay noted Wolsey's difficult position. The divorce case would determine his fate, and the ambassador could foresee no solution.[77] Chapuys developed the picture.[78] From the moment he arrived at Henry's court, he understood that Anne had replaced Wolsey as the most influential court politician. In his first letter to Charles V on 1 September 1529, Chapuys wrote:

> It is generally and almost publicly stated that the affairs of the cardinal are getting worse every day. The cause of this misunderstanding between the king and the cardinal can be no other than the utter failure of the measures taken in order to bring about the divorce, on which failure those parties, who for a long time have been watching their opportunity to revenge old injuries, and take the power out of the cardinal's hands have founded their attacks to undermine his influence with the king, and get the administration of affairs in their own hands.[79]

Three days later, Chapuys had a better grasp of details and wrote that the moment of triumph for the Boleyn faction had arrived. Wolsey was absent from court; the dukes of Suffolk and Norfolk transacted all state business, 'And if the said Lady Anne chooses, the cardinal will soon be dismissed.'[80] Even George

---

[75] Ibid. p. xviii; Scarisbrick, *Henry VIII*, 231. Murphy also argues that the question of public honesty, which Scarisbrick suggests could have furnished a way out for Wolsey and the king did not figure in the divorce debates: Murphy, *Divorce Tracts*, p. xvii; H. A. Kelly, *The Matrimonial Trials of Henry VIII*, Stanford, CA 1976, 66; Scarisbrick, *Henry VIII*, 184–97.
[76] Ibid. 228–40.
[77] *LP* iv/3. 5210.
[78] It is conventional for every scholar working on the divorce to warn against using Chapuys as a reliable source of information. It is also conventional, having issued the warning, to ignore it. I have not broken with these conventions, but I have used Chapuys only when I can corrobor-ate his statements ideally from at least two other independent sources. For a full discussion of Chapuys and the problems he presents see Warnicke, *Rise and Fall*, 1–3. *Caveat emptor!*
[79] *CSP Span.*, iv/1. 189–90.
[80] Ibid.

Cavendish, Wolsey's gentleman usher, understood which way the wind blew, for he wrote of Anne Boleyn that 'It was by and through all the court, of every man that she being in such favour with the king might work masteries with the king and obtain any suit of him for her friend.'[81]

Finally, in October 1529, Wolsey's defences collapsed. On the 22nd DuBellay wrote that 'Wolsey has just been put out of his house, and all his goods taken into the king's hands . . . he is quite undone . . . the duke of Norfolk is made chief of the Council, Suffolk acting in his absence, and, at the head of all, Mademoiselle Anne.'[82]

The surrender and transfer of Durham House, Wolsey's magnificent London mansion, to Thomas Boleyn symbolised deep political dislocations. The cardinal lost much more than his house. He gave up the Great Seal and yielded most of his lands, possessions, and offices. Before leaving London to retire to his archbishopric of York, Wolsey signed under compulsion a confession in which he acknowledged his transgression as papal legate of the Praemunire statutes. All that remained, including his life, now stood within the compass of the king's pleasure. The last year of the cardinal's life found him in the unfamiliar position of a suitor, relying on Cromwell to sustain his fading dreams of glory. While Wolsey slowly moved toward his archbishopric, Cromwell in London prepared to defend the cardinal's interests.

Cromwell faced a difficult challenge, with no allies, against hostile opponents. The Boleyns regarded Wolsey's fall from power as the first stage in a campaign which saw the cardinal's death as an acceptable alternative to his return to royal favour. Cromwell attempted to soften their fatal resolve. He appealed to various faction members, pleading with them to consider the cardinal's past service and future potential. Wolsey, he argued, might still prove useful, and there was nothing to fear. More directly, Cromwell used Wolsey's remaining financial resources to pursue George Boleyn. An annuity of £200 from the lands of the bishopric of Winchester and another 200 marks from the temporalities of St Alban's to win Boleyn's support seemed a reasonable price to pay.[83] But the attempt to bribe Anne's brother held no promise. Both Cromwell and Wolsey knew that aside from the king, whom they could not reach, only one person mattered. The cardinal had written in his own hand that 'If the pleasure of my lady Anne be somewhat assuaged, as I pray God the same may be, then it should be devised by some convenient mean she be further laboured, for it is the only hope and remedy.'[84]

Cromwell never stopped trying to convince the Boleyns that Wolsey had abandoned politics, although Wolsey, himself, did not furnish much evidence for this claim. Despite repeated warnings that only complete submission would preserve his estate and his life, Wolsey refused to remain passive. He resisted every royal command, dragged his feet at every request, and treated the Boleyn faction with imperious disdain. The cardinal, a shadow of his former self, yet

---

81 George Cavendish, *The Life and Death of Cardinal Wolsey*, ed. Richard Sylvester, London 1959, 35.

82 *LP* iv/3. 6019.

83 *SP* 1/56/149–54 (*LP* iv/3. 6115).

84 *State Papers during the Reign of Henry VIII*, 11 vols, London 1830–52, i. 352 (*LP* iv/3. 6114).

would not compromise his patronage rights to curry favour with the Boleyns. He demanded that they pay his debts with crown revenues or the spoils of their triumph.[85] His behaviour and demeanour gave weight to the Boleyns' fears that Henry would recall him. They did their best to prevent even a hint of reconciliation between king and cardinal. Norfolk warned Wolsey through Cromwell to be content with his life and not to 'molest the king'. Henry told Cromwell that Wolsey should forthwith cease to sow sedition between himself and Norfolk. And Anne declined to act as Wolsey's intermediary, refusing to deliver the cardinal's letters to the king.[86] The Boleyns responded to Cromwell's entreaties in polite phrases, but their message was clear. Cromwell could expect neither compassion nor mercy from Anne or those closest to her. Veiled words offered little comfort or assurance.

Unable to penetrate the Boleyns' resolve, Cromwell redoubled his efforts to keep Wolsey from fatal miscalculation. He well knew the danger of anything but full compliance with demands from the king or his new favourites. Time and time again, he begged Wolsey to forebear any political activity, to give way before the onrushing Boleyn tide. Cromwell did manage in February to secure a pardon for Wolsey and the discharge of all suits against him. He also saved Cardinal's College at Oxford, renamed first King's College and later Christ Church. He could not, however, perform a similar miracle at Ipswich, Wolsey's other educational foundation.[87] Neither, it seemed, could Cromwell comfortably sustain his efforts on behalf of Wolsey. The financial costs as well as the emotional strain kept rising, and Cromwell confessed that, alone, he could no longer bear the expensive burden. 'I am', he wrote to his mentor, '£1,000 worse than I was when your troubles began.'[88] Still, Cromwell pressed on, spending his own money, risking his political capital, futilely, to protect his friend and patron. Nothing availed; nothing could avail, it seemed, without Anne. Her influence with Henry might have relieved the pressure, but no Cromwellian initiative, argument, promise, or bribe moved Anne to relent.

Finally, on 18 August 1530, Cromwell wrote a long letter to Wolsey in which he set out an entire summary of the cardinal's status at court. Putting on as good a face as possible, Cromwell began with a review of positive accomplishments. The pardon granted by the king remained 'in good and perfect effect'. Wolsey would not be further threatened by the fear of losing his temporal and spiritual goods. No additional suit would be necessary to protect the cardinal's life or property; the king could be trusted. 'And doubt ye not but his highness is your gracious and benign sovereign lord and would in no wise that ye should be grieved, molested, or troubled.' In these circumstances, Cromwell continued, Wolsey should behave and order himself, 'to attain the good minds and hearts of the people'. Enemies awaited, and Wolsey must not give them cause to renew their attack. It was a time for caution and for prudence:

[85] R. B. Merriman, *Life and Letters of Thomas Cromwell*, 2 vols, orig. pub. Oxford 1902; Oxford 1968, i. 327.
[86] Ibid.
[87] Elton, *Reform and Reformation*, 94–5.
[88] Merriman, *Life and Letters*, i. 327.

Sir, some there be that doth allege in that your grace doth keep too great a house and family, and that ye are continually building. For the love of God, therefore, I eftsoons as I often times have done, most heartily beseech your grace to have respect to every thing and, considering the time, to refrain yourself for a season from all manner buildings more than mere necessity requireth, which I assure your grace shall cease and put to silence some persons that much speaketh of the same.[89]

Cromwell entrusted more specific concerns to the discretion of the bearer, but he included in the letter his own sense of Wolsey's future and the lessons to be drawn from his fall:

I do realise your grace right happy that ye be now at liberty to serve God and to learn to experiment how ye shall banish and exile the vain desires of this unstable world, which undoubtedly doth nothing else but allure every person therein, and specially such as our Lord hath most endowed with his gifts to desire the affections of their mind to be satisfied. In finding and seeking whereof most persons besides the great travails and afflictions that men suffer daily being driven to extreme repentance and searching for pleasure and felicity find nothing, but sow trouble, sorrow, anxiety, and adversity. Wherefore, in mine opinion your grace being as ye are, I suppose would not be as ye were to win a hundredth times as much as ye were possessed of.[90]

Cromwell closed by apologising to Wolsey for not being with him in person: 'And though I am not with you in person, yet be assured I am, and during my life shall be with your grace in heart, spirit, prayer, and service to the utterest of my poor and simple power.'[91]

But try as he might, Cromwell could not save the cardinal. Wolsey's patience frayed; caution deserted him, and he pursued foolish schemes in an effort to regain Henry's favour. When the Boleyns and their adherents recognised that their old enemy would not fit himself to the quiet life, they convinced the king to authorise his arrest. Only death interrupted Wolsey's progress to the Tower of London. He died at Leicester Abbey on 24 November 1530.

The Boleyns, perhaps, had convinced the king to remove the cardinal, but Thomas Cromwell survived the coup against his friend and patron. Rumours of arrest and his execution, which surfaced soon after Wolsey's fall, proved false, but Cromwell realised the need for an accommodation with the Boleyn faction. He was not without resources for the enterprise. Cromwell had earned at least a measure of respect from the duke of Norfolk for the thorough manner in which he had defended Wolsey. This respect led the duke to intervene with the king, who promised Cromwell his good will if he entered parliament. Sir William Paulet, an ex-colleague from Wolsey's household, now the king's Master of the Wards, furnished the seat at Taunton, and Cromwell entered the Reformation Parliament hoping to salvage his shattered career.

---

89 Ibid. 332.
90 Ibid. 333.
91 Ibid. 333–4.

Cromwell did not have to start from scratch either with the king, who knew him well as Wolsey's chief lieutenant, or with the Boleyn clan with whom he had often rubbed shoulders. Their first recorded contact, at the end of 1527, concerned a lawsuit in which Cromwell represented Alice Clere, Thomas Boleyn's sister. Cromwell, unable to furnish a legal remedy, advised Sir Thomas to move Wolsey to intervene in the case.[92] Now, three years later, Cromwell on his own placed himself at the disposal of the king and the Boleyns, quickly making himself indispensable. By the spring of 1531 Cromwell was sworn of the king's council and extended significantly his political relationships. He also began to meet and to renew ties with religious radicals such as Thomas Cranmer and Edward Foxe.

Cromwell's rehabilitation by the Boleyns indicated their confident hold on power in the wake of Wolsey's fall. Control also brought considerable profits. With the cardinal out of the way, the Boleyns celebrated their victory, using their access to royal patronage to unloose a stream of grants, jobs, and offices. Family members reaped the richest harvest. James Boleyn came to the 1529 parliament from Norfolk.[93] William Boleyn, appointed archdeacon of Winchester in 1529, attended the convocation of the province of Canterbury.[94] In the same year he acquired the parish churches of Egillistlyse, Durham,[95] and Winwick, Coventry and Lichfield, one of England's most valuable rectories.[96] In February 1529 George Boleyn secured the chief stewardship of the honour of Beaulieu (Essex), and the office of keeper of the New Park there.[97] In July the king appointed him governor of St Mary of Bethlem, near Bishopsgate, London.[98] Six months later, he followed his father as Lord Rochford, and soon afterwards embarked for the French court at the head of an English diplomatic mission.[99]

Thomas Boleyn most conspicuously attracted royal patronage. Grants in the summer of 1529 yielded a share of the presentation to the rectory of All Hallows ad Fenum, alias 'The More', London,[100] and custody of the lands and tenements in Lathingdon, Essex.[101] On 8 December 1529 Rochford was granted the combined earldoms of Ormond and Wiltshire with an annuity of £30 to support his rank:[102] it had been a good year. On 24 July 1531 the new earl of Wiltshire replaced Cuthbert Tunstall in the office of Lord Privy Seal with 20s per day.[103] Additional grants of lands, offices, and privileges throughout 1531 and 1532 endorsed Wiltshire's growing political stature.[104]

---

[92] SP 1/46/36–9 (LP iv/2. 3741).
[93] LP iv/3. 6043(2).
[94] Ibid. 6047.
[95] Ibid. 5815 (g. 3).
[96] Ibid. 6072 (g. 24).
[97] Ibid. 5248.
[98] Ibid. 5215 (g. 27).
[99] DNB ii. 781.
[100] LP iv/3. 5815 (g. 28).
[101] Ibid. 5906 (g. 4).
[102] Ibid. 6085.
[103] Ibid. 6163.
[104] Ibid. 6709 (g. 1).

As befitted a victorious faction leader, Anne collected the lion's share of the spoils. In May 1530 Henry signed a warrant to Lord Windsor, keeper of the Great Wardrobe, to deliver to Lady Anne Rochford a quantity of equestrian tack sufficient for dozens of horses, ornamented with gold, silver, velvet, and silk, obviously of substantial value and clearly intended to uphold her public role.[105] Earlier, probably in 1528, she had been granted custody of the lands of the late William Carey, during the minority of his son, with the wardship and marriage of the said heir.[106] In 1532 Anne accumulated vast material rewards. By January she had been installed in the queen's apartments at court with a retinue comparable to that which attended Catherine. She acquired two Middlesex manors in June,[107] and on 1 September in an elaborate ceremony, Anne was created marchioness of Pembroke in her own right.[108] With the title came an annuity of £1,000 a year.[109] George Taylor, John Smyth, and William Brabazon received the commission to take possession of the lands in her name,[110] and Thomas Cromwell exercised general supervision over the collection of the rents, farms, and fees. Brabazon wrote to Cromwell in 1533 to report that he had visited Anne's properties, and that 'The tenants have given my lady at her entry as much as has been heretofore given.'[111] Further grants of land awaited Catherine's official departure. In the meantime there were parcels of gilt plate; one worth £1,188 11s 10d given by the king in December 1532;[112] two more in January 1533 were obtained from the estates of Henry Guildford and William Compton.[113] While she enjoyed these gifts, Anne could anticipate more to follow, including a treasure trove of jewels from Catherine to seal her triumph.

The patronage rights to major offices also fell into Boleyn hands. They had lucrative gifts to bestow. Still prestigious after Wolsey's fall, the lord chancellorship had lost some of its lustre. Anne, perhaps, considered giving the Great Seal to Gardiner.[114] Master of Trinity Hall since 1525, Gardiner served as Wolsey's secretary until the cardinal left London in disgrace. Cromwell remained loyal to his mentor. Gardiner, a man of intrigue, known for his secret purposes, abandoned his patron in good time. With Boleyn patronage, he made the transition from Wolsey's household directly into royal service. Henry employed him as ambassador to Clement VII throughout the early stages of the divorce proceedings. Anne added her favour, sending Gardiner cramp-rings as a token of her thanks.[115] More tangible rewards followed in the form of the archdeaconry of Worcester, a post he held in July 1529, when Henry made him

105 Ibid. iv/addenda. 256.
106 Ibid. v. 11.
107 Ibid. 1139 (g. 32).
108 Ibid. 1274, 1370 (g. 1 & 2).
109 Ibid. 1370 (g. 3); 1499 (g. 23).
110 Ibid. vi. 74.
111 SP 1/74/221 (LP vi. 200).
112 SP 1/73/9–13 (LP v. 1685).
113 LP vi. 6 (E 101/421/9).
114 Friedmann, Anne Boleyn, i. 99.
115 SP 1/53/173 (LP iv/3. 5422).

principal secretary. On the rise, Gardiner hedged his bets and consolidated his
position. Ever cautious, he checked the political winds, found them not to his
liking, and sought safe harbour. He allied himself to the duke of Norfolk, served
his king and earned just rewards, a manor here, an archdeaconry there.[116]
Patience paid dividends. In September 1531 Gardiner secured the bishopric of
Winchester, England's wealthiest diocese, an ideal anchorage for his waiting
game.

Additional changes brought factional unity to royal administration. Sir
William Fitzwilliam, Anne's cousin, succeeded Thomas Boleyn as Treasurer of
the Household and also received the chancellorship of the Duchy of Lancaster.
Cuthbert Tunstall, an active supporter of Catherine, found himself pushed out
of London. He lost his bishopric of London to John Stokesley, an early but
rapidly cooling advocate of the divorce, and the office of Lord Privy Seal to
Anne's father. Tunstall retired to his new diocese of Durham, also to await a
change in the political climate.

The vacant chancellorship went to Sir Thomas More. Henry selected More
in the mistaken belief that he could be won over to agreeing to the divorce.
The king assigned Edward Lee, Nicholas de Burgo, and Thomas Cranmer, then
a Boleyn chaplain and fellow of Jesus College, Cambridge, to convert More to
the royal cause. Their inevitable failure forced a realignment of Wolsey's political structures. Opposition to the divorce isolated More from the Boleyn faction's most pressing concern. Formal council sessions proceeded under More's
circumspect leadership, but policy meetings now moved to court, where Henry
and the Boleyns directly shaped the strategy and details of governmental business. More was left to defend his beliefs in the orthodox faith and the liberties
of an independent Church, while the Boleyn faction took up the pragmatic
problems of government.[117]

Other friends and supporters also profited from the Boleyn victory, but the
faction which came together to oppose Wolsey did not long survive the cardinal's fall. Cross purposes and conflicting ambitions soon surfaced. The need to
form a new government sent tremors through the hierarchy of the anti-Wolsey
faction. Norfolk and Suffolk both had claims to the leadership of the council,
but apparently Norfolk's greater competence and, perhaps, his closer ties to
Anne proved decisive. Norfolk was Anne's uncle; his sister, Elizabeth, was
Anne's mother. Thus family connection, Henry's love for Anne, and her political fluency placed the duke's star in the ascendant. He could even dream, at
least briefly, that marriage between his son and Princess Mary might crown the
achievements of his life.

Changes in personnel, however, did not resolve the King's Great Matter.
Common hostility toward Cardinal Wolsey's rule helped to define the Boleyn
faction and had facilitated its rise to power. Now, the need to develop effective
policy to secure the divorce dissolved the bonds of uneasy unity. Suffolk had
nothing to gain from the divorce; he was sulking over his defeat by Norfolk,
and he resented the pretensions of the Boleyns almost as much as he had

---

[116] James A. Muller, *Stephen Gardiner and the Tudor Reaction*, London 1926, 31.
[117] See below ch. iii.

disliked those of the cardinal. Even Norfolk's passion had cooled. His ambitions had been realised; consolidation of power in a quiet atmosphere would have suited, and the divorce project promised to upset the status quo he longed for. While Norfolk might talk about stripping the Church of its splendour, he remained steadfast in his determination to defend its liberties and position in the realm. And while he acquiesced in the king's desire for a divorce, he resented his political eclipse by his niece. Moreover, his wife favoured Catherine and hated Anne. Others, including Fitzwilliam, Guildford, the comptroller, Tunstall, and More opposed the divorce and refused to lend their considerable talents to the cause. In fact, opposition to the divorce promoted new factional activity. Catherine's loyalists began to organise. Effective when directed against Wolsey's dominance, factional unity collapsed in its absence. If the Boleyns were to hold on to their hard won pre-eminence, they would have to identify themselves with new issues and recruit new personnel. Only by broadening the base of their support could they maintain factional supremacy in a political system which provided no place for second best.

Reformed religion produced both ideology and sources of new adherents to the Boleyn cause. The continental Reformation had gained a foothold in England during the decade of the 1520s, but no more, and the loose sand to which it clung offered no guarantee of permanence. Despite native centres of critical dissent and a growing anticlerical spirit which furnished some support, Lutheranism in its early stages presented no more than a minor threat to orthodoxy. Even so, the ecclesiastical hierarchy exhibited a continuing concern that new and old heresies would merge. Episcopal activity against Lollardy from the beginning of the century resulted in 365 'processes' for heresy from 1504 to 1517, and twenty-seven of those convicted suffered death at the stake.[118] Official hostility stood ready to meet any and all religious innovation.

The initial Lutheran impact manifested itself at the universities, particularly at Cambridge. Proximity to the coastal towns of Norfolk allowed Luther's writings, conveyed in merchant ships, to reach the university. The county itself earned a reputation for nurturing heresy. Bishop Nix of Norwich noted in 1530 that merchants and coastal residents in his diocese were greatly infected with heresy. He laid much of the blame for the epidemic on Cambridge University, particularly Gonville Hall which produced 'no clerk who had lately come out of it, but savoureth the frying pan'.[119] In fact, a solid Norfolk–Cambridge reform connection prompted Nix's concerns. Thomas Arthur, John Lambert, Robert Barnes, Matthew Parker, Nicholas Shaxton, Thomas Bilney, Thomas Forman, John Thixtell, Thomas Becon, and Richard Taverner had all come up to Cambridge from Norfolk, and they joined other young scholars to form the group known as 'Little Germany' which regularly met at the White Horse Inn in St Edward's parish.

The first meetings held to discuss the newly arrived Lutheran theology probably date from 1520. Robert Barnes, warden of the Austin friars, organised the group. William Tyndale provided the intellectual focus. Thomas Bilney

118 Philip Hughes, *The Reformation in England*, 3 vols, London 1950–4, i. 126.
119 M. E. Simkins in *The Victoria History of the County of Norfolk*, ed. William Page, London 1906, ii. 253.

brought to the group spiritual inspiration and evangelical fervour. Many of the participants would go on to play key roles in the English Reformation. Thomas Cranmer and Matthew Parker became archbishops of Canterbury. Hugh Latimer, Nicholas Shaxton, Simon Haynes, John Skipp, Edward Foxe, and Miles Coverdale all served on the episcopal bench.

In the 1520s, however, offers of promotion did not flow in the direction of the White Horse. Rather, ecclesiastical authorities viewed with alarm the importation and discussion of heretical ideas, and they acted with vigour to detect and suppress any sign of the new religious ideology. The bishops especially feared that if university students and graduate fellows made Lutheran books and vernacular Scripture available, older groups of religious dissidents would distribute them throughout the realm. United, old and new heresies might sweep away traditional ecclesiastical loyalties. Conservative bishops energetically responded to the threat posed by any deviation from orthodoxy. Recantations encouraged by public executions attended heresy proceedings. Norwich, Lincoln, London, and Ely witnessed keen efforts against the new religion. Bishop West of Ely and Longland of Lincoln kept watchful eyes on Cambridge and Oxford respectively, believing that the universities must be kept orthodox whatever the cost. Tunstall's London and Nix's Norwich were ports through which Lutheran books could be smuggled and also required vigilant attention.

Wolsey permitted the work of conservative prelates to go forward, and they quickly used their opportunity to begin a vigorous attack against heretical literature and those involved in its dissemination. Soon after Bishop West sponsored the burning of Lutheran books at Cambridge at the end of 1520, censorious flames lit up the London sky. At St Paul's Cathedral on 12 May 1521, the bishops flanked by eminent peers and foreign ambassadors, with Wolsey present, demonstrated to an enormous crowd England's official opposition to Lutheranism. At about the same time, he distributed a circular letter to magistrates everywhere, commanding them to aid in the detection of heretical activities.[120]

The early reaction against the importation and dissemination of Lutheran books and tracts, however, did not succeed. By 1525 episcopal concern and their calls for more effective measures had multiplied. Again the universities provoked the deepest disquiet. Oxford now joined Cambridge as a principal cause for unease and began to receive closer scrutiny. Archbishop Warham recommended to Wolsey that Fisher and Tunstall conduct a special visitation at Oxford. In January 1526, Longland initiated a series of secret book searches and tried to stop the trade in heretical literature by asking Wolsey to bind merchants and stationers to foreswear any further involvement in the smuggling of illicit books from the continent. Longland also wanted a public demonstration of orthodoxy and suggested to Wolsey that a Paul's Cross sermon, followed by the burning of heretical works, would help to stem the flow of forbidden literature. Wolsey concurred, and on 26 February the ceremony took place with Fisher delivering the sermon. Barnes, some London booksellers, and

[120] A. G. Dickens *The English Reformation*, London 1964, 68.

a handful of German merchants appeared as penitents. And all watched in pleasure or sorrow as the flames consumed great numbers of prohibited books.

A few weeks earlier, at Cambridge, Thomas Forman of Queens' College thwarted a surprise raid by warning no less than thirty suspects from the White Horse circle to conceal or dispose of any illicit writings in their possession. Even before the fires had cooled, and with the elaborate pageants against heresy still fresh in people's minds, printing presses in the Low Countries laboured to produce new material for English dissidents. In March 1526 the first folios of Tyndale's translation of the New Testament began to appear at the universities, in coastal towns, and in London. For whatever reason, the bishops were slow to react. Not until October did Tunstall preach an elaborate sermon at St Paul's to mark his determination to stop distribution of the work. Once they began, however, the bishops acted in concert and with conviction. Tunstall ordered his archdeacons and city authorities to search for Tyndale's book and to confiscate all copies. He backed his injunction with his own money, buying up as many copies as he could find to keep them off the market. Warham followed Tunstall's lead, issuing the same instructions to all bishops within his province. Longland and West went even further by requiring suspected priests to take a special oath not to spread the teachings of Luther before allowing them to take up their benefices within their dioceses, a policy they continued until 1532.

Pressure against individuals mounted as well. Tyndale had been forced to flee the country in 1524. John Frith did the same and worked with Tyndale for a time. Robert Barnes, who had recanted in 1526, broke his penance and escaped to Wittenberg. The bishops forced Hugh Latimer and Edward Crome to submit themselves and to temper their activities. Richard Taverner bought freedom in the same way, but Thomas Bilney, who had converted both Barnes and Latimer, found himself convicted of heresy on flimsy evidence, a prelude to his eventual execution in 1531. Some of the Oxford reformers died in 1528, victims of the epidemic of the sweating sickness that swept the country in that year. It began to seem as if the persecuting tactics had broken the back of English Lutheranism, a victory for orthodoxy. But the forces of orthodoxy had not reckoned on the king's overweening passion for Anne Boleyn. Nor could they know that the Boleyn faction, so splintered after their defeat of Wolsey, would find new strength as champions of religious reform.

Political expediency alone cannot explain the Boleyn connection to reformed religion.[121] The family, prior to Anne's arrival at court, had identified itself with prominent reformers. Thomas Boleyn and Erasmus exchanged letters before support for reform had any specific political value, and Sir Thomas was the recipient of three dedications from the prince of humanism.[122] In August 1527 Erasmus wrote to Rochford, praising his love for learning and including a commentary on a psalm originally suggested by Boleyn as a suitable topic.[123] Their correspondence apparently continued over the years, for in

---

[121] See for example Pollard, Henry VIII, esp. 223–41.
[122] The De praeparatione ad mortem (1534); the Enarratio in Psalmum XXII (1530); and the Explanatio symboli (1533). See James K. McConica, English Humanists and Reformation Politics, Oxford 1965, 61.
[123] LP iv/2. 3345.

1533 Erasmus responded to Wiltshire's request for an exposition of the Apostle's Creed. The scholar recognised that Wiltshire had asked for it, not for himself, 'who needs no teaching from Erasmus, but for persons less in-structed', and he adapted his language and argument to 'the most ordinary comprehensions'.[124] After 1527, of course, Boleyn's role as a patron of often radical reformers is more difficult to separate from questions of political self-interest. There is, however, no sign of any discomfort between the Boleyns and their evangelical clients. In fact, many of those charged with heresy between 1520 and 1527 found relief and sustenance in the Boleyn household and advanced with their patronage to notable careers.[125]

Anne's personal commitment to reformed religion is also clear. As a starting point, it is logical to assume that she shared her parents' religious orientation. The vicious attacks on her mother's reputation by Nicholas Sander strongly suggests that Lady Elizabeth Boleyn must have sympathised with the reformers. There is little to be learned about Anne's religious orientation from her educa-tion, which was typical for her gender, social position, and times.[126] When recalled from France to England in 1521, at the age of thirteen or fourteen, her religious views would have reflected childhood. As she matured, Anne, most likely, increasingly absorbed the spiritual values of her family, and after 1527, strong feelings against the papacy added enthusiasm to her loyalty to the new religion.

Anne Boleyn also became a patron of reformed religion, with even greater resources, as queen, than her father enjoyed. Historians are fond of quoting Chapuys's charges that Anne and her father were 'more Lutheran than Luther himself'; and that Anne, alone, was 'the principal wet-nurse of heresy'.[127] With these partisan political epithets, Chapuys perhaps attempted to tie endorse-ment of Catherine's cause to the maintenance of the 'true religion' in order to reinforce the importance of the defence of the marriage in the mind of Charles V. Context, then, robs the ambassador's characterisations of analytical utility, but his opinions of Anne found widespread accord among Catherine's adher-ents who also believed that Anne's domination of Henrician court life aided and abetted heresy.

The king himself brought together the issues of reformed religion and his own marital cause. Until the pope had begun to frustrate his efforts to obtain the divorce, Henry had been a staunch defender of orthodoxy and papal supremacy. Thwarted, however, his conflict with Rome set Henry on new intellectual and spiritual paths which made him more receptive to voices denouncing the guile and greed of the clergy, and asking him to intervene to bring right order to the Church. When Cardinal Campeggio arrived in London in 1528, he noted the flood of 'Lutheran' books and warned Henry against the dangers to the Christian commonwealth posed by heretics, but the king in the summer of 1528 welcomed almost any new ideas, as long as they upheld his position on the divorce. Rather than condemning heretical books out of hand,

---

[124] Ibid. vi. 1598.
[125] See below ch. iii and passim.
[126] Warnicke, *Rise and Fall*, 27–8; Ives, *Anne Boleyn*, 22–4; Dowling, *Humanism*, 231–4.
[127] CSP Span., 96.

Henry encouraged by Anne, turned his attention to William Tyndale's *The Obedience of a Christian Man*, Simon Fish's *A Supplication for the Beggars*, and other radical works. Not only did he read these books, he found much to admire in them.[128]

Friends of Catherine, unable to criticise the king in any case, blamed the Boleyn faction for sponsoring and circulating books and pamphlets critical of the established Church.[129] Certainly they had cause for their concern. The political ascendancy of the Boleyn faction encouraged like-minded men to make public their commitment to religious change in various ways. Even Norfolk and Suffolk had openly announced their intention to follow up their victory over Wolsey with an attack on clerical privilege and wealth. Most importantly, Anne herself, from the moment she reached the court, played a leading role in advancing evangelical ideas in England. Her early activity revolved around attempts to protect men involved in the circulation of pro- hibited books, and her advocacy produced successful results.

The defence of orthodoxy in the 1520s had concentrated on impeding the importation of illicit texts written by continental reformers or Englishmen in exile. Almost from the inception of printing, England offered an attractive market for religious literature, mostly written in Latin to aid clergymen in the performance of their parochial duties, or to teach piety by examples drawn from saintly lives. But before long, less conventional works began reaching English shores, at first a trickle and then in more substantial volume. Encouraged initially by Lollards and other native dissidents, the trade in heretical books rapidly expanded as Luther's reputation grew. Parts of London gained notoriety as centres for the distribution of Lutheran propaganda, and by the mid-1520s, extensive episcopal efforts at suppression made the smuggling of heretical books a dangerous enterprise.[130]

Anne mitigated some of the perils by offering protection to those who came to grief in the service of reform. For those unfortunates who got caught, she represented the last best hope for relief. One of these otherwise obscure indi- viduals, Thomas Alwaye, petitioned Anne, shortly after Wolsey's death. He asked her to intercede to restore his freedom to do business throughout the realm. Apparently a merchant, Alwaye had run foul of the law when he attempted to smuggle into the country 'English testaments and certain other books prohibited'. Arrested with the illicit goods in his possession, Alwaye came before Cardinal Wolsey who committed him to the Tower. Bishops Tunstall and Longland examined the guilty merchant and sentenced him to remain within the diocese of Lincoln for one year. In particular they warned him against setting foot in either London or the university towns. In his petition to Anne, Alwaye appealed against the sentence which had caused him a good deal of economic hardship. He hoped that Anne's intercession would release him from the provisions of his probation.[131] It is of the utmost signifi- cance that a man such as Alwaye recognised that Anne had the power to help

---

128 Dickens, *English Reformation*, 99.
129 Garret Mattingly, *Catherine of Aragon*, Boston 1941, 279.
130 Dickens, *English Reformation*, 28–30.
131 BL, Add. MS 1207.

him, and that he knew that in contrast to Tunstall or Longland, her sympathies were on the side of reform and those who promoted it.

Anne's support for men who traded in Protestant literature, from 1528, helped to weaken the official campaign of suppression and offered aid and comfort to those individuals in trouble with the law. In the summer of 1528, Anne wrote to Wolsey, beseeching him to remember the parson of Honey Lane.[132] Thomas Forman was rector of the London church called All Hallows, Honey Lane, and Thomas Garret served as curate. Both men had need of protection. Forman, a graduate of Queens' College, Cambridge, and later its president, regularly joined the White Horse circle and often found himself in trouble with the authorities. On one such occasion he was accused of concealing and keeping Lutheran books scheduled for burning.[133] In this case, however, Anne was probably most interested in shielding Thomas Garret.

Garret had received his academic training at both Oxford and Cambridge, took up the curacy at Honey Lane, but earned a far greater reputation among friends and enemies as a bookseller, enthusiastically involved in distributing William Tyndale's *New Testament* and other prohibited texts. Constantly in danger, Garret became a hunted fugitive until captured and placed in Wolsey's hands. Perhaps through Anne's timely intervention, the cardinal treated Garret gently, employing him to copy documents. Twelve years later, Garret was not so lucky; he was executed with Barnes and Jerome in the wake of the passage of the Six Acts.[134] William Betts and Nicholas Udall were also implicated in 1528 as allies of Garret. Neither suffered permanent damage, and both earned Anne's patronage. Betts became Anne's chaplain in 1533. Udall, after recanting to purge charges against him, returned to Oxford, received his MA in 1534, and with his friend John Leland, wrote verses to celebrate Anne's coronation. Afterwards, he became headmaster of Eton.[135]

Anne herself promoted forbidden books at court. As queen she commissioned at least one merchant to bring gospels and other religious works back from the continent,[136] but her interest in reformist literature had come to court with her, and by 1528 Lutheran books, printed abroad and smuggled into England from the Low Countries, circulated freely, albeit discreetly, among members of Anne's retinue, reaching even the king by indirect means. As the story is repeated by Strype, Anne had given a copy of Tyndale's, *Obedience of a Christian Man* to Anne Gainsford, a gentlewoman in her company. George Zouch, her suitor, borrowed it and was so moved by its message that he read it wherever he went. One day, Richard Sampson, dean of the Chapel Royal, spied Zouch reading the book, noticed the title, and snatched it from the startled young man. Mindful that Wolsey had commissioned church officials to be vigilant against such texts, Sampson delivered it to the cardinal. When Mrs

---

[132] BL, Cotton Vespasian F iii, fo. 34 (*LP* iv/addenda. 197).

[133] H. C. Porter, *Reformation and Reaction in Tudor Cambridge*, orig. pub. Cambridge 1958; Hamden, Connecticut 1972, 42–6.

[134] Dickens, *English Reformation*, 75–6.

[135] Maria Dowling, 'Scholarship, Politics and the Court of Henry VIII', unpublished PhD diss., London 1981; Cf. Dowling, *Humanism*, 82.

[136] Idem., 'Scholarship', 133; BL, Add. MS 43,827.

Gainsford told Anne what had happened, Anne realised that Wolsey might use the incident in an effort to undermine her relationship with Henry. And thus, before Wolsey could act, Anne went to the king, asked him to help her to retrieve the book, and 'besought his grace most tenderly to read it'. According to Strype, the king delighted in the book, 'had his eyes opened to the truth', and thus inspired, delivered his subjects 'out of the Egyptian darkness, and Babylonian bonds, that the Pope had brought him and his subjects under'.[137]

Strype's sense of historical causation should fill us with caution if not dread, but the evidence for Anne's commitment to reformed religion is clear and clearly connected to the question of the divorce. A field of mutual interest began to take shape. The Boleyns sought supporters of their cause among reformers seeking their patronage. As the Boleyns became prominent at court, their reputation as upholders of reform, and therefore, as potential patrons of reformers exercised a magnetic attraction. Traditional politics and radical religious ideology began to intertwine.

---

[137] John Strype, *Ecclesiastical Memorials*, 7 vols, London 1816, v. 171–2.

3

Conservatives and Reformers

Two factions surfaced in the 1530s to contest for power and place in England. Both drew energy and coherence from religious ideology, and each organised, initially, under banners identifying rival candidates for the office of queen. Following the departure of Wolsey, for a decade and more, conservatives and reformers fought bitter and often fatal political battles to determine which factional ideology would drive the mainspring of royal government and administration. The underlying matrix of Reformation, never far from the surface, promised no end of combustible fuel. From 1530 to 1533, when the Act of Appeals put the Royal Supremacy into effect, the issue of the divorce burned at the core of factional conflict. The political stakes could not have been higher. If conservatives prevailed, Henry's domestic life would remain clouded, but England would remain within the Christian commonwealth, and Rome would continue to guide the religious experience of English subjects. If, however, the reformers won, Anne Boleyn would be queen, and the means used to achieve the divorce and remarriage would shake the realm to its very foundations.

During 1530 and 1531 the king unwittingly helped to promote this factional conflict by failing to act on his own well-rehearsed arguments for the divorce and the schemes developed to see it achieved.[1] These were not years without policy; they were years bereft of political will. Henry would not yield to conservative pleas that he submit to Roman jurisdiction, but neither did he commit himself beyond theoretical agreement to the radical policy of schism and reform increasingly advocated by the Boleyn faction as the best method for securing the divorce.[2] And so, until the end of 1531 Henry talked about schism, made diplomatic efforts to gain the support of France, and hoped, quite unreasonably, that the pope could be brought around to allow the divorce trial to take place on English soil. So long as the King's Great Matter remained unresolved, conservatives and reformers had good reasons to compete for factional supremacy.

The Boleyn faction found itself in disarray after Cardinal Wolsey's fall. Its leaders, with access to royal patronage, hoped to amplify their strength by binding themselves to forward positions in the movement for ecclesiastical reform. The radical solution to the divorce crisis, translated into action by

---

[1] See below.

[2] Murphy (*Divorce Tracts*, p. iii) argues that because Henry participated in the debate over the divorce, he began to direct government policy personally from 1527. There is no necessary connection on the evidence presented by Murphy, and we should be cautious about assuming that intellectual activity is equivalent either to the formulation or the realisation of policy. Cf. Elton, *Reform and Reformation*, 116; and J. A. Guy, 'The Privy Council: revolution or evolution?', in Coleman and Starkey, *Revolution Reassessed*, 69.

Cromwell, and Anne's willingness to respond to the needs and interests of English Protestants, not only enhanced the faction's attraction for potential adherents, it also shaped the concerns and personnel of the opposition. The conservative faction had little to encourage it in its unequal, uphill fight. They had inherited Wolsey's fatal dilemma. Henry would have Anne Boleyn as his wife. There would be no retreat. Yet there would be no divorce in communion with Rome. If the divorce took place in schism the Boleyn faction would triumph. Reformation would bring changes no conservative could welcome or tolerate. The anger of men, frustrated by events, burned bright at times and smouldered beneath the surface at other times, but it never fully abated.

Thomas More's brief career in the office of Lord Chancellor illustrates the hardening of the conservative position along ideological lines. Thanks to recent scholarship,[3] we know a good deal about More's chancellorship. In bare outline it seems that More accepted his post in government in the mistaken belief that he could use the office to promote the cause of humanist reform while safeguarding the liberties of the clergy and the doctrine of the Church. As isolated issues, perhaps, anticlericalism could be addressed and heresy might be discouraged, but the divorce crisis took away any hope of this. The Boleyn faction viewed Catholic constitutional structures as a major obstacle raised against the divorce, and thus they encouraged attacks on ecclesiastical liberties. More, having placed principle before political accommodation, had none but conservative ground on which to stand. In these circumstances, reluctantly or not, More placed himself squarely on the side of those who supported Catherine and opposed the Reformation. He turned his attention to the detection and prosecution of heresy, while trying in the council to stop the accelerating slide toward schism. He lent his name, reputation, and advice to those dissidents seeking to organise resistance to the growing power of the Boleyn faction.

More's campaign against heresy has been treated as an aberration, an abnormal contradiction in 'so reasonable and balanced a man'.[4] From a factional perspective, however, his actions appear both logical and deliberate. The Boleyn faction had been seeking and winning the support of people traditionally and unequivocally classified as heretics. If More could check the rise to power of radical religious enthusiasts and limit the influence of their writings and sermons he might be able to defend the integrity of papal supremacy in England. If the Boleyns could not, then, call upon reformed religious doctrine to argue for the divorce, schism could be averted. Wolsey had not fully explored this avenue. In More's eyes the cardinal had neglected to exploit his position which combined the powers of lord chancellor with those of legate a latere. Rather, the cardinal's lax handling had allowed heresy to flourish to the point where it threatened to undermine the Christian commonwealth so important to More.

3 Elton, Reform and Reformation; J. A. Guy, The Public Career of Sir Thomas More, New Haven 1980; Alistair Fox, Thomas More: history and providence, New Haven 1982; Richard Marius, Thomas More, New York 1985.
4 G. R. Elton, 'Sir Thomas More and the opposition to Henry VIII', in Studies, i. 171. Cf. Marius, Thomas More, 386–406; Fox, Thomas More, 128–46; Guy, More, 103–10.

The cardinal had with reluctance burned books when conservative bishops such as Longland and Nix demanded that he burn people. Men branded as notorious and dangerous, Wolsey merely consigned to prison, or, as often, released after they had recited words of recantation. Thus important reformers escaped, fled for a time to continental havens, and far too frequently, conservatives believed, returned to England to continue their heretical activities. Furthermore Wolsey had used his legatine authority to restrict the harsher proposals of those bishops eager to bring inquisitorial tactics to England. Deliberately then, and with little charity or mercy, More set about reversing Wolsey's policy of restraint. Between August 1531 and April 1532 numerous persons were apprehended for heresy; five were executed. Most notably, Thomas Bilney, the Cambridge evangelical leader, died on 16 August 1531. His convert, Hugh Latimer, despite strong Boleyn connections was investigated and imprisoned by Archbishop William Warham.

More also took a hard line against heretical books. Two proclamations,[5] one issued on 22 June 1530, the second later in the same year, testified to More's determination to end the dangers posed 'by blasphemous and pestiferous English books, printed in other regions and sent into this realm, to the intent as well to pervert and withdraw the people from the Catholic and true faith of Christ'.[6] All crown officers were to employ themselves in the detection of heresy; forbidden books were to be surrendered. Those who refused to submit would be subject to the existing penalties of medieval heresy legislation. It is difficult to evaluate the impact of More's pursuit of heresy in all its forms. His resignation from office in May 1532 argues that the hard line approach failed to work as a political tactic. Some might have trembled when they heard More's name. Many books met their end in flames; people died. Who knows what might have happened if More had had sufficient time without challenge to carry through his campaign against heresy? But More had little room to manoeuvre, and no time to act, because the Boleyn faction had come to the fore.

Now ideologically committed to reform, the Boleyn faction rapidly coalesced. Faction members increased their influence in all political venues. Anne's personal relationship with the king flourished, and she had established her own identity as a substantial politician. As such, Anne became a visible target for reformers, including many regarded by More as heretics. They sought employment and sway at the heart of affairs. Anne's brother George was prominent in the privy chamber, and her father occupied a leading position among members of the council. Support from her uncle, the duke of Norfolk, had waned. He had little stomach for reform, but he remained something of an asset, an aristocratic presence, still powerful and for the moment compliant.

Those who had served the king and Anne in the debate over the divorce received generous rewards for their intellectual or diplomatic contributions. Bishoprics left vacant by Wolsey's death or otherwise, furnished important patronage resources. Stephen Gardiner and John Stokesley, respectively, received the sees of Winchester and London. John Salcot or Capon went to

[5] See *Tudor Royal Proclamations*, ed. Paul L. Hughes and James F. Larkin, 3 vols, New Haven 1964–9, i. 181–5, 193–6.
[6] Ibid. 194. Cf. Elton, *Reform and Reformation*, 127–8; Guy, *More*, 171–3.

Bangor to try on his episcopal mitre. Edward Lee secured the archbishopric of York. None of these men, appointed in 1530 and 1531, developed much enthusiasm for religious novelties in later years, but temporarily they gave added weight to the factional efforts to obtain the divorce, and they never challenged the policy which established the Royal Supremacy.[7]

Other men who had helped to prepare tracts which upheld the divorce also profited from their labours. Nicholas de Burgo, formerly in Wolsey's service, received monetary grants, the promise of a benefice, and denization. He continued to work as one of the chief writers in the king's cause.[8] Edward Foxe also went on to participate in the pamphlet debate over the Royal Supremacy. Born in the mid-1490s, Foxe had already established himself before the storm over the divorce broke. By 1527, perhaps earlier, Foxe had obtained a secretarial position in Wolsey's household. The cardinal used him on the initial diplomatic missions concerning the divorce, and Henry relied on Foxe as one of the principal writers in the first stages of the debates on the legality of his marriage to Catherine. Although Foxe did not join the episcopate until 1535, he did not want for promotions. The king appointed him his almoner. In November 1527 with Wolsey's favour he received the prebend of Osbaldwick, York and the mastership of the hospital of Sherburn, Durham. The following year he was elected provost of King's College, Cambridge and presented to the rectory of Combe Martin in Devonshire. In 1531 Foxe secured the archdeaconry of Leicester, and in 1533 he added the archdeaconry of Dorset.[9]

Thomas Cromwell supplied the Boleyn faction with their most valuable ally. His work in the Reformation Parliament brought Cromwell respect and promotion. He entered royal service early in 1531. The king's servant first, as he had been Wolsey's, Cromwell quickly became a mainstay in the legal and financial business of the crown. Frequent access to the king added political potential to his role and endowed him with an aura of loyalty and competence, virtues in short supply among Wolsey's successors. Attendance at court as Henry's agent brought him into close contact with the Boleyns and extended his knowledge of the most pressing factional concerns. In 1531 Cromwell did not participate directly in the formulation of policy for the divorce, but well-placed to glean threads of information, he must have followed with interest the work of Foxe, Stokesley, and de Burgo on policy for the Royal Supremacy which would become the rallying point for the Boleyn faction's future.

Between the early summer of 1530 and the late summer of 1531, the principal members of the team, put together to argue the theological case for the divorce, turned their attention to politics.[10] Stymied by Pope Clement and

[7] Gardiner, Stokesley, and Lee were part of the circle of scholars working on the divorce debate. Each wrote at least one tract and all were active in the public campaign for the dissemination of the royal arguments: Murphy, *Divorce Tracts*, p. xxii. Capon helped to argue the divorce case at Cambridge: *DNB* iii. 931.

[8] Murphy, *Divorce Tracts*, p. xx.

[9] *DNB* vii. 553–4.

[10] Murphy suggests that there is a connection between the documents of the divorce debate and the *Collectanea*. 'It now seems likely that a similar collection of materials to that developed in the Collectanea had been compiled for the debate over the Divorce, a document which has

Cardinal Campeggio at Blackfriars, the way to the divorce through Rome seemed blocked. In fact, panic began to set in among Henrician councillors. Henry had been cited to appear in Rome. His case, adequate perhaps in an English court, had no chance of persuading papal judges. Certainly, their verdict would favour Catherine. Faced with imminent defeat, the king instructed Edward Carne and William Benet to delay the proceedings, and Henry began to solicit opinions from foreign universities.

At home, and with speed, a new policy designed to bypass Roman jurisdiction began to appear. The king's writers produced the *Collectanea satis copiosa*.[11] Initially, according to Graham Nicholson, who has developed this evidence, Edward Croke and Stokesley gathered material from continental libraries, responding to instructions from London relayed by Gardiner and Foxe. Later in 1530 Benet and Carne joined in the search for more sources. With the material in hand, Foxe, linked with the divorce from the beginning, probably performed the task of compilation.[12] Painstakingly culled from diverse sources, the *Collectanea* provided a summary of arguments which led to the political theory that the king was autonomous in his own realm and thus immune from outside interference. According to conclusions drawn from the assembled authorities, kings should rule their Churches. Rome had no right to revoke cases from provincial jurisdictions to its own. Throughout the 1530s, reformers drew on the copious resources of the *Collectanea* for their tracts, sermons, and statutory preambles. Broadcast throughout the realm, arguments which supported the case for Henry's proposed marriage to Anne evolved into a general theory of Royal Supremacy.[13]

Cromwell's participation in the process of elevating a series of intellectual propositions to the status of royal policy is a subject of renewed controversy among scholars.[14] There is no question that he knew of the polemical discourse taking place. The fierce pace of intellectual activity, Cromwell's presence at court with the king and the Boleyns, his early connection to Edward Foxe in Wolsey's household, all suggest Cromwell's familiarity with the ideas presented in the *Collectanea*. More significantly, publication brought to notice most of the conclusions about the divorce which had been circulating since 1527. Thomas Berthelet, the king's printer, issued *Censurae academiarum* in the spring of 1531.[15] This treatise, containing university opinions on the divorce, was translated into English and published in November 1531. At about the same time

---

not survived or which perhaps has not yet been identified. Indeed, such a compilation may well have been the inspiration and model for the *Collectanea*': p. xxiii.

[11] Cited by Elton, *Reform and Reformation*, 135–6; and Guy, *More*, 131–2. Both rely on an unpublished thesis by Graham Nicholson, 'The Nature and Function of Historical Argument in the Henrician Reformation', unpublished PhD diss., Cambridge 1977, 74–110. Cf. Nicholson, 'The Act of Appeals and the English Reformation', in Claire Cross, David Loades, and J. J. Scarisbrick (eds), *Law and Government under the Tudors*, Cambridge 1988, 19–30.

[12] Ibid. 25.

[13] Ibid. 19. Nicholson argues that the *Collectanea* suggests that there was 'a largely consistent direction in policy from the autumn of 1530 to Archbishop Cranmer's declaration of nullity of the king's marriage to Catherine in May 1533'.

[14] Elton, *Reform and Reformation*, 136; Guy, *More*, 130–45; Nicholson, 'Act of Appeals', 28.

[15] Date of publication supplied by Murphy, *Divorce Tracts*, p. iv.

appeared the *Glasse of Truth*, which announced in print the independence of English kings from Roman jurisdiction.[16]

The air at court must have resonated with the debate. There was no need for secrecy in the work of research and compilation. Reformers and other up-holders of the king's cause must have discussed with relish each new discovery, giving hope and comfort to those anxious for encouraging news. Cromwell travelled in just such circles, as did Anne Boleyn. The arguments of the *Collectanea satis copiosa* became the basis of the policy by means of which the Boleyn faction united marital ambitions and the politics of reform.

The remainder of 1531 and most of 1532 furnished the temporal dimensions of the first phase of the conflict between competing factional interests, newly arrayed in ideological garb. The physical arenas in which the battles were waged included parliament and the council chamber but were not limited to these venues. More or less articulate citizens also had opinions about the King's Great Matter. Both reformers and conservatives sought to influence popular perceptions and positions. While no call ever issued for a trial of the divorce judged by public opinion, there were serious attempts to convince the political nation at least to take up positions for or against the Royal Supremacy.

The Boleyn faction could more easily exploit their advantages. Henry's love for Anne opened doors for reformers. The divorce question and Reformation, two sides of one coin, brought men through those doors. Anne, her family, and increasingly Thomas Cromwell, worked to ensure that access to sources of royal patronage resulted in suitable promotions for loyal friends. The Boleyn house-hold operated as a breeding ground and nursery for the new religion. Boleyn household chaplaincies often marked the start of important ecclesiastical careers. Most of the Boleyn chaplains came from Cambridge; all shared evan-gelical sympathies and enthusiasm for religious change. They saw in Anne Boleyn an answer to their material and spiritual prayers – a vehicle had been delivered to carry simultaneously career ambitions and their dedication to reform. It is always difficult to separate interest and conviction, but there is a distinct pattern in Anne's patronage of radical clerics that convincingly dis-plays their mutual attraction to similar religious values. The Boleyn faction began to add ideological substance to its quest for the divorce.

The Cambridge connection, most importantly, brought Thomas Cranmer to the Boleyn faction. Stephen Gardiner and Edward Foxe introduced Cranmer to Henry VIII in August 1529, perhaps for the purpose of inviting the then unknown theologian to discuss his plan to have the universities of Europe judge

---

[16] Nicholson convincingly concludes that material from the *Glasse* was drawn from the *Collectanea*: 'Act of Appeals', 26-7. If Murphy, then, is correct in her opinion that both works are connected to a source collection which also supplied the *Censurae*, our picture of the intellec-tual position of the crown from the inception of the divorce to the Act of Appeals would be fully developed. It should be noted, however, that the important work of both Nicholson and Murphy does not speak to the political question of the translation of policy into the legislation of the 1530s. Nor does it testify to the role played by Cromwell in this process. Nicholson's effort in this regard (p. 26) is largely speculative and unsatisfying. It is one thing to assert, as he does, that the *Collectanea* established that in theory the king was independent of Roman jurisdiction in issues relating to royal marriage; it was quite another thing to argue and to implement a theory that held the English Church independent of the universal Church.

38

the divorce case. Cranmer, a member of the White Horse group, had already established a Lutheran reputation. Soon after his royal interview Cranmer was working for the king. In October 1529 he met Henry and received a commission to write a pamphlet favouring the divorce. During the two months he took to complete the book, Cranmer stayed at Durham House, the new London residence of Thomas Boleyn. So began the close association between Cranmer and the Boleyn faction. At the end of the two months, Cranmer, by then a Boleyn family chaplain, had finished his work, and on 21 January 1530 he joined an embassy to the pope and to the emperor, led by Thomas Boleyn, which also included Edward Lee, John Stokesley, and Edward Carne. Their mission, undertaken to persuade Clement and Charles to drop their opposition to the divorce failed, but it served to tighten the bonds of attachment between Cranmer and the Boleyns. Upon returning from the diplomatic assignment in Italy in October 1530, Cranmer took up residence at court and continued to work for the Boleyns on behalf of the divorce.[17]

At the end of June 1531, Cranmer wrote to Wiltshire from Hampton Court with his evaluation of a book written against the divorce by Reginald Pole. In his letter Cranmer expressed the concern that Pole's arguments might be difficult to refute, and that if the common people heard them it would be impossible to convince them that Pole was wrong. Nevertheless, Cranmer attempted to counter Pole's arguments and made several suggestions to Boleyn concerning measures to be taken to convince Englishmen of the justice of the king's cause. Cranmer had other things to tell Boleyn, but he declined to put them into writing or even to send a verbal message with his bearer. Rather, 'the rest of the matter I must leave to show your lordship by mouth when I speak with you, which I propose God willing, shall be tomorrow, if the king's grace let me not'.[18]

Cranmer's presence with Henry and Anne as a permanent member of the royal entourage is in itself significant, representing an important source of direct influence and a communication link between faction members in London and both Henry and Anne. The close connection between Cranmer and Anne held firm until the day of her death; that of the king and his future archbishop remained intact throughout Henry's lifetime, regardless of sharp political and religious tremors which often threatened to shake Cranmer loose from royal favour. The steadfast personal friendship between Cranmer and the king helped to preserve the reform faction even as its leaders, Anne Boleyn and Thomas Cromwell perished.

More immediately, however, Cranmer's growing influence led to his unexpected appointment to the archbishopric of Canterbury. When William Warham died in August 1532, the king passed over several obvious men, including Stephen Gardiner, to select Thomas Cranmer for the office; this despite the facts that Cranmer held only a minor church office, had a wife

---

[17] Cranmer probably spent at least part of the next fifteen months translating the *Censurae* into English. It appeared in print in November 1531 as *The Determinations of the Mooste Famous and Mooste Excellent Vniuersities of Italy and Fraunce*: Murphy, *Divorce Tracts*, pp. v, 21. Cf. Jasper Ridley, *Thomas Cranmer*, orig. pub. 1962; Oxford 1966, 35.
[18] *Cranmer's Letters*, 229–31. Cf. Ridley, *Thomas Cranmer*, 35–7.

whom he had to put away, and, at the time of his selection had to be recalled from diplomatic service at the court of Charles V at Mantua. Obviously, the Boleyns had worked hard to secure the archbishopric for their most dependable adherent. Cromwell, too, welcomed Cranmer and did what he could to hasten his return. And Henry showed his enthusiasm by installing Cranmer at Canterbury as soon as he arrived from Italy on 10 January 1533. Cranmer had consistently voiced his opinion that the divorce case could be decided in England; now he began the process. Within two weeks of his consecration on 30 March he had asked for and had received licence to examine, determine, and judge the King's Great Matter.[19]

As the reform component of the Boleyn faction began to take definite shape and to expand, men in favour brought like-minded friends to court. Cranmer, for example, introduced Hugh Latimer to Anne Boleyn, obtaining for him an invitation to preach in favour of the divorce in March 1530. Pleased with Latimer's efforts, Anne became his staunchest ally, a noteworthy relationship because of Latimer's well-established reputation for religious radicalism. Latimer, also a member of the White Horse circle while at Cambridge, often found himself in trouble for his preaching. In 1525, Nicholas West, bishop of Ely, banned Latimer from preaching at the university or within the diocese. Latimer, using a loophole, transferred his preaching activities to the local Augustinian monastery, exempt from the bishop's authority. He thus evaded West's displeasure, but not that of Cardinal Wolsey who summoned him and forced him to disown any Lutheran connections by oath before granting him licence to preach throughout the realm. In 1529 Latimer again found himself in trouble for preaching radical sermons, but his support for Henry and Anne in the matter of the divorce shielded him and brought him eventually to the Boleyn inner circle, where he met or renewed his acquaintance with other reformers, including Nicholas Shaxton. The two became favourites, not only with Anne but also with the king. They frequently dined at Anne's table, and they were often joined by Henry who delighted in debating points of doctrine with the two Protestant clerics.[20]

Shaxton had first come to notice through Gardiner, who marked his enthusiasm for the divorce. Shaxton had studied at Cambridge, part of the Norfolk–Gonville Hall connection. He also frequented the White Horse Inn, and espoused unambiguous opinions about purgatory and clerical celibacy. These ideas brought him into conflict with the conservative bishop, Richard Nix of Norwich, who forced Shaxton to take a special oath to renounce the errors of Wycliffe, Hus, and Luther before he received licence to preach in the diocese. Shaxton's radical views did not disturb Anne. She appointed him her chaplain and almoner in the summer of 1531, and at her urging Cromwell appointed him to the parish church of Fuggleston in Wiltshire and to the office of Treasurer of Salisbury. But rather than residing either in his parish or the cathedral, Shaxton remained in the new queen's household and preached from time to time at Paul's Cross. In 1534 he gained a canonry in St Stephen's,

19 Ibid. 35–7.
20 Allan G. Chester, *Hugh Latimer, Apostle to the English*, Philadelphia 1954, 111.

Westminster, and the following year he became bishop of Salisbury, joining on the bench of bishops his friend, Hugh Latimer, elevated to the see of Worcester in August 1534.[21]

Neither Shaxton nor Latimer could take up their preferments until they had made arrangements to pay their first-fruits. Henry withheld his formal assent to their promotions, and in the end it was Anne who paid. No better demonstration exists of Anne's firm friendship to the Reformation than the practical means by which she assisted reformers. In this case she advanced to Latimer and Shaxton £200 each out of her private funds. These generous loans, not repaid during her lifetime, could still be found recorded among her outstanding debts two months after her death.[22] Throughout their rapid advancement, both Latimer and Shaxton benefited from the unified interest and close co-operation of Anne and Cromwell who shared leadership roles within the reform faction. Anne had brought them both to court and encouraged their promotion. Cromwell handled the business of patronage and employed the talents of both men on behalf of royal policy.

The Barlow brothers also benefited from their factional connections. John Barlow, one of at least four brothers, made the initial contact with the Boleyn family. A cleric, Barlow held the Essex livings of South Banfleet, Great Bentley, and Hawkswell from 1521 to 1527. We know no details, but sometime between 1525 and 1528 he entered the service of the Boleyn family and became chaplain to Sir Thomas Boleyn. Much employed in connection with the divorce and highly partisan, Barlow became well-known as Anne's servant, a member of her household.[23] Through Boleyn auspices, Barlow received a royal chaplaincy in 1531.[24] Never a bishop himself, loyalty and his utility to the Boleyn faction created opportunities for his brothers. E. G. Rupp tells a fascinating story about Roger Barlow, who is described in 1526 as a merchant, trading in Spain. He went on an expedition to South America with Sebastian Cabot, returning finally to Bristol in 1528. He hoped, once home, to persuade the king to sponsor a project to find a route to the Indies across the North Pole.[25] Unfortunately, the story goes no further. The proposal if ever heard by the king failed to generate sufficient interest. Roger stayed in Bristol and later became involved in the Barlow clan's efforts to reform the diocese of St David's.

John Barlow also introduced his brother William to the Boleyns, an action of much greater significance. William Barlow can be seen as the archetypal member of the Boleyn faction, an ideologue who saw in politics an instrument for the reform of English religious life. In addition, the conflicts which attended each of his promotions are characteristic of the factional struggles in regional centres over ecclesiastical doctrine and the forms of religious worship which gave shape to Henrician politics after 1529.

Barlow was born in Essex just before the turn of the century. He studied at both Oxford and Cambridge, took vows as an Augustinian, and by 1524 had

---

21 *DNB* xvii. 1390–2.
22 *LP* x. 1257 (ix).
23 Rupp, *English Protestant Tradition*, 64.
24 *LP* v. 82 (g. 58).
25 Rupp, *English Protestant Tradition*, 63.

advanced to the office of prior of Bromehill in Wetting, Norfolk. He must have met Cromwell, at least by 1528, when the minister, then Wolsey's servant, suppressed the priory to endow the cardinal's college at Oxford. Temporarily unemployed, Barlow began to experiment with Lutheran doctrine, and for a time he engaged in writing tracts against the existing ecclesiastical establishment. Seizing the opportunity presented by his brother's connections, Barlow attached himself to the Boleyn interest and established himself as a tireless labourer on behalf of the divorce. Between 1529 and 1531 he shuttled between London, Paris, and Rome, building up considerable credit for himself with Cromwell and Anne who became his principal patrons. In 1534, as marchioness of Pembroke, Anne granted Barlow the small priory of Haverfordwest from which port he embarked on his Protestant mission.[26]

Barlow proved to be a fiery preacher, and he shocked conservative Welsh sensibilities. Led by the bishop of St David's, Richard Rawlins, the local clergy espoused traditional religion, and the laity responded for the most part to the directions of their parish priests. Economically, the cathedral church and many lesser sites of shrines benefited from pilgrims drawn from all of Wales, but Barlow argued that the diocese wallowed in superstition and idolatry. He called on three of his brothers to help him to reform the diocese and began a series of antipapal sermons which infuriated the local clerical hierarchy.[27] Rawlins sponsored charges against Barlow before the king's council. Anne and Cromwell guarded him from prosecution, and Barlow continued his partisan attack. He denounced both the hostility of the clergy and the backwardness of St David's, and he proposed to redress the 'misordered living and heathen idolatry' that had plagued the cause of reform. The Boleyns heartily agreed with him and tried to advance him to a suffragan bishopric in the diocese. So fierce was the opposition, however, that Cromwell could not win the necessary consent from the bishop and his officers.[28]

To compensate Barlow, perhaps, or to take St David's off the boil, Cromwell removed him from Haverfordwest to the priory of Bisham, a Berkshire foundation of much greater value. Later in 1535 the minister sent him on an ambassadorial mission to Scotland to induce James V to abandon the pope. Still at his diplomatic post in January 1536, Barlow learned that he had been promoted to the bishopric of St Asaph. But, before he could leave the Scottish court, Bishop Rawlins died, and Cromwell appointed Barlow to succeed him at St David's. Barlow's allegiance now resided solely with Cromwell. The bishop survived Anne's fall unscathed and returned full sail back to St David's. His consecration in the summer of 1536 shattered the uneasy peace which had prevailed since his departure. Within six months he had made clear his intention to reform his diocese. He planned to endow grammar schools and to sponsor Protestant preachers. First, however, he would subdue opponents in his cathedral chapter by moving the see from St David's to Carmarthen. The old canons would be

[26] *DNB* i. 277.
[27] Glanmor Williams, 'The Protestant experiment in the diocese of St David's', in *Welsh Reformation Essays*, Cardiff 1967, 111. Cf. SP 1/91/167–8 (*LP* viii. 466); BL, Cotton Cleopatra E iv, fo. 107 (*LP* viii. 1091).
[28] SP 1/90/113 (*LP* viii. 412).

excluded; reform could proceed. Barlow's plan to translate his see failed, but he continued throughout his career to deliver consistently useful service to faction and the cause of reform.[29]

Boleyn patronage succeeded well in bringing important reformers to influential offices. Another Boleyn chaplain, Matthew Parker, did not bloom as a prominent public figure until much later. He was years younger than most of his colleagues. His presence in Anne's household confirms her support for young, Protestant clerics, an effort which helped to ensure continuity among personnel within the reform faction. William Betts, John Skipp, William Latimer, and Robert Singleton completed the company of Anne's chaplains. Betts and Skipp commenced their journeys to preferment from Gonville, that early hotbed of heretical views that also produced Shaxton. Betts had been implicated with Thomas Garret in the illicit book trade.[30] John Skipp followed Shaxton as Anne's almoner on the former's election to the see of Salisbury. He combined continuing education with active work on behalf of the Royal Supremacy and gained several preferments for his loyal service, assisted by both Anne and Cromwell. In 1534 Skipp became vicar of Thaxted, Essex and received a canonry in Westminster Abbey. Two years later, he was collated to the rectory of Newington, Surrey, and to the archdeaconry of Suffolk. In 1539 he succeeded to the bishopric of Hereford, vacated by the death of Edward Foxe.[31] William Latimer, another younger man, was engaged in bringing Anne books from abroad. When Thomas Starkey died in 1538, one of his livings, the college of Corpus Christi, London, worth almost £80, went to Latimer. Later, in the reign of Elizabeth, he wrote a manuscript life of his first patron, Anne Boleyn.[32]

The least known of Anne's chaplains was Robert Singleton, a Lancashire cleric who held the vicarage of Preston from boyhood and attended both Oxford and Cambridge. Singleton did not reside in his benefice, but worked in London and Kent as Anne's chaplain and as a Cromwellian agent in Dover. He survived the falls of both of his patrons, but not for long. By 1543 Singleton, discovered among a group of heretics in Kent, was forced to recant. In 1544 he was executed, ostensibly for treason.[33]

Boleyn chaplaincies furnished tangible approbation for a limited number of clerics. Anne's determination to base factional policy on religious ideology, however, reached far beyond provisions for personal chaplains. The success of the few stimulated the ambitions of many others. Some hoped that a shared religious purpose would lead to personal advancement. Some hoped that their factional connection would promote the cause of Reformation. The result seemed to suggest, particularly to conservatives, that heresy had become official policy. Support for the divorce served as a protective talisman, allowing the most notorious heretics to roam freely throughout the realm, enjoying the protection and patronage of the Boleyns and Thomas Cromwell. Laws did not

29 Williams, 'Protestant experiment', 114–20.
30 Dowling, *Humanism*, 81.
31 *Alum. Cant.*, iv. 86.
32 Dowling, *Humanism*, 89.
33 Christopher Haigh, *Reformation and Resistance in Tudor Lancashire*, Cambridge 1975, 84.

apply equally to conservatives and reformers. Chapuys noted in March 1531 that the most learned Lutheran preacher had been arrested and lay in danger of being executed as a heretic, but, he complained, the priest suffered no penalty and was released from prison none the worse for his experience. During the examination, at which the king presided, the first article alleged against the priest was that he had preached that the pope was not the sovereign chief of the Christian Church. Henry seized on this statement and agreed with it. Slapped lightly on the wrist, the preacher promised, 'one of these days', to preach a sermon retracting some of those doctrines which disturbed Henry's sense of orthodoxy. Chapuys concluded by citing 'the general opinion' which held that Anne and her father had been the principal instruments of the priest's release from prison.[34]

Even Robert Barnes returned to the king's good graces if not his outright favour. Barnes had signalled his desire to return to England in 1531. His *Supplication unto the most gracious prince Henry VIII* combined advocacy of caesaropapism with a defence of several Lutheran theological tenets. Convinced by Cromwell that Barnes could be useful in the dispute with Rome, the king granted him a safe-conduct to visit England. Cromwell was never able to secure for his client more than a Welsh prebend, but Barnes served on various diplomatic missions. At home, he preached frequently, often overstepping all bounds of circumspection. As long as he had a buffer between himself and his enemies, Barnes pursued a vigorous career. When Cromwell fell, Barnes, lacking a protector, was quickly condemned on a charge of heresy and died at the stake on 30 July 1540.

The strategy of the Boleyn faction had clearly emerged by the beginning of 1532. Schism would produce the divorce; a comprehensive political offensive would produce the schism; opposition would be stifled. The new Church of England would bring continental theology and forms of worship to England. Zealous reformers carried the Boleyn programme to the political nation by all available means. The numbers of radical preachers multiplied under the Boleyn aegis, and the countryside resounded to their calls for reform of 'superstitious practices' and 'false doctrine'. Increasingly, as well, ever louder demands could be heard for an end to the exercise of papal authority in England. Not surprisingly, this factional barrage provoked a conservative response. Conservatives were well represented in all centres of power, and as long as the king did not announce his factional preference their resistance could proceed unrestrained. Individuals, particularly Thomas More, exercised great personal caution. Otherwise, there was little to choose in energy between the competing factions.

There were, however, differences in factional structure between conservatives and reformers. The Boleyn faction had a comparatively well-known leadership which provided a measure of vertical integration. Policy and patronage came from the top, and those on lower factional rungs looked upward to Anne Boleyn and Thomas Cromwell for ideological direction and support. Throughout his career in royal service, Cromwell extended and enriched this

[34] *CSP Span.*, iv. pp. ii, 352.

44

network, which with the passage of time penetrated ever deeper into the social fabric of the realm.[35]

In contrast, conservatism seems to lack identifiable structure, comprised of splintered groups with diverse goals, united only by their common programme of opposition to the dominance of the Boleyn faction and reformed religion. The conservative faction had several centres of influence. Their leading lights could be discerned, but they illuminated limited domains. Chapuys, the imperial ambassador, had contacts in the House of Lords, including Bishop John Fisher, the earl of Shrewsbury, and Lord Darcy. A hardcore group of doctrinaire Catholic MPs in the House of Commons became the Queen's Head group, named after their favourite tavern. Some members of the lower house of convocation defended Catherine's interests and Catholic orthodoxy, as did bishops Tunstall of Durham, Nix of Norwich, and Archbishop Warham. Most vehemently, Franciscan Observants in Greenwich and the Bridgettines of Syon in Richmond took on the task of countering in kind radical sermons and pamphlets. Looking at this amorphous pattern of conservative factionalism, it seems futile to try to identify or to label precisely a single, central nucleus.[36] In fact, the soft focus of the conservative faction might have been its greatest asset. Lack of formal links and multiple clusters made difficult targets of individuals under fire. Yet the whole pattern of conservative opposition had some definition. Various individuals met regularly to share information and to plot their moves. We have evidence of this substructure of factional coordination from two separate sources. Cromwell himself, in September 1535, explaining the executions of Fisher and More to Gregory da Casale referred to them as leaders of an organised opposition, a conspiracy, which from as early as 1529 had been active against the king's policies.[37]

The second witness, Sir George Throckmorton, furnishes more substantial evidence of the conservative faction working effectively to block Boleyn initiatives. In a document from 1537, discovered by J. A. Froude,[38] Throckmorton, a staunch Catholic MP from Warwickshire, is seen consistently fighting against the divorce, the Royal Supremacy, and all reform measures. In 1537 under some unspecified political duress, Throckmorton, commanded by Cromwell, wrote to Henry VIII confessing to his career as a dissident. It is difficult to discern purpose in Throckmorton's confession. He claimed that he had been blinded by the 'sayings and counsels' of men who had led him astray. He hoped that

---

35 Peter Clark, *English Provincial Society from the Reformation to the Revolution: religion, politics and society in Kent, 1500–1640*, Hassocks 1977, 49–50. Clark furnishes a clear example of this process operating through what he calls party networks, a web of patronage and deference woven from the parish to the centre of political influence.

36 For material about conservative groups and their tactics see Guy, *More*, 140–2; Elton, *Studies*, i. 155–72; idem. *Reform and Reformation*, 122. Elton writes of an Aragonese faction with two centres, one formed around Eustace Chapuys, which included the Queen's Head group, Bishop Fisher, and other conservative peers; the other consisting of Catherine's chaplains. Guy sees a more diverse factional structure, but he agrees with Elton in calling conservatives 'Aragonese', a label which unnecessarily limits the scope of their activity and ignores continuity of programme and personnel after Catherine's death in January 1536.

37 Merriman, *Life and Letters*, i. 427–31. Cf. Elton, *Studies*, i. 165–9.

38 Ibid. 166–7, 167 n. 1.

Henry would consider that 'I have opened the secret part of my conscience, which was the ground of all my misdemeanors to you and all your affairs.' Cromwell had repeatedly warned him, but, Throckmorton ruefully noted, he had not heeded. Lately, however, the message had been recalled, and that, along with some recent reading, had convinced Throckmorton that he had acted wrongly, 'for the which I humbly beseech your highness of pardon'. In short, Sir George claimed to have undergone a Protestant conversion and now had his feet on the right path. The books that inspired him were the New Testament and *The Institution of a Christian Man*. His language – the metaphor of blindness, the confession of human weakness, and the unsupported plea for forgiveness – certainly bespeaks a religious context for the confession if not its inspiration in his conversion.[39]

To a sceptical eye the body of the confession downplays Throckmorton's initiative. It is unlikely that the naive figure Sir George portrayed himself as could have played the role described or have survived in active opposition for so long. Otherwise, Throckmorton's story rings true. We cannot say with certainty why he revealed his secrets, but it is even more difficult to imagine why he would have lied about substantial matters five years after their occurrence; too many hostile witnesses still lived. The question of veracity is important, because if Throckmorton told the truth about his connection to various conservatives, we have a remarkably clear picture, at this decisive moment, of conservative factional opposition to the Boleyn plans for the divorce and all that might follow from it.

During the critical months of 1532,[40] Throckmorton visited and had dealings with men from every centre of conservative factionalism. Shortly before the parliamentary session, he met Friar William Peto from the house of Franciscan Observants in Greenwich. Then, after doing his part to oppose the Act for the Submission of the Clergy, Throckmorton was called to speak with Thomas More who thanked him for his effort and encouraged him to 'continue in the same that ye began and not be afraid to say your conscience'. More told Throckmorton that he was deserving of God's reward, and that with time, the king too would make known his gratitude. Sir George also had several meetings with the bishop of Rochester. John Fisher filled him with reactionary fire and advised him to speak to Nicholas Wilson, formerly the king's confessor, now a bulwark of Catherine's cause, 'and so I did, and come home to his house diverse times'. Finally, Throckmorton travelled to Syon, where he listened to Richard Reynolds's threats of damnation. Reynolds insisted that Throckmorton continue to speak in parliament, even if it did no good, because, he said, 'I did not know what comfort I should be to many men in the house to see me strike in the right way, which should cause many more to do the same.'[41]

Committed to the papal supremacy and dedicated to fighting against legislation directed against clerical liberties, Throckmorton enmeshed himself in factional politics. He worked with the Queen's Head group, planning

---

[39] The text of Throckmorton's confession (SP 1/125/247–56) is printed in Guy, *More*, 207–12. Cf. J. J. Scarisbrick, *The Reformation and the English People*, Oxford 1984, 63–4.
[40] Guy has sorted out the problems of chronology raised in the confession: *More*, 198–9.
[41] Ibid. 207–12.

parliamentary opposition, and he seems to have represented the Commons resistance in his discussions with the members of other factional clusters. From his movements we get a sense of the way in which the conservative faction went about its political business. Selected individuals in parliament and convocation confronted and worked against legislation introduced by Cromwell and the Boleyns. Some conservative writers countered the reform propaganda with their own books and tracts against the divorce and the Royal Supremacy. A vigorous preaching offensive took every opportunity to promote the conservative cause. Thomas More handled the debate in the council and either orchestrated the opposition, or, at least, kept a watching brief over all. There does not seem to have been a definitive hierarchical political structure to the conservative faction, nor a single cohesive policy directing the various activities, but this did not diminish their effectiveness.

The best documented area of conservative resistance is that which issued from the Franciscan convent in Greenwich, where William Peto and John Forest with others mounted an aggressive campaign against the royal divorce. Observant friars had been granted land adjoining the palace in Greenwich by Edward IV. In 1486 Henry VII confirmed the grant and founded the house, which became a favourite refuge for Catherine of Aragon. Often, it is said, she would awaken at midnight to join the friars in their devotions. Forest, who later succeeded Henry Elstow as warden of the convent, had served as the queen's confessor. Peto, provincial of the order, was Princess Mary's chaplain. During the divorce crisis, Forest, Peto, and many of the friars steadfastly maintained their loyalty to Catherine and put their talents to work in her defence.[42]

Throughout 1532, Peto lived on the edge of personal peril in his efforts to bring the conservative case to public attention. On Easter Sunday 1532, at Greenwich, Peto preached with the king in his audience that the projected divorce would result in tragedy. In addition, suspicions ran strong that he had organised a scheme to smuggle abroad for printing at least two of Bishop Fisher's seven treatises against the divorce. Throckmorton's confession adds texture to Peto's activities. Sir George stated that Peto sent for him shortly before the opening of the parliamentary session. The friar at the time found himself imprisoned in Lambeth, but he refused to remain silent. When Throckmorton arrived, Peto told him of the Easter sermon he had preached to the king. He also revealed a conversation afterwards between himself and Henry in which he said that he had argued that the king could never remarry as long as Catherine lived, because their marriage was valid. Peto supported the queen's statement that she had never consummated her marriage to Arthur. No words to the contrary could be true

> for he said such [i.e. Catherine] should best know it of any living creature, and that such had received the sacrament to the contrary. And such being so virtuous a woman there ought to be more credence given to her than to all the other proofs. And as to all the other proofs, he said these were but upon

[42] *Original Letters Illustrative of English History*, ed. Henry Ellis, 11 vols in 3 series, London 1824–46, ii. 245–6.

presumptions save the saying of Prince Arthur that he had been in the middle of Spain, which he supposed was but light word spoken of him.[43]

It seems surprising that Peto would have flown this argument in Henry's presence, but according to Throckmorton, the friar's impudence was mere prologue to outright slander. 'And further said he that he did show your grace that ye could never marry Queen Anne for that it was said ye had meddled with the mother and the sister.' So powerfully did Peto influence Sir George to whom he was related, that later, in 1533, Throckmorton, himself, used similar words to the king in an interview which Cromwell also attended. When the king meekly responded, 'never with the mother', Throckmorton claimed Cromwell had to add, 'nor with the sister neither, and therefore put that out of your mind'. Even from his confinement, Peto encouraged Throckmorton to remain active in Parliament against the divorce, 'to stick to that matter as I would have my soul saved'.[44]

While Peto risked all by directly confronting the king, John Forest worked to keep the friars in Greenwich firmly aligned to the conservative position. Forest's activities in the convent are known through the reports of Richard Lyst, a lay brother, one of the few Boleyn advocates in this furnace of conservative factionalism. Before he joined the friars in Greenwich, Lyst had been near powerful people without much personal gain in position or influence. He described himself as a former servant in Cardinal Wolsey's household, but he could not have been prominent, since he was unknown to Cromwell at the start of their correspondence in November 1532. Lyst lived in Cheapside and maintained a business as a grocer and apothecary. During this time, he met Anne Boleyn. Perhaps, as later, he prepared special waters for her after she came to court.[45] Anne maintained the connection, sending money on several occasions to Lyst's mother. It must have been Anne who alerted Cromwell to the advantages of having a loyal client in place to report the friars' movements and plans. Lyst had been writing to Anne before he began a series of letters to Cromwell. The Act for the Submission of the Clergy had not been easily received, and it makes sense that Anne, knowing the need to gauge resistance from Greenwich, asked Lyst to write directly to Cromwell. And so, on 7 November Lyst introduced himself to Cromwell as 'your poor beadman, as yet unknown to you'.[46] He then began to discuss the internal conflicts taking place at the Greenwich convent.

Despite his dual relationships with the friars and Anne Boleyn, Lyst has not had much attention or respect. Regarded as a gossip or as a neurotic by some modern scholars, he nevertheless filled a major gap in Cromwell's intelligence network. Earlier, he had sent Richard Curwen, a royal chaplain, to Greenwich to plead the king's cause. He also recruited John Lawrence, a Boleyn loyalist, from within the house to defend official policy. But Curwen's advances were

---

[43] Guy, *More*, 210.
[44] Ibid.
[45] SP 1/76/85 (*LP* vi. 512).
[46] BL, Cotton Cleopatra E iv. fo. 29 (*LP* v. 1525).

repelled, and Lawrence immediately came under attack.[47] Only Lyst continued to report the factional struggle at a time of intense anxiety and significance for all concerned.

The major focus of Lyst's scrutiny was John Forest, well known for his opposition to the Boleyns and the 'king's matter'. In his initial letter to Cromwell Lyst accused Forest of trying to supplant or expel John Lawrence in order to bring the convent fully to the support of Catherine. 'And his original and chief cause is, because he knoweth that Father Lawrence is provided, and also will preach the king's matter whensoever it shall please his grace to command him.' According to Lyst, Forest refused the command to preach himself in favour of the divorce. Neither would he allow Lawrence to do so. Believing that Forest, to keep Lawrence silent, was planning to have him expelled from the convent in Greenwich, Lyst pleaded with Cromwell to move the king to intervene, 'for that shall be to the king's honour and to the comfort of us that doth favour the king's grace and cause'.[48]

Two against many, Lyst and Lawrence could have been friends. Admiration for Lawrence came easily to Lyst's pen. He praised the friar for his learning, preaching, and politic wit, hoping that Henry would recognise and appreciate Lawrence's value, 'for he hath a common custom in his preaching ever to draw the hearts of the king's subjects to favour his grace'. Lyst well understood the role played by the Greenwich Observants against the divorce. He had written earlier to Anne and trusted that she had informed both Cromwell and the king of the dishonour and displeasure brought by the unfaithful indiscretions of Peto, Henry Elstow, and Forest. Now he wanted to tell Cromwell directly about Forest, whom, diverse times, he had heard 'report that you dare not displease him for fear lest he should bark against you and your deeds in his preaching'.[49]

Lyst complained that Forest shamed himself by promising the king to take his part and then preaching against his cause. 'I suppose your mastership did hear of the last indiscreet sermon that Father Forest made at Paul's Cross, where I was present myself with him; how indiscreetly he used himself, more like barking and railing overlarge of the decay of this realm, and of pulling down of churches.' Filled with a sense of self-importance, Lyst recommended that Forest be restrained from occupying the pulpit at St Paul's. 'In my judgment it is more convenient for him to sit at home with his beads than to go forth and preach.' Fully expecting that his report would be highly regarded both by Cromwell and Anne Boleyn, Lyst claimed to 'have other things pertaining to our religion which very few do know of which secretly I do intend to show unto you or the king's grace when I might have convenient time and place'.[50]

Lyst must have received sufficient encouragement. Cromwell sent Thomas Goodrich, a royal chaplain and future bishop of Ely, to interview him. Goodrich carried word back to the king, Cromwell, and the Boleyns, and Lyst continued his reports from Greenwich. On 4 February he wrote separately both

[47] See David Knowles, *The Religious Orders in England*, iii, Cambridge 1961, 207–8.
[48] BL, Cotton Cleopatra E iv. fo. 29 (*LP* v. 1525).
[49] Ibid.
[50] Ibid.

to Anne and Cromwell. To Anne he expressed satisfaction that the king now knew the whole situation, 'howbeit I have great marvel that the matter is slenderly looked upon as yet'. He reminded Anne of the troubles in the convent and his own sacrifices in defence of her cause. For himself, Lyst, derisively called Anne's chaplain, took rebuke as a badge of honour; 'but all that I have suffered in that cause and for your sake, hath been rather comfort and pleasure unto me than otherwise; and so it should be in the cause of his friend'. For remedy against abuse of Anne, Lyst seized on a plan that had been in the air for about a year. He thought it a good idea to move the friars from Greenwich to Christ's Church in London, thus breaking their power to oppose royal policy. Greenwich, he argued, could be put to use as a college, and all would benefit from the transformation.[51]

Lyst carried the same themes into his letter to Cromwell. He stated that if the king would order the move he might do so without substantial offence against God, or any great note of the people:

> for if there had been a place of our religion in London, by the reason thereof there should have been avoided many inconveniences that hath chanced by our brethren against the observance of our rule, and so all such inconveniences against the observance of our rule in time to come should be avoided if there were a place of our religion in London.

Cromwell and Anne, to be sure, did not need Lyst's policy suggestions, but his letter, otherwise, contained useful information about Forest's 'unkindness and duplicity'. Lyst charged his superior with the murder of brother Raynscroft and the continued suppression of John Lawrence. He himself felt so threatened, 'that scant two nights a week I can take my natural rest; and if my troubles should continue long, I fear some inconvenience of sickness to chance unto me'.[52]

Lyst's delation of Forest began to bear fruit. On 18 February he wrote again to Cromwell, reporting that Forest had returned from a meeting with the king, at which 'his grace laid certain things against him, and with him his grace was not content'. Forest, however, unchastened, regarded the charges against himself, as a general factional attack on the order, initiated and sponsored by Cromwell. He began to crack down on Lyst and other Boleyn adherents within the house, looking for 'our particular knowledge, because he would have us punished'. The friars passed a statute among themselves, 'so that what brother soever there be that doth manifest or show any act or deed done secretly in our religion . . . yet all shall be grievously punished if that may be particularly known'. Fearful that if Forest discovered him as Cromwell's spy he would suffer 'unmerciful punishment', Lyst trusted that the king and Cromwell would 'be good unto us, and not suffer us to be punished for speaking and showing the truth'.[53]

Nevertheless Lyst believed that his letters had been worth the risk their writing entailed. If, he said, the king and Cromwell had not admonished Forest,

---

[51] Ibid. fo. 28 (*LP* vi. 115).
[52] Ibid. fo. 30 (*LP* vi. 116).
[53] Ibid. (*LP* vi. 168).

preachers from the convent would have openly supported Catherine in sermons against the divorce. Now, however, the king and Cromwell had been alerted to the danger, and the brothers feared 'in so much now that none of us all, as far as I can perceive, dare neither say nor do anything that should offend the king's grace, your mastership, or yet any that belongeth unto the king's grace or you'. Yet, despite his feelings of confidence, Lyst asked Cromwell to burn his letters after receiving them to avoid any chance of retaliation from Forest, apparently a real concern.[54]

With the co-operation of Elstow and Richard Reynolds of Syon, Forest began a purge of malcontents. Five friars had been ordered to France and instead had left the religion. Lyst himself felt the heat of Forest's vengeance. He informed Cromwell that Forest and Elstow 'have made labour to have me out of this house and to have me sent to Southampton, and if I should be sent to any other convent far off, as they do intend, I am in a doubt how I should be ordered, because Father Forest hath put me in such an infamy and note among the friars, and set the religion against me'. Again, Lyst appealed for Cromwell's protection and promised even greater effort on behalf of the king's cause: 'And so I am the king's and yours, and shall be to the extremity of my power with the grace of Jesu.'[55]

Lyst continued to write from Greenwich until 20 May 1533. By that time the Act in Restraint of Appeals had become law, and the King's Great Matter had been resolved. Lyst observed that Father Forest, 'your little friend and less lover and mine also for all his great cracks he is now far enough from us'. Forest had been sent to a convent in the north. Lyst, without a mission to sustain him, hoped to be delivered from Greenwich. Even with Forest absent, the other friars continued to plague him, and he wrote that he could get no rest. Hoping to change his state, he asked Cromwell to remind the king and Anne Boleyn of his service and to furnish substance for his plans to depart. He sent a gift to Anne through Cromwell requesting, as well, that she remember his 'poor mother'.[56]

Indeed Anne and Cromwell remembered Lyst, who left Greenwich in the late spring of 1533. By October the former lay brother wrote that he had lately been a student at Clare Hall, Cambridge, and most recently had been at St Audrey's, Ely, where he took his first orders. Lyst would probably have pursued this path to the priesthood much earlier, but until death abrogated an obligation to marry, he could not do so. Now he intended 'to proceed further and become a secular priest and to serve God, I trust, better and with more quietness than I have done or might be suffered in time past among the friars'.[57] Cromwell saw Lyst's ambitions to a successful conclusion. First, he tried to secure for him 'a poor fellowship of Clare Hall'. He wrote to Master Creyford on Lyst's behalf but received no answer, and in March 1534 Lyst beseeched Cromwell to pursue the suit.[58] Soon afterward, however, he received

[54] Ibid.
[55] Ibid.
[56] SP 1/76/85 (*LP* vi. 512).
[57] SP 1/79/186 (*LP* vi. 1264).
[58] SP 1/82/269 (*LP* vii. 302).

satisfactory reward. He was presented to the vicarage of St Dunstan's in the West, London and held the benefice until his resignation in 1556.[59]

The other Greenwich principals fared less well. Throughout 1532 William Peto and Henry Elstow continued to oppose the divorce. They both spent time in prison, and Henry briefly considered bringing them to trial. They were released, however, and immediately left England for Antwerp, where they remained until 1555. Then Queen Mary revived the convent and invited the two aged friars to live out their days at Greenwich.[60] John Lawrence, Lyst's ally, asked for a dispensation from orders in 1532. Nothing further is known of him.[61]

John Forest did not survive to enjoy a Marian retirement with his colleagues. Already sixty-two years old in 1532, Forest hastened his death by his intransigent opposition to the divorce. Pushed by Lyst's denunciations, Forest lost his office as warden in 1533 and was sent either to Newark or Newcastle. By 1534 he was back in London, implicated in the Elizabeth Barton affair. He found himself in custody, expecting to die within three days. He abjured and survived this crisis, joining the convent of Grey Friars in London in 1536. By 1538, however, he was back in prison for advising penitents to resist the Royal Supremacy. Cromwell produced evidence of heresy; Cranmer examined and condemned Forest who was burnt in a fire started with the wooden image of Llandarvel.[62] Eroded by the passage of time and the relentless force of the Boleyns, the first wave of conservative factionalism could not offer effective resistance to the implementation of policy for schism and reform.

Parliamentary approval of the Act in Restraint of Appeals in the spring of 1533 changed the nature of conservative resistance. Factional control of government made impossible an equal contest for control of policy. The Boleyns with ideological form and direction had won this important round; they had given the king what he wanted most. Cranmer had been appointed to the archbishopric of Canterbury on 10 January 1533, a trigger for events. The secret marriage of Henry and Anne took place on 25 January. Cranmer pronounced the king's marriage to Catherine null and void as soon as legally feasible. Cromwell had firm control over policy, although his status did not accurately reflect his power. Granted the office of Master of the Jewels in April 1532, he did not become principal secretary until April 1534. He had, however, comprehensively vanquished Thomas More, who, surrendering to the inexorable tide of events, resigned the chancellorship on 16 May 1532, the day after the clergy made their Submission. Cromwell's nominee, Thomas Audley, was appointed to the diminished office. All the signs indicated the triumph of the Boleyns and reform. The court, the council, the privy chamber, and parliament, all, for the moment, danced to the tempo set by a single drum, and the dominant rhythm of reform, no longer muted, rapidly accelerated.

At the apex of faction, Thomas Cromwell and Anne Boleyn had formed a workable alliance which energised Henrician politics. In 1532, after passing the

59 *Original Letters*, 246.
60 Knowles, *Religious Orders*, iii. 208, 439.
61 Ibid. 208.
62 Ibid. 369–71.

Act for the Submission of the Clergy, parliament restrained annates to Rome. Then, the Act in Restraint of Appeals was followed by the First Act of Supremacy, the Act in Absolute Restraint of Annates and Concerning the Election of Bishops, an Act Forbidding Papal Dispensations and Payment of Peter's Pence, one which annexed First Fruits and Tenths to the crown, and a new Treasons Act. Seemingly at a stroke, papal taxation in England was abolished, Cranmer rose to the head of an English episcopate, the Royal Supremacy was established, and treason legislation defended the new edifice.[63]

Patronage interests helped to link the victorious faction leaders and to keep the wheels of reform turning smoothly. Anne herself had considerable patron- age resources. The grant to support her dignity as marchioness of Pembroke included advowson rights with the rental income. The Queen's Jointure promised additional opportunities for clerical patronage. Increasingly, however, Cromwell manipulated the levers of power for the reform faction. He combined in himself the dual roles of chief patron and principal director of policy. He had drafted the legislation which produced the Royal Supremacy and shepherded it through parliament. With practical assistance and inspiration from Cranmer he began to bring the ideological expectations of the reform faction to the far corners of the realm.

Cranmer and Cromwell developed an easy business relationship which be- came a close friendship. In November 1533 the archbishop wrote to Cromwell, thanking him for securing a royal loan of £1,000. Thomas Goodrich, soon to become bishop of Ely, had delivered the approval which stipulated the terms of the loan to be granted in installments of £500. Cranmer needed the money, but, 'practiced with my lord of Wiltshire', he could not come to London himself. He thus desired Cromwell to give the cash to the bearer of his letter.[64]

In their factional roles Cromwell took charge of broad issues of policy and Cranmer handled many of the details. The blending of responsibilities worked well, allowing Cranmer to set out the religious aspirations of the reform faction from behind the political shield held by Cromwell. In the process Cromwell himself moved increasingly toward the radical religious position espoused by Cranmer. The resultant bonding of politics and religious ideology between the two leaders produced quick results. Past heresy became the new language of factional orthodoxy, and Cranmer left no hint of compromise or apology in demanding access for his reforming voice.

In January 1534 Cranmer wrote to Richard Sampson, then dean of the Chapel Royal, to promote reformed sermons in the services held in the presence of Henry and Anne. First he recommended that Hugh Latimer preach 'before his grace all the Wednesdays of this next Lent ensuing'. The archbishop knew that Sampson would stick at the mere mention of Latimer's name. He told the dean that Latimer had lately been endangered for his preaching, 'and suffered great obloquy'.[65] Cranmer, too, had been criticised for licensing Latimer. Yet, he said, he knew Latimer to be 'a man of singular learning,

---

[63] For a full review of the statutes passed see Stanford E. Lehmberg, *The Reformation Parliament*, *1529–36*, Cambridge 1970, 131–216.

[64] *Cranmer's Letters*, 270.

[65] Ibid. 308n.

virtuous example of living, and sincere preaching the word of God'. Cranmer recited his determination, 'I intended evermore the furtherance of the truth and the pure dispensation of the word of God', to require Sampson to discharge the king's pleasure:

> Furthermore, these shall be heartily to desire you also, that my old acquainted friend, master Shaxton, the queen's grace's almoner, may be assigned likewise to preach the third Sunday in Lent before the king's grace; and that you will forthwith, upon the sight hereof, ascertain me in your letters by this bearer, according to the king's grace's said pleasure and my request.[66]

Cranmer softened the demand by promising to requite the 'favour', but Sampson well knew that he had no choice in the matter. He tried to put his submission in the most useful light. Shaxton, the dean claimed, merely by asking, 'should with all my heart have in Lent what day he would before the king's grace, and yet should have the said third Sunday with no less good will, notwithstanding if it is appointed more than two months past'. Sampson had more difficulty digesting Latimer's appointment. Those dates also had been filled, but Sampson would serve the king's pleasure, even though he, himself, could not abide Latimer's radical preaching:

> I favour him in my mind for his learning. I pray God it may be moderate. The signs are not most pleasant, since that his teaching moveth no little dissension among the people wheresoever he cometh, the which is either a token of new doctrine or else negligence in not expressing of his mind more clearly to the people.[67]

With Sampson's defences in a state of ruin, Cranmer turned toward preparing Latimer to preach before the king, 'whereupon I thought it very expedient for diverse considerations reasonably me moving thereto, to admonish you of certain things in no wise to be neglect and omitted on your behalf in time of your preaching; which to observe and follow according to mine advice hereafter to you prescribed, shall at length redound to your no little laud and praise'. Then, like Polonius to Laertes, Cranmer filled Latimer with advice, warning him not to use the occasion to defend himself against his enemies or to attack his adversaries. Rather he should be circumspect in his choice of text and charitable towards his audience, as long as they received his sermons in like manner. 'Nevertheless', Cranmer allowed, 'if such occasion be given by the word of God, let none offence or superstition be unreprehended, specially if it be generally spoken, without affection.' Next, Cranmer strongly suggested that Latimer occupy the pulpit for no longer than an hour, or at most an hour and a half; 'for by long expence of time the king and queen shall peradventure wax so weary at the beginning, that they shall have small delight to continue throughout with you to the end'. Finally, Cranmer invited Latimer to come early to

---

[66] Ibid. 308.
[67] SP 1/82/47 (*LP* vii. 32).

London to prepare and rehearse under the archbishop's watchful eye.[68] Latimer learned his lessons well. Six months later, he received a commission to visit all preachers licensed by Cranmer to be certain that they 'should neither preach any thing which might seem prejudicial to the said matrimony, whereby the king's issue might come into question or doubt amongst the vulgar people, nor likewise reprehend in their sermons any such ordinances, act, or statutes, heretofore made, or by the said high court of parliament hereafter to be ordained'.[69]

The strength of the reform faction, exemplified by the ease with which Cranmer exercised his dominance, spelled disaster for the conservative faction. Their parliamentary cadre could offer nothing more than token opposition to the avalanche of reform legislation. Monastic strongholds had been breached: Peto, Elstow, and Forest were gone. Episcopal resistance had been fragmented: Warham was dead; Tunstall was in Durham; Gardiner was on his way to France. Convocation never recovered from its submission. Thomas More, the most visible conservative, lost his battle in the council and resigned. Much worse was to come. In the summer of 1533 Cromwell and Cranmer struck and brought down Elizabeth Barton, the Nun of Kent. All conservatives were tainted by her fall. Oaths, demanding formal allegiance to the succession and the Supremacy, furnished the instruments which broke conservative leadership. Fisher, More, and several Carthusians died at the hands of various executioners. As the power of the Boleyn faction became greater, opposition at the centre stilled to the point where attention could be paid to partisan voices from the countryside.

If the English Reformation is understood as a process, rather than an event, there is no contradiction between the desperate ideological conflict in London in the early 1530s and the relative calm in outlying areas of the realm.[70] Unfortunately, some scholars recently have taken the apparent disparity of an overheated centre and cooler edges as evidence that 'The English Reformation was in only a limited sense popular and from "below".'[71] They have looked at 'events' and have concluded that since none by itself was sufficient to cause or to be defined as the Reformation, no Reformation occurred, at least at the level of the general laity. Proponents of this 'revisionist' strategy have argued that their approach has undermined the work of Professor Dickens and others who have been seeking the origins of English Protestantism in the 1530s. According to Christopher Haigh, 'The existence of long term religious discontents can be disputed, the significance of Protestantism as a progressive ideological movement can be doubted, the continuing popularity and prestige of the Catholic Church can be stressed, and the political Reformation can be explained as the outcome of factional competition for office and influence.'[72]

---

[68] *Cranmer's Letters*, 308–9.

[69] Ibid. 297.

[70] For a discussion of popular religious ferment in London see Susan Brigden, *London and the Reformation*, Oxford 1989; idem. 'Thomas Cromwell and the "brethren" ', in Cross, Loades and Scarisbrick, *Law and Government under the Tudors*, 31–89.

[71] Scarisbrick, *Reformation*, 1.

[72] Christopher Haigh (ed.), *The English Reformation Revised*, Cambridge 1987, 3.

Without for a moment accepting the convoluted reasoning which seeks to revise English history along with English historiography, it is, nevertheless, well to note that the pace of Reformation politics throughout much of the realm did not reflect the intensity experienced in London and the universities. Haigh has shown that in Lancashire the quality of the parochial clergy was so poor that they could not be properly ordered in any orthodoxy, Catholic or Protestant. Moreover, these priests, or more often clerical assistants, had little or no contact with the reformist ideas of London or the university towns.[73] Large parishes, numerous chapels unattractive to an educated, resident clergy, created formidable problems in diocesan administration in Lancashire. Predictably then, in more remote areas of England, machinery for introducing and enforcing religious change did not function with efficiency.[74]

As a result of obstacles faced by the reform faction in isolated parts, conservative preaching could not be completely suppressed. Nicholas Wilson, for one, transferred his activities to the north when London became too dangerous for militant conservatives. A friend of Thomas More, supporter of Catherine of Aragon, and defender of papal authority, Wilson helped to keep conservatism alive in Lancashire, Cheshire, and Yorkshire in the early 1530s.[75] John Ainsworth, another fiery advocate of Catherine's cause, was less fortunate. In the months immediately following the marriage he could safely say in his sermons that the Roman church was 'Our Holy Mother Church'. But by the end of 1538, authorities prevented him from preaching in York, and when he nailed up copies of his inflammatory sermon he was apprehended, tried for treason, and executed.[76] He had ignored the reality of political geography in attempting to preach in the city of York, a provincial capital. Equally, he failed, fatally, to note that by 1538 Cromwell, despite the challenge from Calais,[77] was playing a much stronger government hand.

Closer to the seat of factional power in London, opposition met determined scrutiny much earlier. On 7 November 1535, for example, William Oxenbregge, who described himself as the queen's servant, reported that the vicar of Rolvynden, Kent had preached openly that his parishioners 'should not follow the saying of evil princes nor evil rulers, but rather put on your harness and fight against them'. Oxenbregge, discharging his duty to inform Cromwell, asked for instructions to resolve the matter.[78]

The one area that Cromwell and the Boleyns could not control was the unlearned discourse of the lower orders. Public opinion reflected an imperfect understanding of hierarchical, factional politics. People everywhere, during and after the divorce crisis, chose their favourite candidate for queen, and often their enthusiasm could not be contained. Serious consequences might follow.

73 Idem. *Tudor Lancashire*, 30.
74 Ibid. 44–5.
75 Ibid. 111.
76 Ibid. 111–12.
77 See below.
78 SP 1/99/9 (*LP* x. 786). Efforts to enforce the Royal Supremacy and to extend Reformation throughout the realm are discussed in subsequent chapters.

Susan Brigden tells of the London popular reaction to news of the divorce in which rumour and fact combined indiscriminately. First, in 1527 rumours swept the city that Henry would repudiate Catherine for a French princess. The king called on the mayor to put an end to this talk on pain of his royal displeasure. When it became known that Henry's love had found Anne Boleyn, so great was the popular reaction that by 1530 diplomats were reporting the rumour that a rebellion of Londoners would inevitably and immediately follow the proposed marriage. And in 1531 the story of a strange riot was dispatched as fact: 'A riot of London women (and men disguised as women) seven or eight thousand strong attempted to seize Anne Boleyn, but she escaped.'[79]

Most popular public opinion went unnoticed; much of it took place in taverns under the influence of strong ale. Obviously, conversations between family members, friends, and neighbours went unreported. Except where the possibility of rebellion might intervene, Tudor politicians paid little attention and gave little heed to the views of the commons. But prison awaited even insignificant men who spoke out on behalf of Catherine or Rome in front of the wrong people. Roger Dyker, a sixty-nine year old war veteran found himself in Marshalsea Prison for saying that the king would not forsake 'so noble a lady, so highborn, and so gracious' to marry Anne Boleyn.[80]

Anne's cause did have its popular champions, although their favour had no greater intellectual foundation or basis in fact than that of her opponents. In 1533 William Glover reported to Anne that 'there was a messenger of Christ that came to me once, and commanded me to come to your grace'. Glover said that he did not believe the heavenly ghost at first, but several additional visits, accompanied by threats of divine retribution, issued by a shade in 'angel form', finally convinced him to deliver the message. And so Glover said that God approved her marriage and would bless it with a child. That Glover wrote to Anne after her coronation, at which she appeared noticeably pregnant, might have somewhat diluted the good news, but against the broad background of less favourable popular attitudes Anne may have welcomed Glover's assurance of divine goodwill.[81]

Cromwell could not do much to stem the tide of popular bruit and rumour, but he did what he could to produce quiet in the realm. He put into place a series of statutes designed to protect Anne, the royal marriage, and royal offspring from slings and arrows as well as more formidable threats. The Act of Succession of 1534 stated that Anne Boleyn was Henry's only lawful wife and England's only queen. Their children would be the legitimate Tudor heirs; Elizabeth replaced Mary in the succession. Another statute in the same year defined as treason the defamation of Anne or her daughter, and oaths demanding acceptance of the Succession were presented to all officials for their subscription.[82] Cromwell did not thus end the popular outcry against Anne. Some

---

[79] Susan Brigden, 'The Early Reformation in London, 1522–1547: the conflict in the parishes', unpublished PhD diss., Cambridge 1972, 18–19; idem. *London and the Reformation*, 208.
[80] SP 1/68/123 (*LP* v. 628).
[81] SP 1/81/69–70 (*LP* v. 1599).
[82] Lehmberg, *Reformation Parliament*, 182–216.

continued to challenge the new regime and the new religion, even at the risk of their lives. Most people never knew that statutes had been passed in parliament. None of this mattered much. Anne could survive if not ignore the threats posed by her factional adversaries and other disaffected people with even less political stature. The attack she could not survive was that launched against her by the king, her husband, and put into motion by Thomas Cromwell, heretofore her factional partner.

4

Cromwellian Ascendancy: Patronage and Reform

After Anne's coronation on 1 June 1533, Cromwell moved into the forefront of the reform faction. Anne was still involved in the patronage and protection of reformers, and her evangelical sympathies continued strong, but Cromwell's handling of factional business and the affairs of state mattered more. Men came to realise that proposals for reform as well as their own careers had first to gain the favour of Thomas Cromwell. Still without significant office himself, Cromwell solidified his personal control of royal patronage when Henry, showing complete confidence in his chief minister, appointed him vicegerent in spirituals in December 1534 with authority to exercise all the provisions of the Act of Supremacy. For all practical purposes Cromwell now became the central figure both in the factional arena and in the Henrician political universe.[1]

During this transitional phase in the history of the reform faction, which ended with Anne's fall and execution in the spring of 1536, there were no overt signs of competition or animosity between Anne and Cromwell.[2] Outwardly, their relationship seemed co-operative, even cordial. Cromwell attended to the queen's business and protected her reputation against popular sedition. Clients understood the connection between the two factional leaders. Hopeful suitors sought the patronage of both with no indication that either had the greater power to grant their requests, and they assumed that information intended for one would become known to the other. In May 1533 Edmund Bonner wrote to Cromwell to ask him to set forth his service with the future queen.[3] Cranmer apologised only to Cromwell for not writing either to Cromwell or to Anne about Catherine.[4] Sir William Courtenay asked Cromwell in July 1533 to review a proposed marriage he had arranged for Cromwell's cousin Richard with a 'nigh kinswoman' of the queen in order to secure the queen's approval

---

[1] Ives's evaluation of Cromwell needs to be read with great care, and his conclusions must be rejected since they are contradictory. For example, on p. 354 of *Anne Boleyn* Ives states that compared to a man like Henry Norris, 'Cromwell was in the second division'. He claims that men like Rochford, Norris, and other 'senior members of the privy chamber circle' regarded Cromwell as a mere functionary. Yet earlier he says that Anne's hopes depended on Cromwell; that his presence represented 'the real originality in the Boleyn camp'; and that 'At last Anne was backed by a first-rate politician' (pp. 186–7). Later, of course, he credits Cromwell, a second-rater, with devising and executing the complex plot which destroyed Anne and a host of 'first-division' politicians associated with her (pp. 355–7).
[2] For a diametrically opposed interpretation of the relationship between Cromwell and Anne see Warnicke, *Rise and Fall*, 104ff.
[3] SP 1/76/15–16 (*LP* vi. 438).
[4] *Cranmers Letters*, 242 (*LP* vi. 496).

for the match.[5] In addition to the appearance of teamwork between Cromwell and Anne, Cromwell also kept a watchful eye on the queen's personal business, including the complicated details of the jointure. A 1533 remembrance contains numerous matters concerning leases which Cromwell needed to discuss with Anne.[6] As money from the leases began to be delivered, Cromwell reviewed the accounts.[7]

Rather than the product of a political struggle or some deep-seated factional division, Anne's eclipse by Cromwell resulted from the successful conclusion of the King's Great Matter. Anne had won! She and Henry were married. She was queen. But victory removed Anne in formal terms from a position in faction to an established place in the structure of the Tudor state. From her new station Anne drifted into activities more traditional to the wife of a king. Shortly after her coronation, she retired to Greenwich to prepare for the September birth of Henry's long-awaited son. And she must have expected that much of her time in future would revolve around the domestic and social responsibilities of court life.

Anne did not completely abandon politics after becoming queen, nor did she forget her friends and coreligionists. Aspects of patronage on behalf of reform continued to engage her interest and energy. She wrote to Bristol corporation on 20 January 1534 for the advowson of the college or hospital of St John the Baptist in Ratcliff Pit within the city. The advowson would go to Sir Edward Bainton, her vice-chamberlain, Nicholas Shaxton, her almoner, and 'to our trusty and well-beloved David Hutton'. Anne did not name her nominee for the next vacancy of the mastership, but she did advise the city fathers that the man she had chosen was a friend of good learning, virtue, and demeanour. She trusted that his preferment would be to 'the pleasure of almighty God', and at the same time would lead to 'the rest, quietness, weal, and benefit' of the town. Her trust, however, had its limits. Anne instructed the corporation to signify its pleasure in writing and to hand the letter to her bearer.[8]

Despite the distractions of her life at court, Anne also remained sensitive to the needs of imperilled partisans. She confidently relied on Cromwell to handle the details. Richard Herman, a merchant doing business from the English House at Antwerp, had been arrested in July 1528 for Lutheran activities. Authorities had found in his possession several letters urging Herman to remain steadfast in his efforts to set forth the New Testament in English. It is not clear how long Herman languished in prison, but his punishment also included expulsion from his merchant company and other economic restrictions.[9] Herman now appealed to Queen Anne for her assistance, and she responded. Anne asked Cromwell in 1534 to restore Herman to 'his pristine freedom, liberty, and fellowship'. Anne also believed the merchant to be an important source for information about Protestant activities on the continent. She

5 SP 1/77/239 (*LP* vi. 837).
6 BL, Cotton Vespasian C xiv, fo. 252 (*LP* vi. 1188).
7 SP 2/0/23 (*LP* vi. 1189).
8 BL, Harleian MS 6184. 766 (*LP* vii. 89).
9 Clark, *English Provincial Society*, 31. This must have been Tyndale's translation.

suggested that Cromwell collect as much news as possible before allowing Herman to depart.[10]

Anne's interest in the fortunes of international Protestantism is not remarkable. Insofar as surviving evidence indicates, she remained attentive to religious issues, and she backed her commitment with her patronage. Her letter in May 1534 to Edward Crome reveals her sense purpose in the exercise of patronage and her impatience with subordinates slow to comply with her designs. Crome, a veteran of the divorce campaign, had impressed Anne with his effective preaching in favour of royal policy for the break with Rome. The queen rewarded him with the rectory of St Mary, Aldermary in the city of London. But as time passed, Anne noted that Crome had not taken up his promotion, 'by which your refusal we think that ye right little regard. . . your own weal or advancement'. Anne reminded Crome that her concern encompassed nothing more than 'the furtherance of virtue, truth, and godly doctrine'. She insisted that the encouragement of these values required residence, and she demanded that Crome take up his benefice at once.[11]

Anne had a long memory and could be relentless when the occasion demanded. The abbot of York, at his preferment, had agreed to allow his chief rival, John Aylmer, to continue his studies at Cambridge. In May 1535 Anne received credible reports that Aylmer had been called back to the monastery where the abbot charged him with sundry duties, 'to the no little disturbance and inquietation of his mind, and to alienate him as much as may be from his said study and learning'. Insisting that the abbot permit Aylmer to return to Cambridge, Anne also required him to furnish Aylmer with 'sufficient exhibition to the maintenance of his study there, else to signify unto us in writing by this bearer a cause reasonable why ye differ to accomplish our said request made unto you in that behalf'.[12]

Since Anne made only sporadic forays into factional politics after 1533, much of the responsibility for leading the reform faction fell to Cromwell. As he emerged from the shadows cast by the divorce, the ideological implications of the six years of struggle between reformers and conservatives began to appear and take shape. During his tenure as Henry's principal minister, which lasted until 1540, Cromwell unveiled an ideologically inspired policy for the Church which defined the Royal Supremacy, dissolved the monasteries, and began the reformation of the Church of England. Between 1533 and 1536 Cromwell gained control of faction and vastly increased his influence in government and administration. Anne had been a leader of the reform faction. Cromwell was much more. As vicegerent, vicar general, and special commissary, Cromwell obtained from the king personal authority to exercise the provisions of the Royal Supremacy, and he used this authority to put forward his programme for the reform of the English Church.

Cromwell's path to unchallenged factional leadership proceeded less directly, guided for the most part by events beyond his control. Politics continued to

---

[10] BL, Cotton Cleopatra E v, fo. 3306 (*LP* vii. 664).
[11] BL, Harleian MS 6148. 79b–80a (*LP* vii. 693).
[12] SP 1/92/169 (*LP* viii. 710).

reflect Henry's passion for Anne. Politicians could only ride the wave through its crest, hoping to stay out of angry waters. Cromwell, well-placed in these conditions, had no need to make risky moves. He and Anne agreed on basic policy and shared mutual interests. If the king's passion ebbed, the minister enjoyed Henry's confidence apart from any influence exercised by the queen. Anne's flood of triumphs ended with the birth of Elizabeth on 7 September 1533. Her supporters could talk of a healthy pregnancy and a future filled with sons, but the birth of a princess boded ill. Henry had expected a son as a sign of God's blessing on his change of wife. The painful process of divorce had been endured, but there was no son. What now? The perfect union began to show signs of tension, and Anne's delighted enemies gathered to work at widening the cracks in the relationship between Henry and the hated concubine. Chapuys, the imperial ambassador, quickly made it known to Cromwell that abandoning Anne would lead to renewed cordiality between the emperor and England. He suggested to Cromwell that since Henry had proved his independence by marrying Anne, he could now take Catherine back without any loss of reputation. The ambassador had earlier reminded Cromwell that Wolsey's fall had resulted from the cardinal's break with the imperial party. He believed Cromwell to be a man who understood reason, and he told Charles that the minister was only waiting for an opportunity to change his whole policy.[13]

Nothing in Cromwell's actions should have given Chapuys much cause for celebration. The minister warned the ambassador that the king's love for Anne had not abated, and, he warned, any intervention by the emperor would lead to disaster.[14] Cromwell not only counselled caution, he practiced it assiduously. No premature word or deed would colour his demeanour. If Chapuys seemed encouraged Cromwell had done his work well. The emperor would remain passive, the minister would keep his options open. There is no sign that Cromwell loved Anne; her role in Wolsey's fall may have kept minister and queen from forming a close personal relationship. They had, however, worked together in successful collaboration, and they shared similar interests in promoting reformed religion. If time ripened circumstance Cromwell would serve his king first, but unless Henry unequivocally signalled his desire to be rid of his queen, Cromwell would leave him to determine his own domestic arrangements. When Cromwell ignored this lesson in 1540, it cost him his life, but now circumspection and pragmatism prevailed. Cromwell bided his time and continued to mask his private thoughts.

Then, slowly at first, the climate began to change. Storm warnings unfurled over the marriage. Henry was seen to pay attention to a young and beautiful lady at court, a doubly dangerous liaison. The new favourite reportedly sent a sympathetic message to Princess Mary which raised hopes that her situation might soon improve. Anne did what she could to remove her rival from court if not from Henry's affection. When direct confrontation failed, Anne used Lady Rochford, her sister-in-law, in an attempt to discredit the interloper. The plan

[13] *CSP Span.*, iv/2, 759–60.
[14] Ibid.

backfired; the plot was detected; the king ordered Lady Rochford to depart the court. Not until February 1535 did the Boleyns succeed in overthrowing the king's mistress. They substituted Margaret Shelton, Anne's first cousin, for the unidentified rival, thus resolving for the moment the political problem for faction if not the personal problem for Anne.

Additional strains began to surface. Anne publicly quarrelled with her uncle, the duke of Norfolk, who retired from the court in a fury after airing his grievances with his niece to any and all who would listen. In the countryside abuse of Anne persisted as a popular if sometimes dangerous pastime. Among the politically powerful, support for Catherine and Mary widened and strengthened. Willing to accept the present queen as the mother of royal sons, they saw no advantage in Anne as the mother of Elizabeth. Not only did Anne offend the religious sensibilities of many lords, they feared for the future should Henry die without a male heir. In that case, Elizabeth, a child, would come to the throne, and a regency dominated by Anne and her father presented a terrifying prospect. Therefore, the news in the autumn of 1535, that Henry had a new love, received a warm welcome from more than a few peers of the realm.

Irony attended the blossoming romance of Henry and Jane Seymour. Two years after the birth of Elizabeth, Anne was again pregnant; a son could follow, and Henry must have felt elation at the prospect. But on 10 September, while on progress through the south-western counties, Henry decided to stop for the night at Wolfhall in Wiltshire, the family seat of John Seymour. Seymour's daughter Jane, a former attendant to Catherine, captured the king's heart – so the story goes. In any case the French ambassador reported the liaison between Henry and Jane three weeks later. Anne could not have been happy about the new affair, but she had survived at least two of Henry's mistresses, and the prospect of a son offered a measure of comfort and reassurance. Anne could not yet have known that the delicate hold she retained would soon break.

Catherine's death on 8 January 1536 furnished the opening act to Anne's fall and execution. At first sight, the death of Catherine seemed a godsend to Anne and the Boleyns. Without a royal rival, Anne's followers might have been excused for believing that opposition would soon die out, and that Anne would eventually attract the popularity which had been Catherine's. Fisher and More were dead. The Royal Supremacy was the law of the realm. Disarray weakened the conservative faction. Without strong leadership to guide their path, and with no cause to pursue beyond the claims of Mary to a place in the succession, the collapse of factional opposition seemed the next logical development; joy at Catherine's death seemed the most logical emotional response. Then, the joker fell out of the pack.

Quickly the Boleyns came to understand the negative implications of Catherine's death. As long as she lived, the former queen limited Henry's domestic alternatives. Even Henry could not afford the luxury of two ex-wives, each a queen, each with offspring. The king could stay married to Anne, or he could divorce her and take back Catherine. If he could win her he could have Jane Seymour as a mistress, but not as his wife. Catherine dead, however, multiplied the possibilities both for the king and for enemies of the Boleyn faction. Henry could now find an excuse to declare his marriage to Anne invalid, and he could then take Jane as his wife and queen. Anne's rule and the strength of her faction would be broken. Conservatives allied with the Seymours would bring England back to the Roman communion. Reform with all it portended would become but a memory. The hopes of both factions seemed suspended by slender uterine threads. In Anne's pregnancy lay her future, and perhaps, as well, the future of reform in England.

On 29 January 1536, in the fourth month of her pregnancy, Anne miscarried of a boy. For all practical purposes this finished her. Henry showed no sympathy, despite Anne's claims that fear for Henry's safety after his fall from a horse had caused her to lose the baby.[15] The king viewed the loss as God's condemnation of his marriage. His love for Jane Seymour ran hot. He treated Anne with marked and observed coldness. Following her confinement, Anne, accustomed to being always with the king, remained at Greenwich. Cromwell, sensing the trend, began to distance himself, breaking the factional partnership. His testing time had arrived! If he could manage events to the satisfaction of the king, Cromwell's immediate future would be assured. If he failed, however, Wolsey's fate might be his own. The similarities in their circumstances could not have escaped Cromwell as he struggled to position himself for the coming political crisis. Filled with anticipation tinged with a measure of fear, he took charge, as he had once before, of the process by which Henry would be relieved of another unwanted wife.

Anne, however, presented problems that went much deeper than a divorce on grounds of domestic discord. Now that Henry had withdrawn support, Anne no longer possessed political credibility. Her fall, then, threatened to bring down the reform faction too. Many of her opponents saw her departure as the first step towards reconciliation with Rome and the waning of Cromwell's authority. After all, he had been closely associated with the queen. As Anne went, so Cromwell might follow. To survive, Cromwell had to tread surefootedly through treacherous political terrain.

Too much weight has been given to Thomas Cromwell's participation in the fall and execution of Anne Boleyn. It would be well to remember that Anne was Henry's wife and queen, and that the king had both an interest in his own marriage and the power to make his choices manifest. Historians go too far who would use factional analysis to explain Anne Boleyn's fall. The evidence will not bear out their preference. Ives and Starkey are the main proponents of a factional approach to Anne's fall, citing each other to support arguments which assume the political advantages to Cromwell as sufficient cause for his pursuit of the queen to the death. Since he would gain from Anne's departure, they conclude, he must have been personally responsible for initiating the plot which brought her down.[16]

It is true that Cromwell had much to gain politically from Anne's fall – sole control of faction and exclusive position as Henry's principal minister. It is also true that Anne alive represented great danger to Cromwell. Divorce would remove Anne from the court. Her father and brother would suffer a sharp

---

[15] For the broader implications of Anne's miscarriage see Retha M. Warnicke, 'Sexual heresy at the court of Henry VIII', *Historical Journal*, xxx (1987), 247–68.

[16] Ives, *Anne Boleyn*, 335–83; idem. 'Faction at the court of Henry VIII', 169–88; Starkey, 'From feud to faction', 16–22.

decline in political status, and much applause might attend the retreat of the Boleyns, widely regarded as arrogant usurpers of place and privilege. The very act, however, of casting out Anne and her family could cause unimaginable strife at the moment when Cromwell needed the consolidated resources and the energy of a united faction to give substance to his policy for the radical reshaping of the English Church and commonwealth. With Anne alive, Cromwell could never be sure of the undivided loyalty of men whose careers had been nurtured and promoted by the Boleyns. Unless he broke apart the family nexus of faction, reformers would continue to look to the Boleyns as a possible alternative to his own leadership. His men, after all, were also her men. Anne, by her mere survival, could become a dangerous rival, a centre around which political intrigue might cluster and grow.

It has been argued then, that Cromwell's only safe course, the rational alternative, required Anne's death. If George Boleyn could be eliminated too, so much the better. And if at the same time Cromwell could use the occasion to destroy additional centres of potential opposition, what more could be hoped for? Hindsight helps to develop this pattern of argument. Henry Norris and Francis Weston, along with George Boleyn, held influential positions in the privy chamber. Their execution removed a source of institutional competition that had plagued both Wolsey and Cromwell. No further challenge emanated from the privy chamber during the balance of Cromwell's ministry.[17]

Other victims of Cromwell's attack, however, cannot as easily be seen in terms of a purely political explanation. William Brereton, for example, carried little political weight, and it requires some imagination to regard his death as part of a Cromwellian scheme to strike at the power of the duke of Norfolk by executing Brereton, who served as deputy to the duke of Richmond.[18] Yet the case has been advanced that Brereton held the key to set down 'Norfolk's pretensions'. The duke had been encouraging Henry's bastard son 'to flex his muscles', especially in his marcher lordships. Parliament, at Cromwell's urging, had just passed a statute abolishing marcher liberties, but, it is claimed, Norfolk would not be likely to allow independence to pass away without a fight. If Brereton was destroyed, more 'reliable' men could be appointed to his offices to facilitate implementation of the statute. Intimidated, Norfolk would accede to Cromwellian policy without further demur.[19]

Clearly, some historians exhibit Machiavellian instincts much stronger than those which, they claim, moved Cromwell. If his vision toward potential political threats could project so deeply as to bring men such as Brereton to their deaths, what prevented Cromwell from seeing the more obvious dangers posed by Gardiner, Norfolk, Tunstall, and a host of other factional opponents determined to overthrow his ministry with its radical religious programme? London Bridge would have rained conservative heads if *Realpolitik* prevailed.

Unless we put Henry back into the foreground of the picture our efforts to

[17] For Starkey's fullest discussion in print of the privy chamber see his 'Representation through intimacy', in Ione Lewis (ed.), *Symbols and Sentiments*, London 1977, 187–224. Cf. idem. 'The King's Privy Chamber, 1485–1547', unpublished PhD diss., Cambridge 1973.
[18] Ives, 'Faction at the court of Henry VIII', 18.
[19] Ibid.

understand the reasons behind the selection of the victims arrested with Anne and the viciousness of the whole process can only be frustrated. If on the other hand, we recognise Henry as the moving force and a principal planner of Anne's fall, the elements of the tragedy take on purposeful perspective.[20] There well may have been political ramifications to the scenario. Anne did threaten Cromwell's leadership of the reform faction, and the permanent separation of Anne from the king did him no harm at all. It is also possible to speculate on the basis of our own sense of friendship that Cromwell was not sorry to see Anne dead for personal reasons. He treated her as the Boleyns had dealt with Cardinal Wolsey, Cromwell's patron, mentor, and friend. Unmerciful herself, Anne could expect little in return, but it seems likely that Cromwell acted as a royal instrument, not as an independent agent in the events leading up to Anne's execution.

The others who went to their deaths with the queen were George Boleyn, Henry Norris, Francis Weston, William Brereton, and Mark Smeaton. Thomas Wyatt and Richard Page were also arrested and spent time in custody, but escaped with their lives. The original list of suspects probably came from Henry, since Cromwell laboured long and hard to secure the release of Wyatt, a longtime friend, and Page, who had close connections with the favoured Russells and Fitzwilliams. If Cromwell had had power to order the arrests, he would not have arrested Wyatt and Page unless he intended to have them tried with the others.

Once the decision had been made, Cromwell struck with devastating speed and accuracy. Charges of adultery and incest, believable or not, alienated Anne and those accused with her from any potential group of defenders in the realm. Cromwell used Mark Smeaton against Anne as he had used Richard Rich against Thomas More – to put the 'evidence' before the responsible tribunal – and he brought those closest to her at court to the same bar as defendants, rather than allowing them to appear as witnesses for the defence. A wide net was cast, pulling in those men who participated with Anne in the social swirl of court life, those who played the games of courtly love and kept the tongues of gossips wagging. What the victims had in common, however, was a lack of solid political support. No one came forward to dispute the patently false and salacious charges brought against Norris, Weston, Brereton, George Boleyn, and Smeaton.

Anne's friends also melted away as the charges against her became known. Only Thomas Cranmer, who owed so much to the Boleyns, stepped forward to defend her. Cromwell, understanding Cranmer's sympathies, had kept the archbishop out of the plot and away from the court. Ordered by the king to remain at his palace at Lambeth, Cranmer heard only rumours. On 3 May, therefore, he began a letter to the king, 'in such perplexity that my mind is clean amazed'.

---

[20] Warnicke's argument about Anne's deformed foetus, if correct, puts Henry in the centre of the process. It adds evidence to the analytical conclusion that restores Henry to the role of principal player in his own domestic life, a position he occupied in the dissolution of his first marriage. It also returns a measure of consistency to our understanding of Cromwell as a man who rarely if ever attacked his factional enemies with violence. See Warnicke, 'Sexual heresy', esp. pp. 255–61.

An honest man, if politically isolated from events, Cranmer could not reconcile what be believed to be two contradictory truths. The king would not lie, and so Anne must be guilty; but Cranmer also believed Anne to be innocent of crimes of incest and adultery,

> for I never had better opinion in woman, than I had in her; which maketh me to think, that she should not be culpable. And again, I think your highness would not have gone so far, except she had surely been culpable. Now I think that your grace best knoweth, that next unto your grace I was most bound unto her of all creatures living. Wherefore I most humbly beseech your grace to suffer me in that, which both God's law, nature, and also her kindness, bindeth me unto; that is, that I may with your grace's favour wish and pray for her, that she may declare herself unculpable and innocent.[21]

Anne, of course, needed more than a character witness, but even Cranmer had all but conceded her cause. If he could not help to salvage Anne, perhaps he could help to ensure the survival of reform. Cranmer recognised danger in the connections between Anne's position and the fate of reformed religion in England. He claimed, in fact, to have 'loved her not a little for the love I judged her to bear towards God and his gospel'. Unequivocally, Cranmer stated his position, placing Anne, if guilty, beyond the pale of the reform faction:

> So, if she be proved culpable, there is not one that loveth God and his gospel that ever will favour her, but must hate her above all other; and the more they favour the gospel, the more they will hate her: for then there was never creature in our time that so much slandered the gospel; and God hath sent her this punishment, for that she feignedly hath professed the gospel in her mouth, and not in her heart and deed.

Significantly Cranmer asked Henry in his conclusion to continue his support of reform, 'forasmuch as your grace's favour to the gospel was not led by affection unto her, but by zeal unto the truth'.[22]

Thus Cranmer established the order of his concerns. His commitment to reform far outweighed his personal attachment to Anne and George Boleyn. The strongest Boleyn ally had cast his lot with Cromwell and the reform faction. The vicegerent had satisfied the king's purpose without creating significant opposition in the ranks of reformers. The Boleyns fell without interrupting Cromwell's leadership of the reform faction. He weakened the conservative faction by destroying the focal point of their discontent. With Anne removed from the frame, conservatives took much time to regroup, time which Cromwell used effectively. Most importantly, Cromwell gave the king what he wanted most, a new wife and the prospect of sons to follow. All this he accomplished without making new enemies and without disrupting the

---

[21] *Cranmers Letters*, 324.
[22] Ibid.

business of reform which proceeded almost as though Anne Boleyn had never lived or died.

Anne's execution in May 1536 left Cromwell without serious rival in either faction or government. Until the conflict over Calais[23] began to limit the range of the minister's authority, he firmly exercised ascendancy over ecclesiastical policy and the programme for its enforcement. Deliberately, Cromwell set about to extend the Royal Supremacy in order to achieve the factional goal of reshaping the English Church and commonwealth. Recognising that the introduction and administration of fundamental reform without the coercive power of a professional army or paid bureaucracy demanded the most careful practice of the arts of political persuasion, Cromwell counted on patronage to build consensus for his ecclesiastical policy.

The Boleyn faction, under the dual leadership of Anne and Cromwell, had effectively used its patronage to bring key men into the episcopacy, and Cromwell continued the practice of furnishing bishoprics to important adherents. Other than this monopoly of episcopal presentations, however, Cromwell found himself handicapped in his attempts at patronage. Ecclesiastical England encompassed more than 8,000 parishes. Cromwell could appoint to few of these livings and had no foreknowledge of vacancies. The diverse interests of individuals and groups produced conflicts and delays. Each act of patronage could become a major test of Cromwell's patience and determination.

The religious orders dominated parochial patronage. In the diocese of Lincoln, for example, between 1495 and 1520 heads of monasteries presented to 1,331 of the 2,760 parochial vacancies. The crown, during the same period, granted Lincoln churches to 123 priests, while the two bishops had only eighty-five livings to confer. No other group or individual played a significant patronage role. Advowsons were widely dispersed among the laity, and were subject to the unpredictable incidence of vacancy.[24]

Between January 1535 and July 1540 the crown made 158 presentations by letters-patent to benefices in England and Wales.[25] This number, an average of thirty per year, was supplemented by advowsons executed by the crown without the use of letters-patent. Thus, in Hereford during the same five years, the crown made two presentations which appear on the patent roll and nine others recorded only in the episcopal register.[26] The general absence of records which identify patrons of ecclesiastical benefices makes impossible an accurate estimate of the number of crown livings. Certainly, the total was small. In the years of Cromwell's vicegerency, the crown presented to twenty benefices in Lincoln diocese, an average of less that four per year, a figure which corresponds to that

---

[23] See below, ch. vii.

[24] Margaret Bowker, *The Secular Clergy in the Diocese of Lincoln, 1495–1520*, Cambridge 1968, 67.

[25] Geographical breakdown by diocese: Bath and Wells 5; Canterbury 6; Chichester 2; Coventry and Lichfield 13; Ely 1; Exeter 13; Hereford 2; Lincoln 27 (includes 7 Windsor prebends); London 21; Norwich 8; Rochester 1; Salisbury 12; Winchester 3; Worcester 8; York 13; Welsh Dioceses 10; Unidentifiable 15. Total 158.

[26] *Registrum Caroli Bothe, Episcopi Herefordensis, 1516–35*, ed. A. T. Bannister, London 1921, 377–81, 384–5.

of five per year compiled from the Lincoln episcopal registers between 1495 and 1520.[27]

Rights of presentation enjoyed by the crown through outright ownership of the advowson were augmented by others that came to the king by virtue of prerogative or by gift. The parish church of Whitforde was at the king's disposal in January 1536 because the see of St Asaph[28] was vacant, and the crown had the right to appoint to vacancies in the absence of the bishop. Henry Moxon, incumbent of the parish church of Saresden, in the diocese of Lincoln was attainted, and his benefice passed to the crown with his other property.[29] When the suppression of the monastery of Stanlegh, Wiltshire, temporarily vested its advowsons in the crown, the king presented his nominee to the parish church of Rye.[30] Richard Trobyfylde gave the advowson of the parish church of East-alington in the diocese of Exeter to the king *hac vice*, probably to obtain royal good will in some other matter.[31] The parish church of Hirstmonceux, in the diocese of Chichester, came to the king through the minority of Thomas Fynes.[32]

From haphazard sources such as these emerged the fibres from which Cromwell fashioned the threads of patronage. By letters-patent, during his vicegerency, he presented to thirteen suffragan bishoprics, twenty-three canonries, six hospitals, fifty-nine livings described as parish churches, twelve rectories, nine vicarages, ten chapels, six chantries, and twenty miscellaneous benefices which are singular or impossible to identify.

These livings greatly varied in value. The parish churches, rectories, vicarages, and prebends ranged in worth from about £5 to about £55 with an average near £25. The more valuable benefices – colleges, hospitals, and deaneries – awaited men particularly useful to reform faction interests. The college of Corpus Christi, London, worth £79 17s 10d, was held first by Thomas Starkey, then by William Latimer.[33] Starkey's work on behalf of reform is well-known.[34] Latimer served as Anne's chaplain. John Incent, a competent and loyal ecclesiastical administrator, succeeded Richard Pace as dean of St Paul's with a stipend of £210 12s 1d.[35] Thomas Legh, one of the principal monastic visitors, secured the hospital of Burton Lazars, Lincoln, worth £265 10s ½d.[36] The wealthiest non-episcopal benefice in Cromwell's gift, Thomas Beckett's hospital in Southwark, went to Thomas Thirleby who later advanced to the bishoprics, first of Norwich, then Ely, in the reign of Edward VI.[37]

---

[27] Bowker, *Diocese of Lincoln*, 67.
[28] *LP* x. 80 (g. 18).
[29] Ibid. xiv/1. 534 (g. 19).
[30] Ibid. 533 (g. 12).
[31] Ibid. x. 326 (g. 16).
[32] Ibid. viii. 239 (g. 23).
[33] *VE* i. 387.
[34] For Starkey's career and writings and the environment in which he worked see J. K. McConica, *English Humanists and Reformation Politics*, Oxford 1965; W. G. Zeeveld, *Foundations of Tudor Policy*, Cambridge, Mass. 1948; Thomas Mayer, *Thomas Starkey and the Commonweal*, Cambridge 1989.
[35] *VE* i. 363.
[36] Ibid. iv. 152–3.
[37] Ibid. ii. 61.

Under law Cromwell shared patronage of crown livings with Lord Chancellor Thomas Audley.[38] He had a statutory right to present to all benefices valued under £20. The Boleyns had brought Audley to the Woolsack in 1532 to succeed More, and his appointment emphasised the decline of the office. A lawyer and judge, Audley had little to recommend him as a major player. Subservience to Cromwell defined his tenure. He rarely concerned himself with the politics of patronage. But Audley could not be completely ignored. The chancellor could be a tough fighter when self or family interest stirred him to act. For example, he vigorously battled to get the deanery of Exeter for Thomas Brerewood,[39] because Brerewood had promised to provide a prebend for his kinsman.[40]

Cromwell's ability to present to livings formally assigned to the chancellor required him to maintain a harmonious relationship. Usually, Audley followed the secretary's lead in dispensing royal patronage, but Cromwell never developed the easy, informal relationship with Audley that he had with others. The chancellor might be manipulated and directed. He could not be ignored or bypassed, as some found out to their cost. John Hilsey, bishop of Rochester, discovered in Audley a fierce adversary. Hilsey's chancellor had obtained a benefice with an estimated value of £20 from Cromwell by royal grant. At the time of presentation, however, Audley learned that the actual value of the living was £15 8s. Properly claiming that the living lay within his gift, the lord chancellor intervened. He blocked Hilsey's suit and gave the benefice to the archbishop of Canterbury to dispense at his pleasure. 'And whereas', complained Hilsey, 'the said lord of Canterbury is content that my said chancellor shall have the said benefice, yet my lord chancellor will in no wise suffer my poor chaplain to enjoy the same neither at the king's hand nor at his hand.'[41]

Early in his ministry Cromwell himself experienced the frustration of counting on Audley's compliance without first asking for his consent. Cromwell had tried to institute a clerk to an unnamed crown benefice in Audley's gift. Feeling slighted, Audley asserted his patronage rights, forcing the embarrassed vicegerent to spend valuable time sorting out the mess. An angry Cromwell charged Audley with ingratitude for not allowing the original institution to stand. Audley replied with regret at Cromwell's sudden displeasure, particularly because the world had considered them to be friends, and now, 'ye set forth a demonstration to the contrary'. The accusation of 'ingratuity' hurt him most of all. The chancellor had believed that 'amongst friends that love sincerely, one friend may debate and defend his own commodity gently and honestly without loss of friendship'.[42]

On the substance of his conflict with Cromwell, Audley contended that

---

[38] For Audley's career and an evaluation of the lord chancellor's life see Stanford E. Lehmberg, 'Sir Thomas Audley: a soul as black as marble?', in A. J. Slavin (ed.), *Tudor Men and Institutions*, Baton Rouge 1972, 3–31.
[39] Brerewood eventually received the deanery: J. Le Neve, *Fasti Ecclesiae Anglicanae*, 12 vols, London 1962–7, ix. 5.
[40] BL, Cotton Titus B i, fos 384–5 (*LP* xii/1. 764).
[41] SP 1/100/117 (*LP* ix. 1153).
[42] BL, Cotton Titus B i, fos 365r–v (*LP* ix. 528).

although the benefice in question was his to dispense, he stood ever willing to accomplish the king's commandments and his vicegerent's requests. The chancellor asked only that he not be interrupted in the exercise of his office against his will. Audley well understood that his political future hinged on accepting his subordination to Cromwell. He recognised without rancour the significant decline of the office of Lord Chancellor in the new scheme of things: 'I have served his grace truly and his people indifferently. I meddle with as few things as ever did chancellor. I am not so changeable to the people as chancellors have been. I think never chancellor less set by, and yet I am right well content with the little meddlings that I have.'[43] Since he did not dispute the waning of his office, or his own diminished status, Audley stated that he could not understand the unkind words meted out by Cromwell. He had no thought to vie for power. He upheld royal policy and factional interest and desired only to be used in a friendly, honest fashion, reckoned to be worth a polite request.[44]

This interchange between lord chancellor and vicegerent casts light on Cromwell's predominance in patronage matters. Technically, benefices appropriated to the crown resided with the king or the lord chancellor, but Cromwell alone took charge of the distribution of royal patronage. He entered the office of vicegerent with control of crown livings as a foundation, and immediately set about to increase his limited supply of benefices. The need was great. Supplicants for benefices far outstripped vacancies. Cromwell's position as a patron marked him as the target for the aspirations of many clerks. The great mass of the secular clergy differed little from their medieval counterparts. They served their cures for better or worse, collected their fees, and quietly merged into the social landscape. Those with more ambition and the right connections could aspire to financial security and a measure of status. They occupied positions in the diocesan hierarchy or as chaplains to aristocratic magnates. But, when clerical tastes demanded the best from the ecclesiastical vineyard, Cromwell held the only key to the cellar.

Loyal servants looked to Cromwell for steady advancement and the augmentation of their ecclesiastical incomes. Often, these men, while engaged in the performance of their duties, kept at least one eye sharpened to opportunities for personal gain. Their employment by the crown placed them on the inside track with potential patrons eager to please, an advantage not ignored. And, if ambition ran up against an unwillingness to part with valuable benefices, Cromwell could be called upon to forward their suits.

Thomas Bedyll was one of the most self-serving and least attractive of Cromwell's servants. A generation older than most of his factional colleagues, Bedyll had enjoyed a long career. After proceeding BCL from New College, Oxford, in 1508, Bedyll became secretary to Archbishop Warham, a post he held until 1532. Praised by Warham for his 'approved fidelity and virtue', Bedyll entered royal service after the archbishop's death. As a counsel for the king, he took part in the interrogations of Fisher and More, and assisted in the visitations of the monasteries. Also clerk to the council from 1532, Bedyll

43 Ibid.
44 Ibid.

repeatedly surfaces in accounts of diverse examinations, state trials, and inspections. At all times, he carried out to the letter instructions from his superiors.[45]

A hard worker for the crown, Bedyll exerted equal or greater effort in promoting his own career. On learning of Edward Foxe's elevation to the bishopric of Hereford, Bedyll acted swiftly to win for himself some of the new bishop's abandoned benefices. He wrote to remind Cromwell of his devotion and service, complaining that his duties had increased his expenses, putting him at great charge. Many of the livings he held had been converted to pensions, and Bedyll wanted Cromwell's patronage. To facilitate the minister's work on his behalf, Bedyll appended to his letter a list of Foxe's livings, including the prebend of Osbaldwick in York, the hospital of St Nicholas in Salisbury, the archdeaconry of Leicester, and many other benefices of good value.[46]

'Sir the time is ever now during my life to do you pleasure with all that ever I have as ye shall prove it, at all times upon my truth.' Here Bedyll wanted Cromwell to help him to secure a valuable benefice in the gift of the archbishop of York. Bedyll did not doubt that Cromwell could obtain the benefice, but he feared that Edward Lee might stick at giving up a living reserved for one of his own chaplains. To prevent conflict and delay, Bedyll proposed if necessary to trade one of his London livings, worth £40 a year, for the preferment in York. 'This is the thing which I had rather have than any bishopric in England.' The suit failed, and although a pluralist on a grand scale, Bedyll died in 1537 with no living grander than that of the archdeaconry of London.[47]

Friendship with Cromwell, when combined with competent performance, gave clerks a telling advantage in their suits for advancement. Richard Layton, one of the principal monastic visitors, exemplified the hard-working, well-rewarded Cromwellian friend and factional adherent. Crown livings marked the growth of their relationship. Layton acquired the archdeaconry of Buckinghamshire in October 1534,[48] the rectory of Sedgefield, Durham[49] and the rectory of Brington, Northamptonshire in 1535.[50] In the same year he obtained clerkships in chancery[51] and the privy council.[52] Subsequently, he was collated to the rectory of Harrow-on-the-Hill in July 1537,[53] appointed to the prebend of Ulleskelf (York) in June 1539,[54] and capped his career in July 1539 with receipt of the deanery of York.[55]

Layton's frank, informal request for Cromwell's support in pursuit of a benefice shows the lengths to which men would go in their quests for ecclesias-

---

45 David Knowles, always judicious, has described Bedyll as 'one of the least attractive of Cromwell's minions': *The Religious Orders in England*, iii. 274.
46 *LP* ix. 24.
47 SP 1/92/189 (*LP* viii. 730).
48 *Ath. Cant.*, i. 535.
49 Ibid.
50 Ibid.
51 *LP* ix. 816.
52 Ibid. viii. 858.
53 Ibid. xii/2. 747.
54 Emden, *University of Oxford*, 346.
55 Ibid.

tical promotion. Layton had received a letter from Stoke College, Essex, obviously prearranged, which informed him that the master there, Robert Shorton, was in *articulo mortis*. The dean's health meant little to Layton. He wanted one of Shorton's Durham benefices. Bishop Tunstall had promised to grant it to Layton as a favour to Cromwell, 'at his great business that ye quit him of, whereas ye stuck unto him all other his friends foresaking him'.[56] Now Layton wanted Cromwell to write to Tunstall to harvest the undertaking. He did not distrust the bishop, but, Layton stated, Tunstall needed letters from the king and Cromwell for the benefice at the time it became vacant. Layton himself could not personally handle the matter. Monastic visitations kept him far from London. So he had commissioned a servant to obtain the requisite letters and to deliver them to Tunstall when Shorton's death seemed imminent.[57]

Layton then asked Cromwell to send Ralph Sadler to the king to prevent Henry from interfering in the business on behalf of some other candidate. One final contingency needed attention. Fearing that Shorton might be dead before the complicated transaction had been completed, Layton proposed an alternative course of action:

> I suppose the said Doctor Shorton, the dean of Stoke, will be departed before this letter ever unto you. If you do write for me unto my same lord, master Richard I trust will be my surety for the first-fruits till I am to London there to discharge him with other sureties, so that my servant that goeth may take possession for me, if ye make such a clause in your letter to my lord that ye be answered for the fruits.[58]

Because he enjoyed Cromwell's friendship, Layton had no need to advertise himself. He concentrated on technical details in the patronage process. Men away from the bright lights of court life had to struggle to gain Cromwell's attention and co-operation. William Turner, for example, wrote to Cromwell, frustrated because his work on behalf of royal interests had not received sufficient reward. He complained that Cromwell gave livings 'to them which his highness did never see and which never take pains or labour for his highness'. Unsure that his image was clear in Cromwell's memory, Turner rehearsed his career, citing his continuous effort in the service of reform. Lately allied with Edward Foxe, Turner claimed to have been active in favour of the divorce, 'without any profit or certainty of living'. Cromwell had, he stated, at their last meeting spoken comfortable words that 'the king's highness shall look better upon you within this twelvemonth'. Now Turner hoped that Cromwell would deliver on his promise, because he could expect no help from Foxe, his principal patron. Newly elected to the bishopric of Hereford, Foxe faced great expenses in furnishing and setting forth his episcopal dignity. Turner calculated that it would take six or seven years for the new bishop to be able to make

---

[56] SP 1/98/26r–v (*LP* ix. 632).
[57] Ibid.
[58] Ibid.

sufficient provision for his immediate servants. Thus, he had no choice but to put his whole trust for his well-being into Cromwell's hands.[59]

Crowds of hopeful suitors came forward, seizing the smallest opportunity to ask Cromwell to extend his blessings in their direction. Some relied on intangible connections or the force of their words to sponsor their claims to livings. The benefice of Poyning in the diocese of Chichester became vacant on the death of its incumbent, and the advowson in wardship passed to the crown. Anne Hilles asked for the living for her son, George, and she recited the several reasons why he should be preferred. Cromwell was George's godfather; the living would allow him the means to the increase of virtue and learning. She described herself as a widow dependent on Cromwell to 'vouchsafe this my rude letter in good part and to oblige the king's most gracious bill assigned for the said benefice to the use of my said child'.[60]

Richard Bulkley petitioned Cromwell on behalf of his brother. Dr Arthur Bulkley, chaplain to the duke of Suffolk, held a position in the Court of Arches. Now, with help from his brother, he sought livery in Cromwell's service with sufficient promotion for his support.[61] Other candidates needed Cromwell's help in obtaining benefices outside the vicegerent's gift. John Wilkinson, already vicar of Grantham, aspired to pluralism. He persuaded the rector of Manton to resign the living only to himself, probably in exchange for a pension. The dean of Lincoln, however, blocked his way. He held the advowson. In return for his promise to pray daily for Cromwell's heart's desires, Wilkinson asked the minister to write to the dean to cause him to permit the transaction.[62]

Patronage rights could often be quite confusing, and Cromwell rarely knew in advance what response his support for a clerk might produce. He nominated a priest named Lawe to the parish church of Stockport in the county of Chester and immediately received a complaint from the countess of Derby that a clerk bearing his letters had interfered with her right to present to the living. The countess stated that she had secured the advowson from the patron, Laurence Warren, 'for the use of my well-beloved chaplain, Thomas Bradshaw'. She claimed that Lawe had obtained a second advowson, and induced the incumbent to resign. He then, according to the countess, took Cromwell's letters and with them persuaded the bishop's officers to grant him institution and induction. To stop Lawe from putting her chaplain from his right, the countess intervened, demanding that no presentation be made until a commission could determine the lawful holder of the advowson.[63]

Cromwell's advancement of clerks to benefices triggered bitter conflicts as his nominees ran up against men and women reluctant to surrender their patronage. Cromwell asked William, Lord Sandys for the advowson of a benefice in his gift for a Mr Browne. Sandys flatly refused. He appointed his

59 SP 1/103/116r–v (LP x. 654).
60 SP 1/96/209 (LP ix. 406).
61 SP 1/126/35 (LP xii/2. 998).
62 SP 1/106/248 (LP xii/1. 628).
63 BL, Cotton Vespasian F xiii. fo. 168 (LP xi. 51).

own chaplain to the living. In reply to Cromwell's request, he not only declined to yield his right to present, he insisted that Cromwell drop his suit.[64]

Economically motivated applications for Cromwell's patronage and persistent disputes over rights of presentation strongly suggest that the attraction of benefices often had little to do with callings to serve spiritual needs. Each church office had a fixed monetary worth. Advowsons were, then, valuable as property. They could be used, as vacancies permitted, to furnish income for friends and relatives. They could be traded for political influence or financial advantage. Understandably, holders of advowsons struggled anxiously to protect their rights.

Cromwell asked Thomas Sparke for the advowson of the vicarage of Giggleswick in Yorkshire. Since he had recently appointed Sparke to a suffragan bishopric in the diocese of Durham, Cromwell could not have anticipated anything less than grateful compliance. Sparke did try to co-operate. He obviously wanted to encourage his patron's continued favour, but Sparke could not completely abandon his financial interest in the vicarage. He granted Cromwell the next presentation to Giggleswick, but begged to retain the rights to the advowson held in perpetuity. Sparke even offered to pay the incumbent £10 or twenty marks for his good will, and thus he prayed Cromwell to be content.[65]

The attraction of benefices appreciated in the estimation of careerist clerks when there was no residence requirement. The regular income, even after provision of an adequate deputy, offered much to ambitious clerks. Time and money from the non-resident living sponsored a search for more lucrative places at court, in the household of a noble family, or within the diocesan administrative establishment. Elizabeth Darrell asked Cromwell for his help in securing a suitable position for her son, Richard. Otherwise, he would be forced to reside on his benefice.[66]

Inevitably, offers of rewards accompanied appeals for patronage. Men who doubted their own qualifications or the strength of their political connections fortified their suits with promises of cash payment. Robert Androys wrote to Cromwell, 'beseeching your mastership to remember the bishopric of St David's and my promise shall be performed – viz. 500 marks'.[67] Fulke Salisbury, dean of St Asaph, coveted the diocese's vacant bishopric. Doubtful whether his service to Henry VII would be remembered, he proposed to surrender to Cromwell the deanery worth 100 marks if elevated to the see of St Asaph valued at 250 marks. Caught up in his financial calculations, Salisbury compared for Cromwell the various amounts the exchange would yield and promoted the profits which would result from his advancement.[68]

Neither Androys nor Salisbury succeeded in their efforts to bribe Cromwell. The value of ecclesiastical patronage could not be counted in coin. Potential

---

[64] SP 1/93/173r–v (LP viii. 924). Sandys later surfaced in Calais as a member of the group which opposed initiatives of Cromwell and Cranmer to reform the Pale.

[65] SP 1/106/198 (LP xi. 877).

[66] SP 1/143/1 (LP xiv/1. 14).

[67] LP x. 378.

[68] SP 1/94/15 (LP viii. 1015).

service to faction and to the state mattered more. Cromwell actively sought to recruit clerks committed to reform, and he gained a reputation as a patron of men of talent. His willingness to overlook if not to forget recent political enmity created a climate which allowed him to utilise the intellectual capacities of diverse individuals formerly associated with conservative factionalism.

Thomas Elyot was one who grasped Cromwell's extended hand.[69] Elyot came to court to work on his *Dictionary*, and at Cromwell's urging, the king granted him access to the royal library and the royal printer. The *Dictionary* was published by Berthelet in 1538. Elyot knew that Cromwell had opened the pathway to patronage and asked him 'to continue my good lord in augmenting the king's good estimate of me'.[70] He lived with the perpetual fear that his past association with More would cause Cromwell to withdraw his favour. In a letter to Cromwell Elyot passionately defended his reforming zeal. He hoped

that the king and you might see the most secret thoughts of my heart, surely ye should then perceive that, the order of charity saved, I have as much detestation as any man living all vain superstitions, superfluous ceremonies, 'slanderous' jugglings, counterfeit miracles, arrogant usurpations of men called spiritual, and masking religions, and all other 'abusions' of Christ's holy doctrine and laws.

Elyot positioned himself in favour of 'the king's godly proceeding to due reformation'. He begged Cromwell, 'now to lay apart the remembrance of the amity between me and Sir Thomas More . . . considering that I was never so much addict unto him as I was unto truth and fidelity towards my sovereign lord'.[71] Elyot needed reassurance. He also wanted a grant of land. Holding no living from the crown, Elyot pleaded indigence and promised in return for Cromwell's help in moving the king, continuous service and payment of first-fruits.[72]

Cromwell's short political memory and lack of vindictiveness, so costly in the long-run, helped him in the early days of his ministry. Demanding only acceptance of the Supremacy, Cromwell brought a host of learned men to the reform faction. He directed a massive campaign to convince the nation to accept Henry VIII's new order. The capable committee of Cromwellian clients included Elyot, Thomas Starkey, Richard Moryson, Richard Taverner, Leonard Cox, Thomas Paynell, John Rastell, Stephen Vaughan, Robert Wakefield, William Marshall, Thomas Swynnerton, Richard Sampson, Edward Foxe, and David Clapham.[73]

[69] Elyot's political relationships are discussed in Alistair Fox, 'Sir Thomas Elyot and the humanist dilemma', in Fox and Guy, *Reassessing the Henrician Age*, 52–73. See also S. E. Lehmberg, *Sir Thomas Elyot, Tudor Humanist*, Austin, Texas 1960.
[70] Thomas Wright, *Three Chapters of Letters Relating to the Suppression of the Monasteries*, London 1843, 140.
[71] Ibid. 141.
[72] Ibid. 142.
[73] This aspect of Cromwellian patronage has been extensively developed in a host of books. Among the best are the following: Zeeveld, *Tudor Policy*, McConica, *English Humanists*; Whitney R. D. Jones, *The Tudor Commonwealth, 1529–1559*, London 1970; Fritz Caspari, *Humanism and the Social Order in Tudor England*, Chicago 1954; Lehmberg, *Sir Thomas Elyot*;

Cromwell also patronised less gifted men of ideas. Unsolicited suggestions abounded. The Reformation inherent in the uprooting of Roman jurisdiction inspired a multitude of dreams and schemes. Cromwell recognised and encouraged popular enthusiasm for reform. Although private suggestions from unconnected individuals made no visible impact on policy, Cromwell welcomed their efforts, seeing, perhaps, in men like John Parkyns future citizens of the English commonwealth.

Parkyns presented Cromwell with a plan for the reorganisation of the universities, bishoprics, abbeys, priories, almshouses, and parishes – no mean feat. He wrote to Cromwell from jail. Late in 1536 he had charged two abbots with treason, but the king's commissioners treated him as the guilty party. Appealing to Cromwell for his release, Parkyns offered proof of his allegiance to reform. He furnished a vast array of proposals for the improvement of the commonwealth, most of which envisaged the increase of royal wealth and power.[74] The master of every college in Oxford or Cambridge would be replaced by a qualified non-cleric appointed by the king to serve at his pleasure. The fellows and scholars would also selected by the crown and, corporately, the universities would be responsible for the religious well-being of the surrounding territory.[75]

Turning to the dioceses, Parkyns thought it well that the lands of the bishoprics should be divided among the king's 'true subjects'. Fixed annuities would supplement episcopal spiritualities. Besides first-fruits and tenths, the king should have all unnecessary plate, jewels, and money.[76] Abbots and priors would also exchange their lands for a fixed stipend, and would be responsible for the goods of their houses. They were to live in cloisters with their brethren, hearing each Sunday a sermon to teach the religious their duties to the king. Again, all moveable monastic wealth along with first-fruits would go to the king. Parkyns than pushed his general scheme through all levels of the ecclesiastical hierarchy, compensating the lower clergy for their pains by allowing them to keep wives.[77]

Cromwell did not adopt Parkyn's radical proposals, but he found useful the contribution to the anticlerical mood. When Parkyns cried, 'Do not cast me away in my old age, do not desert me now when my enemies have conspired to lay snares for me', the minister responded and secured his release from prison.[78] Cromwell's cultivation of the 'common man' in his casual extension of aid to Parkyns continued to produce fruit long after the minister's appetite had been

---

G. R. Elton, *Reform and Renewal: Thomas Cromwell and the commonweal*, Cambridge 1973; and Thomas Mayer, 'Faction and ideology: Thomas Starkey's Dialogue', *Historical Journal*, xxviii (1985), 1–25. All work touching writers previously classified as humanists must now be considered in the light of Alistair Fox's contributions, particularly his 'Facts and fallacies', 9–33. See also Mayer, *Starkey*, 200–46.

[74] SP 1/115/95–102 (*LP* xii/1. 261(1)). For the full story of John Parkyns, 'The Fool of Oxford', see G. R. Elton, *Star Chamber Stories*, 2nd edn, London 1974, 19–51.

[75] SP 1/115/95–102 (*LP* xii/1. 261(2)).

[76] Ibid.

[77] Ibid. (*LP* xii/1. 263).

[78] Ibid.

satisfied. Parkyns showed up uninvited in London with a long written account of his recent travails. He asked that Cromwell obtain the freedom of his servant still imprisoned in Oxford.[79] For himself he desired employment. Cromwell allowed Parkyns to come to court and willed him to be content with his present life. His offer of £100 for the mastership of Savoy went unnoticed and Parkyns never appears again in the historical record.[80]

A serious point is illustrated by the brief relationship between John Parkyns and Thomas Cromwell. Committed to reform himself, and heartened by popular demands for change, Cromwell exerted the full range of his resources on behalf of ecclesiastical reform. He skillfully used his patronage to extend policy to the dioceses and parishes, where, with his help, dedicated reformers fought equally dedicated conservatives for dominance over local ecclesiastical institutions and the power to determine the ideological direction of the Church of England.

Statute provided the direction for the minister's first step. Expansion of his ecclesiastical patronage depended upon early knowledge of vacancies. The act drafted by Cromwell which transferred payment of first-fruits and tenths from the pope to the king contained a provision for each bishop to forward the name and value of every church or other spiritual promotion vacated after 1 January 1535, with the name of the inductee. In addition, the statute prohibited collations to benefices until first-fruits were paid or agreement had been reached on a method of payment. Cromwell established commissions in each diocese to oversee the process.[81] Ostensibly designed as a straightforward auditing procedure, the statute created the institutional means to alert Cromwell to opportunities to increase his control over appointments to ecclesiastical livings.

The deaths of faction members also expanded Cromwell's patronage assets. He carefully attended these occasions, grimly gathering up the benefices which passed from his servants with their final breaths. Capable men stood waiting to serve the king and the cause of reform, and Cromwell could not afford to neglect their careers. In 1537 Thomas Bedyll died in possession of his several livings, and Cromwell immediately set about to collect them for his supporters. He wrote to Archbishop Lee to secure the next presentation to the prebend and canonry of Massham in the cathedral church of York. Lee sent the collation with a glass window, merely hoping that the king would bestow it on a resident clerk, 'for no church in England hath more need of residentiaries'.[82] Equally tractable, Bishop John Clerk of Bath and Wells sent the collation of Bedyll's prebend to Cromwell, 'with a blank for his name that shall have it'.[83] Not all requests proceeded as smoothly. Continuing in pursuit of Bedyll's preferments, Cromwell wrote to Sir William Kyngston of Wanstead, Essex for the advowson of the living formerly held by Bedyll. But Kyngston had given it to the bishop of Exeter and John Veysey had granted it to 'one master

[79] Ibid. (*LP* xii/1. 264).
[80] Ibid. (*LP* xii/1. 270).
[81] *Stat. Realm*, iii. 493; *LP* viii. 284.
[82] SP 1/124/211 (*LP* xii/2. 679).
[83] SP 1/124/216 (*LP* xii/2. 683).

Rowsewell'. Anxious to please Cromwell, Kyngston promised to get the advowson back for the minister's use.[84]

The death of another servant, Dr Nicholas Wolman, at about the same time spurred Cromwell to ask John Stokesley for the right to present to the prebend of Islington, vacated by Wolman's death. The vicegerent might have known that dealing with the bishop of London would not be easy. Stokesley was by now no friend to reform. The bishop claimed that Wolman had never held the St Paul's canonry of Islington, but rather had tenure in the cathedral as prebendary of Finsbury. Stokesley said that he had already granted Finsbury to one who had paid first-fruits and taken possession, 'so that it is not in my power now to accomplish the said desire of the king's majesty if it were for Finsbury, though your lordship wrote for Islington'.[85] If Cromwell threw up his hands in frustration at this point we now know why. The records from the Court of First-Fruits show no collation to Finsbury. They do reveal that the prebend of Islington, valued at £10 7s 7d had been granted to John Spendlove, presumably by Stokesley, whose registrar, Matthew Greston, stood as surety for the nominee.[86] Then Stokesley compounded the confusion. Afraid of having offended Cromwell, he sent in the collation of Islington, 'which by chance is now void'. Cromwell could present whom he chose, but Stokesley reminded the minister that he had recently given up to the crown the prebends of Hadham and Fulham. Now he had not a single prebend for his own chaplains, 'whereby I am and of liklihood ever shall be destitute of learned men'.[87]

His efforts to recycle preferments to the benefit of faction members demonstrate Cromwell's resolution to utilise patronage to facilitate ecclesiastical policy. Cromwell looked in every direction for opportunities to augment his storehouse of livings, and he found a rich source in the doomed monastic establishment. Priors and abbots trying to stave off dissolution yielded a number of advowsons, and with minimal effort Cromwell collected a valuable bounty. Obtaining livings from bishops, however, required a much more intensive approach. While the religious orders, considered corporately, were the greatest patrons of church livings, in any single diocese the bishop often held this distinction. They had at their disposal a variety of ecclesiastical positions, some de pleno jure, some by lapse, and some through the judicious application of political pressure.[88] Bent upon tapping into this rich vein of patronage, Cromwell also realised that taking benefices from conservative prelates would benefit the reform faction in numerous ways.

Archbishop Cranmer contributed much to Cromwell's awareness of the interdependence between the careful exercise of patronage and the advancement of ecclesiastical reform. With many preferments in his own gift, and the continuous clamour from friends, servants, and hosts of other suitors, Cranmer rarely consented to satisfy those without merit. In May 1533 he even turned

84 SP 1/124/241–2 (LP xii/2. 706–707).
85 SP 1/124/254 (LP xii/2. 720).
86 E 334/1/6v.
87 SP 1/124/254 (LP xii/2. 720).
88 The traditional sources of crown patronage are mentioned in Peter Heath, The English Parish Clergy on the Eve of the Reformation, London 1969, 301.

down a Cromwellian nominee he felt to be unsuitable for the office of prior of St Gregory's, Canterbury. The archbishop used the occasion to instruct Cromwell on the pitfalls and responsibilities faced by a patron: 'Ye do know what ambition and desire for promotion is in men of the Church, and what indirect means they do use and have used to obtain their purpose; which their unreasonable desires and appetites I do trust that you will be more ready to oppress and extinguish, then to favour or further the same.'[89]

Tested in the same crucible during the divorce crisis, Cromwell and Cranmer had become friends. There must have been a period of tension attending Anne's fall and Cromwell's elevation to ecclesiastical pre-eminence. Their correspondence, however, exhibits friendship and intimacy growing side by side with close professional collaboration and shared factional commitment. Cranmer sent Cromwell numerous letters touching on patronage issues. As benefices became vacant, Cranmer recommended clerks to fill them. More often than not, Cromwell followed Cranmer's advice to institute men of good learning, hardened by experience in reformation politics, capable of contributing to the process and defence of reform.

Cranmer worked particularly hard to find places for his chaplains, and he expected Cromwell's help. He asked Cromwell to present one chaplain, Edmund Campion, to the Somerset parish of Shepton Mallet, worth £26 yearly. Since Campion had been born in that very parish, Cranmer argued that beyond his value as a preacher his chaplain would also help the judgments of his kinsmen and friends.[90] For another chaplain, Dr Barber, the archbishop persuaded Thomas Cave, Cromwell's servant, to vacate his prebend at Oxford University. Seeking the minister's approval for the transaction, Cranmer noted that Barber's qualities and learning, as Cromwell knew, were worthy of recognition.[91]

At all times Cranmer displayed a sophisticated appreciation of the need to establish reform-minded clerks in key sections of the realm. Soon after his own consecration, he argued for Nicholas Heath's institution to the deanery of South Malling, citing the need to plant friends in those parts of the country untouched by reform.[92] The archbishop recognised that important factional interests depended on defeating conservative bishops in patronage conflicts. When the benefice of Sutton Magna, Essex became vacant, Cranmer supported John Gylderde of Rayleigh, Essex, 'a man (as I am credibly informed) both for his literature, good judgment, and honest conversation worthy of commendation and preferment'. John Stokesley, bishop of London, however, instituted Henry Payne, a former Observant friar, whom Cranmer believed 'neither to be of good learning or judgment, but a seditious person'. Payne died soon afterwards in Marshalsea Prison. Before Stokesley could promote another Observant named Roche, Cranmer asked Cromwell to write to the bishop, ordering him to induct Gylderde without further interruption: 'And in thus doing your

[89] *Cranmer's Letters*, 241.
[90] Ibid. 385.
[91] Ibid. 386.
[92] Ibid. 399.

lordship shall do much for the advancement of God's word, which I think is but easily set forward in Essex.'[93]

Cromwell rarely quarrelled with Cranmer or other reforming bishops about patronage, and he often helped to expedite specific presentations. At his election to Worcester, Bishop Hugh Latimer obtained advowsons of two benefices by the deprivation of Silvester Darius.[94] He intended to institute his chancellor, Thomas Bagard and his chaplain, Ralph Bradford. Frustrated by the length of time it was taking, Latimer turned to Cromwell to facilitate the process. In this fashion Cromwell strengthened factional bonds.

The close co-operation between Cromwell and his episcopal allies is underlined by the single recorded instance when the minister's request for a benefice met resistance. On the king's behalf he had asked Nicholas Shaxton, bishop of Salisbury for the advowson of Horton. Shaxton replied that the advowson had already been granted, but something in his answer must have struck a nerve. The vicegerent warned Shaxton of the king's displeasure at having his will denied and issued a clear ultimatum which Shaxton could not dodge:

> Whereas ye write that unless I will upon the receipt of your letters send him the advowson of Horton, etc, his grace will not only dispose that all other prebends and benefices that might be in my gift by his supreme authority that other may learn to put a difference betwixt his highness earnest request and their own fantasies, but repute me a person most unkind toward him.[95]

Accepting these 'heavy words of a prince towards his obedient and loving subject', Shaxton surrendered the advowson.

Cromwell's sharp exchange with Shaxton constituted an incident. His attempt to control or at least to guide the patronage of the conservative bishops went to the heart of policy, an arterial link with his reform programme. The minister's practice suggests that his interference in the exercise of rights of episcopal patronage had a dual purpose. He needed livings for factional adherents, but, perhaps more importantly, he wanted to reinforce his political ascendancy as vicegerent over individual members of the episcopacy.

Conservative bishops well understood the political issues at stake. They tried to keep Cromwell from using livings in their hands to expedite his ecclesiastical policies. Moreover, they argued that they needed benefices for their own servants, who comprised the backbone of diocesan administration. Each conservative prelate attempted in his own way to thwart Cromwell's direct challenge to his independent use of patronage. Archbishop Lee proved most vocal in his complaints about Cromwellian interference. Behind a compliant facade, he nevertheless fought most of the royal requests for advowsons in his gift. He cited the plight of 'my poor chaplains, to whom I have given little or nothing'. And he acted vigorously to keep Cromwellian nominees from displacing his own. Lee resented the weakening of his prerogative. Whenever a

[93] Ibid. 361–2.
[94] 11 Nov. 1536.
[95] SP 1/135/251 (LP xiii/2. 214).

good benefice became vacant, the archbishop complained as early as December 1535, at least one suitor would instantly spring up with letters from the king recommending him for the living. Lee for his part tried to stay one jump ahead of Cromwell. When a servant brought him news that Master Bryton, his steward, was so near death that 'the physicians had foresaken him', Lee acted quickly. He granted Bryton's prebend to his chaplain and personal confessor, Dr Downes, 'and took from him a vicarage, and give it to one Master Cole, for so am I constrained to make shift'.[96]

Just two days later, the king's annointed arrived, expecting to claim the benefice. He obtained instead the smug apologies of the archbishop. 'Truly there was no cause why his highness should grieve with me therefore', wrote Lee innocently, 'for I gave the prebend on Saturday, whereas the king's letters came Monday or Tuesday after.' One would like to believe that Lee fully savoured his moment of triumph. They appeared infrequently. Downes had not enjoyed the archbishop's patronage through his four years of service, and Cole's preferments in the same period consisted of a single prebend worth £4.[97]

Lee's chaplains could never be certain of promotion. Other clerks with Cromwell's favour closely watched benefices in the archbishop's gift which were being served by men of great age. Lee bitterly complained to Cromwell about these practices. 'Surely if I look no better upon my poor chaplains than I have hitherto, it shall be hard for me to get any chaplains to do me service.'[98] Undeterred, Cromwell's intervention in the patronage activities of the conservative bishops intensified, placing the prelates in a delicate dilemma. Outright denial of a Cromwellian request for a benefice was foolish. The vicegerent could make their lives miserable. Tactical delays, however, might serve if in the meantime the press of business deflected Cromwell's attention. Recognising the ploy, Cromwell balanced his priorities and carefully chose occasions to act. Once he had committed himself to a course of action, his tenacity testifies to the importance accorded to ecclesiastical patronage. These conflicts, each narrow in scope, reflected in microcosm the broader political struggle between reformers and conservatives. Every battle over a parochial vacancy carried a message to the future. A victory in one patronage dispute brought advantage in the next. Patronage trends measured current political status and factional strength. The successful implementation of policy required, then, full attention to conflicts over patronage.

Nowhere was Cromwell's determination more pronounced than in his dealings with John Longland, bishop of Lincoln. An articulate and influential conservative, Longland, better than most, grasped the political significance of patronage disputes with Cromwell, and he fiercely resisted attempts to undermine his authority. Longland left no avenue of opportunity unexplored. Like Lee he appealed to Cromwell to allow him means to satisfy his chaplains, but Longland adopted a much fuller set of techniques to frustrate Cromwell's will.

The battle over Sherington in 1535 brought out all Longland's craft as he

---

96 SP 1/99/128 (LP ix. 933).
97 Ibid.
98 SP 1/103/270 (LP x. 841).

tried to deny Cromwell a foothold in Lincoln. On 18 August a priest named Christopher Rookes came before the bishop and asked in the king's name to be presented to Sherington. Longland refused, asking Cromwell to be good lord instead to Thomas Robertson, his chaplain. In addition, he noted, he had not yet proved his right and title to the advowson, a specious claim. Bishops of Lincoln had been patrons of Sherington for 240 years.[99]

These arguments fell on deaf ears. On 11 September Longland received a copy of a letter from Cromwell written on 3 September, 'whereupon I do perceive that you have been informed that I do continually refuse to admit Sir Christopher Rookes to the benefice of Sherington'. Longland asked Cromwell to give no credence to the report. Rookes, he stated, had shown him no letters.[100] The bishop continued to advance Robertson, 'a man of virtue and honesty, and of great learning'.[101] Longland also opened an attack on Rookes, whom he characterised as 'a clerk of bare learning'. Cromwell rejected Longland's appeal and again demanded the institution of Rookes. But Longland was not through. He returned to the issue of the disputed title to Sherington. He proposed that all the interested parties come before the council to air the entire matter for their determination. In the meantime, he suggested, Robertson should be allowed to enjoy the benefice.[102]

Finally Cromwell asserted his full authority and informed Longland that the king had decided that Rookes should have Sherington without further delay or contention.[103] Having lost the skirmish, Longland withdrew from the field battered but unbowed to continue the fight on other days. Patronage conflicts dot the correspondence between Longland and Cromwell throughout the minister's tenure. When Cromwell asked for the prebend of Leighton Bromswold, Longland tried to evade the request in order to keep the living out of the hands of Richard Layton, Cromwell's choice and a personal enemy.[104] And when Cromwell sued Longland for the advowson of the prebend of Mylton, Longland ignored Cromwell's letters for as long as was prudent.[105]

In these as in other instances Cromwell forced Longland to submit. He proved that he could influence the bishop's patronage, even if the process might be arduous. With most of the other conservative bishops the vicegerent had greater impact. To say that Cromwell could present to any living in the realm would not substantially exaggerate the power concentrated under his rule. No man before or after enjoyed such control over ecclesiastical appointments, circumscribed only by his willingness to act and the time necessary to produce results.

Yet barriers remained, and Cromwell always had to consider the costs. At times a benign political climate meant more than forcing a bishop to yield a benefice. Cromwell found it necessary to choose his moments carefully. He

99 SP 1/95/118 (LP ix. 117).
100 SP 1/96/147 (LP ix. 349).
101 SP 1/95/118 (LP ix. 117).
102 SP 1/97/33 (LP ix. 454).
103 Ibid.
104 SP 1/121/29r (LP xii/2. 28).
105 SP 1/124/191–209 (LP xii/2. 662, 678).

chose not to challenge his principal political opponents. Gardiner and Tunstall were never compelled to surrender their patronage rights. They seemed to be competing for much higher stakes in an entirely different game. More importantly, Cromwell soon realised the futility of vying for every vacant benefice. Without systematic control over the patronage machinery. Cromwell took what he could, made his political point, and probably decided to rely on the passage of time to erode the obstinacy of his antagonists. Meanwhile, Cromwell employed his patronage resources creatively to strengthen his factional dominance and to advance his ecclesiastical policy.

5

The Voice of Reform

Cromwell's most pressing concern was to give substance to the Royal Supremacy, the device he had used to resolve the divorce crisis. From the March 1533 Act in Restraint of Appeals until Cromwell's own appointment as vicegerent in December 1534, a steady stream of statutes transferred powers and revenues from the bishop of Rome to the king of England. By the beginning of 1535, the king was in law the supreme head of the Church of England. In fact Cromwell exercised the royal prerogative. As vicegerent, vicar general, and special commissary to the king, Cromwell held in his own right virtually unlimited jurisdiction in ecclesiastical affairs. As long as he continued to enjoy Henry's favour, Cromwell, personally, possessed

> full power and authority from time to time to visit, repress, redress, reform, order, correct, restrain, and amend all such errors, heresies, abuses, offences, contempts, and enormities, whatsoever they be, which by any manner spiritual authority or jurisdiction ought or may lawfully be reformed, repressed, ordered, redressed, corrected, restrained, or amended, most to the pleasure of Almighty God, the increase of virtue in Christ's religion, and for the conservancy of the peace, unity, tranquillity of this realm: any usage, custom, foreign laws, foreign authority, prescription, or any other thing or things to the contrary hereof notwithstanding.[1]

Cromwell's elevation to the vicegerency by law concentrated enormous strength in his hands. Factional goals for reform could now be realised through the minister's use of royal authority. Cromwell soon recognised, however, that hopes for a renewed Church and commonwealth depended on the swift and complete acceptance of the revolutionary shift in ecclesiastical governance made explicit by the Royal Supremacy. This need engaged Cromwell's immediate attention, and it entailed a sustained effort. With typical thoroughness he employed the most effective instruments, first to inform the country of the requirements of the Supremacy, then to begin the laborious process of enforcement.[2] Cromwell led from strength, using his vicegerental authority to issue a

1   C. H. Williams (ed.), *English Historical Documents, 1485–1558*, London 1967, 746.
2   Much of the material in this chapter has been used by G. R. Elton, *Policy and Police*, Cambridge 1972, passim. Professor Elton has employed the complaint literature written during Cromwell's ascendancy to answer questions touching 'the enforcement of decisions, relations between the government and parts of the realm, or the making of policy' (pp. vii–viii). I have looked at the material from a factional perspective with particular emphasis on the religious problems of Cromwell's ministry. Thus I hope to have added political and ideological dimensions to Elton's thorough discussion of the administrative procedures used by Cromwell to achieve consensus in favour of the Royal Supremacy.

series of written orders which disseminated his instructions. Significantly, he employed the most visible members of the reform faction in their episcopal roles as points of entry for his policy. Letters of 3 June 1535 compelled bishops to uphold the Royal Supremacy in a number of ways. They were to preach regularly on the justice of the king's title, style, and jurisdiction as supreme head of the Church. Cromwell also held them responsible for making known the Supremacy to all ecclesiastical persons within their dioceses, and for instructing all schoolmasters to erase the papal title from materials that students might read.[3]

Cromwell anticipated some opposition from conservatives among the episcopacy and devised methods to discourage overt resistance. On 9 June a proclamation instructed sheriffs to report any instance where a bishop acted contrary to the statutes abolishing papal authority in England.[4] On the 25th a circular letter to the same effect went to the country's justices. In addition, at Assizes and Sessions, the justices were to declare to parents and rulers of families the elements of the Supremacy so that they might teach the same to their children and servants.[5] Cromwell left no room for equivocation.

The bishops, enthusiastically or not, quickly reacted to the pressures emanating from Westminster. They well understood that the enjoyment of their sees obliged them to advertise their endorsement of the Supremacy. Cromwell could expect swift and ardent responses from factional subscribers. Roland Lee, newly elected bishop of Coventry and Lichfield, had advanced through Cromwell's patronage. He replied to the commandment to preach against the pope on 7 June by sending for his horses and repairing to his diocese to take up the pulpit, although, he said, he had hitherto never before preached.[6]

Bishops outside the orbit of the reform faction moved less vigorously if at all to the defence and promulgation of royal policy. Many cited various hardships in an effort to protect themselves from Cromwell's displeasure. Robert Sherbourne, bishop of Chichester, old, ill, and soon to die, begged the vicegerent to allow him, 'considering my old age and impotence', to discharge his duty by deputy.[7] John Salcot, bishop of Bangor, expressed his willingness to preach in person against the usurped and unjust authority of the bishop of Rome, but he doubted his effectiveness because he spoke no Welsh.[8]

John Stokesley did not have to cope with a strange language, but he too had never preached because of his 'stammering and bad speaking'.[9] His maiden sermon, at St Paul's Cathedral on 11 July 1535, did not go well. His speech defect, the large audience, and the presence of Cromwell among a host of other dignitaries destroyed his composure. In short order Cromwell severely admonished the bishop for failing in his duty to preach against the validity of the king's first marriage and the usurped authority of the pope. With the memory of

3 David Wilkins (ed.), *Concilia Magnae Britanniae et Hiberniae*, 4 vols, London 1737, iii. 772.
4 Ibid. 773.
5 Ibid.
6 SP 1/93/37 (*LP* viii. 839).
7 BL, Cotton Cleopatra E vi. fo. 269 (*LP* viii. 941).
8 SP 1/93/27, 29 (*LP* viii. 832, 833).
9 *LP* viii. 1019.

the executions of Fisher and More still fresh, Stokesley on 16 July replied to Cromwell's criticism with care. He rehearsed the measures taken in his diocese to implement the provisions of the Supremacy, and he excused his sermon on grounds of poor health and stage fright. He promised greater diligence and hoped for Cromwell's forebearance.[10]

Cromwell exercised less direct supervision of northern prelates. He entrusted the delivery of royal instructions to Sir Francis Bigod, a friend and follower. Bigod also carried letters from Cromwell to Archbishop Lee and Bishop Tunstall which accused them of neglecting their duty to the Supremacy. No mere messenger, Bigod wrote to Cromwell on 11 June that both Lee and Tunstall accepted their letters with great humility. Bigod proposed to be in the city of York to hear Lee preach sincerely and effectively. Should the archbishop fail, Bigod continued, he had brought along Thomas Garret, his personal chaplain,[11] 'ready to say the word of God truly'. If Cromwell entertained doubts about Garret's reliability, Bigod suggested that the minister speak to Latimer, Crome, or Barnes, who could offer proof of Garret's talents.[12]

While deference marked all Lee's responses to Cromwellian initiatives, the presence of Bigod with his official correspondence made little impact on Cuthbert Tunstall, bishop of Durham. He denied that he had been unco-operative and claimed, 'I have been as sore against such usurpations of the bishop of Rome as daily did grow as any man of my degree in this realm, and that I should now look for the renewing of that thing which I withstood heretofore as far as I might when it flourished most, it is not likely.'[13]

Cromwell's major rival, Stephen Gardiner, remained circumspect. Vigorous opposition to Cromwell's ecclesiastical policy lay in the future, and Gardiner continued strong and active in his support for the separation of the English Church from Roman jurisdiction. Replying to his letters from Cromwell and the king, Gardiner asked to be excused from personal responsibility for diocesan oversight. He stated that his Winchester subordinates would handle the necessary tasks specified in the royal recommendations. However, his workload as a councillor and his labours translating literature designed to buttress the Supremacy kept him busy in London.[14]

At this stage in the formulation of policy, the connection between factional interest and national interest held strong. The Royal Supremacy, central to the ideological aspirations of the reform faction, intimately touched Henry's personal and political sensibilities. He would brook no opposition, and the visibility of those in his service permitted no public protest. Fisher and More had challenged the Supremacy. Their severed heads widely broadcast the result. Few failed to hear or to heed. Cromwell's problems for the moment were less

---

[10] SP 1/94/98 (*LP* viii. 1054).

[11] Garret, who appears in various situations throughout this text, was an active advocate of Protestantism from its first appearance on English shores until his death in 1540. He furnishes a good example of a man whose convictions framed his life. Never in the highest echelons of faction, he gave himself, both professionally and personally, to the factional cause. For his career see ch. ii above and Dickens, *English Reformation*, 75–6.

[12] SP 1/93/50 (*LP* viii. 854).

[13] BL, Cotton Cleopatra E vi. fos 252v–253r (*LP* viii. 1082).

[14] SP 1/93/45r–v (*LP* viii. 850).

political than administrative. Obedience to the Supremacy entailed knowledge, understanding, and acceptance of its substance, and Cromwell had scant ways and means at hand to facilitate the programme. In the larger dioceses particularly, bishops found their burdens too heavy to carry alone. Reflecting on his efforts to distribute the king's commandments to the clergy of Lincoln diocese, Bishop John Longland complained 'that all the clerks I have are not able to write them in long process of time'. Longland hoped that printing 2,000 copies of the instructions would speed the process of dissemination.[15]

Far more seriously, the country lacked qualified clerks, resident in the parishes, able to transmit crown policy to the general laity. Archbishop Lee, always anxious to protect himself from royal displeasure, furnished a detailed outline of difficulties he faced in following Cromwellian guidelines, problems which must have been general even in sees ruled by bishops enthusiastic for reform. According to Lee, he had developed a comprehensive programme for his clergy. Cranmer had given him a book which contained matters to be covered by all preachers in their sermons. Lee gathered together all those around him who could write in order to make enough copies for every priest who preached in the archdiocese of York. None could be licensed before receiving this book. Other clerks got written instructions touching their responsibilities, and Lee hoped 'that all curates and others that can perceive it and utter it, may at least read it to their audience'. The archbishop, however, expressed his concern that 'many of the curates can scant perceive it'.[16] Lee's problems were structural. He stated that he had less than twelve secular priests who could preach. The best livings had gone to nonresidents, leaving York with great numbers of poor benefices incapable of sustaining qualified clerks. Lee bemoaned his need to rely on men barely able to read and understand the form of the sacraments.[17]

Formidable problems confronted Cromwell. With some difficulty and much aggravation he exacted public obedience from the bishops. In the short-term, however, he could not completely reorganise age-old patterns of ecclesiastical life. Acceptance of the Supremacy, to say nothing of Reformation, depended upon the minister's ability to forge a favourable national consensus. Bringing conformity to the episcopal bench started the process, but widespread popular ignorance and outright disobedience to the provisions of the Royal Supremacy sharply increased the difficulty of Cromwell's undertaking.

Negative reports came from all parts of the realm, touching individuals from all levels of the social hierarchy. Examples drawn from a voluminous record underline the diversity of the problems that plagued Cromwell. John Salcot, bishop of Bangor, complained to him of a curate who refused the command to declare the usurped power of the bishop of Rome.[18] From Buckinghamshire Sir Francis Bryan wrote that he had detected sedition at the Brykehill Quarter Sessions. One George Taylor had called the king knave, heretic, and rebel

[15] BL, Cotton Cleopatra E vi. fo. 272 (*LP* viii. 922).
[16] Ibid. fo. 243 (*LP* viii. 963).
[17] Ibid.
[18] SP 1/93/107 (*LP* ix. 109).

against the laws of God.[19] Both men resided in prison awaiting Cromwell's disposition of their cases, anxious for their lives.

Cromwellian agents on other business also took pains to advance the Supremacy. Thomas Magnus, archdeacon of the East Riding of York, held commissions from the crown with responsibility for compiling the *Valor Ecclesiasticus* and for assessing the temporal subsidy in the archdiocese. Travelling with an Austin friar, Magnus circulated through his jurisdiction, recording his valuations. At the same time, he sponsored the preaching and teaching of the friar in favour of royal policy. He also delivered 140 copies of a book which declared the Supremacy to all abbots, priors, parsons, vicars, and curates within his archdeaconry. For his efforts he wanted Cromwell to be aware that 'there is not a more quiet jurisdiction in England than is my poor archdeaconry'.[20]

Other letters to Cromwell offered less cause for optimism. Thomas Skipworth accused several priests of St Alban's of ungodly preaching which, he claimed, hindered the pure word of God and threatened the Supremacy.[21] The mayor of Cambridge jailed Martin Bassett, vicar of St Clement's for speaking traitorous words against the king.[22] Arthur Uvedale, patron of the rectory of Wickham, Hampshire, charged John Fisher, the parson, with acting in a treasonous manner, and understandably Fisher fled when confronted.[23] A priest caught in the gears of the Henrician judicial mill might languish in prison for a long time. James Pratt, vicar of Cowley, found himself jailed in Worcester Castle for uttering seditious words. His case remained unheard, and through an intermediary Pratt begged to be released as age and confinement had brought him close to death.[24]

Cromwell apparently encouraged reports of all breaches of the commandments for the promotion of the Supremacy, and the minister must have been kept busy sorting out seemingly trivial complaints, often brought for reasons of malice or in the expectation of personal gain. These aside, clear opposition to the Supremacy manifested itself at all ranks of ecclesiastical activity from the smallest parish to Canterbury Cathedral. Even Cranmer could not preach unchallenged from his own pulpit. On receipt of the king's letters of 3 June 1535, Cranmer returned to Canterbury. Word of mouth commands from the king and Cromwell required that the archbishop persuade the people of the bishop of Rome's usurpation of power, and of the king's rightful title as supreme head of the Church of England. Cranmer's sermons dealt fully with the premises of the Supremacy. The archbishop declared that the bishop of Rome was not God's vicar on earth, but was rather a holiness in name only. The laws of the bishop of Rome were, therefore, not the laws of God, and people gained no remission of sin by observing them. Finally he attacked the ceremonies of

---

[19] SP 1/90/184 (*LP* viii. 278).
[20] BL, Cotton Cleopatra E vi. fo. 285r–v (*LP* viii. 968).
[21] SP 1/91/105–6; SP 1/91/107–8 (*LP* viii. 406, 407).
[22] SP 1/92/187 (*LP* viii. 727).
[23] SP 1/112/176 (*LP* xi. 1265).
[24] Ibid. 176v.

the Roman Church, arguing that Christ's death, not laws or ceremonies, remitted sins.[25]

The archbishop claimed that his preaching was well received 'until the prior of Black Friars at Canterbury preached a sermon clean contrary to them'. Cranmer, of course, had the ability to defend his intellectual ground as well as jurisdiction to restrain the prior if he chose to exercise his authority. Instead, he placed the matter before the king and council for the full weight of their judgment, because, 'if this man, who preached against [Cranmer] in his own church, be not looked on, the king may expende what an example it may be to others'.[26]

As reports arrived in London from the rest of the realm, Cromwell discovered links between resistance to the Supremacy and opposition to Anne. Mindful that support for Catherine remained strong among conservatives, and fearing that personal attacks against Anne might threaten acceptance of the Supremacy, Cromwell investigated thoroughly all incidents which touched upon Anne's reputation and character. Even common gossip engaged Cromwell's attention. Shortly after Anne's coronation, the minister dispatched Thomas Bedyll, a clerk of the council, to Warwickshire to examine Thomas Gebons and Rauf Wendon. Wendon stood accused by Gebons of saying that the queen was a whore and a harlot, and that there was a prophesy that a queen should be burned at Smithfield, and that he trusted it would be the end of the queen. Bedyll conducted a long, detailed examination but no conclusive evidence was found and no formal charges were brought.[27] Mistress Amadas, wife of Robert Amadas, former master of the jewel house, also engaged in prophetic gossip. She foresaw the destruction of Henry, Anne, and all those who took their part. Henry, cursed with God's own mouth, should be banished. Anne should be burned for she was a harlot. Master Norris was bawd between her and the king; the king had kept the mother and daughter; and Thomas Boleyn was bawd to his wife and his two daughters.[28]

In October 1533 William Gardner wrote that Robert Borett, late of London, did rail upon the queen and Archbishop Cranmer. He had said in the presence of others that 'the queen's grace was a churl's daughter and also a whore'.[29] None of these incidents resulted in further action, but Cromwell did act in cases where the status of the accused warranted more careful scrutiny. On 7 October 1533 he ordered the mayor and jurates of Rye to put in safekeeping a friar and a priest of the town who had spoken seditious words against the king and queen. The town officials examined and imprisoned the clergymen to await the king's pleasure and Cromwell's orders.[30] Cromwell acted most decisively when important individuals allowed their dissatisfaction with the

---

25 *Cranmer's Letters*, 325 (*LP* xi. 361). This letter is incorrectly placed in 1536 by the editors of *LP*. Internal analysis of the text suggests that both the sermon and the letter were composed and delivered in 1535.
26 Ibid.
27 SP 6/7/6; SP 1/77/112 (*LP* vi. 733).
28 BL, Cotton Cleopatra E iv. fo. 84 (*LP* vi. 923).
29 SP 1/79/182 (*LP* vi. 1254).
30 SP 1/80/11–12 (*LP* vi. 1329 i, ii).

marriage to challenge the legality of the Supremacy. Early in 1534, Dr Edward Powell denied the validity of the king's marriage and wrote a book against it. He also accused the earl of Wiltshire of being a heretic. An examination ensued, and Powell lost his preferments in Lincoln. Unrepentant, Powell was executed in 1540 for continuing to deny the Supremacy.[31]

Cromwell responded to the threat of widespread resistance with close personal supervision of complaints and the careful use of patronage. Enthusiasm for the Supremacy became a precondition for advancement to important ecclesiastical office. Cromwell appointed men who could be relied upon to carry out policy. During this phase he necessarily ignored concerns about residence and routine details of diocesan administration. His best livings went as rewards to those most loyal and eager to serve his programme for the Supremacy.

Men of proven ability advanced rapidly. Cromwell looked first to factional adherents to fill vacancies. When Nicholas Shaxton was preferred to the bishopric of Salisbury in 1535, John Skipp obtained his canonry in Westminster Cathedral.[32] Skipp typified the clerical nominees needed by Cromwell. A close ally of Cranmer, he had impeccable credentials. He had been educated at Gonville College, Cambridge, where he remained active for twenty years. In 1533 he joined the Boleyn faction as Anne's chaplain and succeeded Shaxton as her almoner. A patron himself, he brought a number of his Cambridge friends to the attention of court and faction.[33] In 1534 Skipp returned to Cambridge with Simon Haynes to preach in favour of the Supremacy, apparently to good effect. Accolades took tangible form. Skipp secured the vicarage of Thaxted, Essex, in 1534[34] and collation a year later both to the rectory of Newington, Surrey and the archdeaconry of Suffolk.[35] Skipp's later career culminated in his election to the bishopric of Hereford following the death of Edward Foxe. From his episcopal dignity Skipp returned to his intellectual pursuits. He had earlier participated in the compilation of the *Institution of a Christian Man*, the *Bishops' Book* of 1537. Later, he revised the 'Epistle to the Hebrews' for the *Great Bible* of 1539, and he contributed to the formative deliberations for the *First Book of Common Prayer*.[36]

Simon Haynes, Skipp's colleague, had also matriculated at Cambridge.[37] He was president of Queens' College from 1528, and he hosted Edward Foxe's mission to the university on behalf of the King's Great Matter. In 1533, at Dunstable, he subscribed to Cranmer's instrument of divorce and became active in defence of the Supremacy. Cromwell repaid Haynes's efforts in January 1535 with the vicarage of Stepney and a Windsor prebend.[38] Then the vicegerent brought him from Cambridge to London where Haynes remained in royal employ until his death.

---

[31] SP 1/82/44 (*LP* vii. 28).

[32] *LP* viii. 239 (g. 9).

[33] *Ath. Cant.*, i. 109.

[34] Ibid.

[35] *Alum. Cant.*, iv. 86.

[36] J. Venn, *Biographical History of Gonville and Caius College*, Cambridge 1898, 20.

[37] Queens' College, Cambridge: BA, 1516; MA, 1519; BD, 1528; DD, 1531.

[38] *Ath. Cant.*, i. 111.

A zealous reformer, Haynes so strongly opposed passage of the Six Articles in 1539 that he was imprisoned for a time. He had written a letter to Dr William Butts in which he maintained that transubstantiation could not be proved as an article of faith without acknowledging on the same grounds the authority of the bishop of Rome.[39] Later, during Edward VI's reign, Haynes, then married, joined Skipp in the preparations for the *First Book of Common Prayer*.[40]

Haynes contributions to reform continued beyond the grave. His will leaves clear evidence of the practical element in his Protestantism. He bequeathed ten marks for the poor and twenty shillings for a learned sermon to be preached at his burial. For his two sons, Simon and Joseph, he left sufficient means along with full instructions to his wife for their upbringing. Simon and Joseph were to attend school until they learned to read, write, and understand the grammatical principles of Greek and Latin. Then, when each reached the age of eleven, they would be sent to a grammar school for instruction under a learned master, 'until they can make a verse and write an epistle, and also have competent sight in the Greek tongue'.[41] At the age of fifteen Joseph would go to Oxford, Simon to Cambridge; they would get a solid grounding in humanist writings and the work of reformers such as Philip Melanchthon. They would study civil law and the laws of the realm:

> Afterward I exhort them to study holy Scripture so as they may be able to be priests and preachers of God's word if they be apt thereto, or else to continue in the study of civil law or laws of the realm if they be apt thereto, or else to depart home to their houses to live by their industry and labour.[42]

The rich Cambridge matrix also produced Simon Symonds and Nicholas Heath. Symonds began his education at Eton, near his home, then continued on to King's College, Cambridge. His clerical career started modestly in 1518 with appointment to the vicarage of Elmden, Essex[43] but quickly progressed when Cromwell discovered his talent for preaching. In quick succession Symonds received a royal chaplaincy and prebends in both the cathedral church of Coventry and Lichfield and in Windsor.[44] He preached in London from 1535, despite charges from the more ardent William Marshall that he was no friend of reform.[45] John Hilsey also mistrusted Symonds, and the bishop asked Cromwell to admonish him before allowing Symonds to preach a sermon at Paul's Cross on Easter Sunday 1537.[46] Cromwell closely supervised Symonds, but he continued to employ him and to furnish him with support, including the dean's office in the collegiate church of Tamworth.[47] Symonds's career offers an example of a man who, though he might have privately entertained conserva-

39 BL, Cotton Cleopatra E v. fo. 58 (*LP* xiv/1. 1035).
40 S. L. Ollard, *Fasti Wyndesorienses*, Windsor 1950, 120.
41 PROB 11/35/29–30.
42 Ibid.
43 I. Harwood, *Alumni Etonenses, 1433–1797*, Birmingham 1797, 129.
44 Ollard, *Fasti*, 59–60.
45 SP 1/106/22r (*LP* xi. 325).
46 SP 1/117/123 (*LP* xii/1. 726).
47 *LP* xiii/2. 282 (g. 21). Valued at £21 in VE iii. 148.

tive religious opinions, rendered loyal service to Cromwell and the crown. That Cromwell could direct the skills of men such as Symonds is a measure of his own considerable abilities.

The career of Nicholas Heath presents additional insight into Cromwell's use of patronage. To look at Heath's career in retrospect distorts the role he played in the 1530s. During Mary's reign, as lord chancellor and archbishop of York, he saw no fewer than 217 people put to death for their religion, all under his writ. Among these were his former colleagues, Cranmer, Latimer, and Ridley. In the 1530s, however, Cranmer was Heath's first important patron. In 1534 the archbishop recommended to Cromwell one 'which for his learning, wisdom, discretion, and sincere mind towards his prince, I know no man more meet to serve the king's highness's purposes'.[48] London-born and a Cambridge graduate, Heath received his first benefice, the rectory of Hever, Kent, officially from the prior of Camberwell,[49] but Cranmer and Anne must have pushed for his presentation to this benefice closest to the heart of the Boleyn family. Heath preached vigorously against Elizabeth Barton in 1534 and soon afterwards secured a royal chaplaincy along with the archdeaconry of Staffordshire.[50] He then took up diplomatic work. He went with Edward Foxe and Robert Barnes on the December 1535 embassy to the German princes gathered at Smalkald. On this occasion he met Melanchthon and Martin Bucer, both of whom praised his learning.[51] Cromwell took advantage of Heath's intellectual talents, putting him to labour first on the *Institution of a Christian Man*, then on the *Great Bible*. In 1542 Heath supervised, at the behest of convocation, the translation of the *Acts of the Apostles*.

Throughout the 1530s, Heath remained closely linked to Cromwell and Cranmer, earning recognition and promotion. From the vicegerent he obtained custody of the priory of Lenton, Nottinghamshire in 1535,[52] the deanery of Shoreham, Kent in the jurisdiction of Canterbury in 1538, and a prebend in the palace of Westminster in 1539.[53] Between 1537 and 1538 Cranmer instituted Heath to the rectories of Bishopsbourne and Cliffe in Kent and the deanery of South Malling, Sussex.[54] In 1539 in a conservative climate John Hilsey resigned the bishopric of Rochester, and Heath moved up to the episcopal bench. He was translated to the see of Worcester in 1543.[55] Though he grew more conservative as time passed, it was not until after Henry's death that he broke with the crown on matters of ritual. He finally lost his see, deprived in 1551, and he was placed in the custody of Nicholas Ridley, then bishop of London, an ironic kindness that Heath failed to repay when their positions were reversed in 1555.[56]

---

[48] *Ath. Cant.*, i. 402–3.
[49] Ibid. 402.
[50] *Alum. Cant.*, ii. 208.
[51] *Ath. Cant.*, i. 403.
[52] *LP* ix. 367 (g. 17).
[53] *LP* xiii/1. 410 (g. 15); *LP* xiv/2. 102 (g. 29).
[54] J. Peile, *Biographical Register of Christ's Church*, Cambridge 1910, 11.
[55] John Le Neve, *Fasti Ecclesiae Anglicanae*, ed. T. D. Hardy, 3 vols, Oxford 1854, ii. 569.
[56] Peile, *Christ's Church*, 11.

Despite the appointment of competent and loyal men to important levels of the ecclesiastical hierarchy, personal patronage by itself had severe limitations. Cromwell lacked both benefices and qualified men to fill them. Preachers, particularly, were in short supply. Responding to the restrictions on his patronage, Cromwell turned again to statute in 1536 to shore up his complex programme for the enforcement of the Supremacy. The Act against Papal Authority confessed in its preamble that notwithstanding the good and wholesome laws, ordinances, and statutes heretofore enacted for the extirpation of the authority of the bishop of Rome,

> yet it is come to the knowledge of the king's highness and also to diverse and many of his loving, faithful, and obedient subjects, how that diverse seditious and contentious persons, being imps of the said bishop of Rome and his see, and in heart members of his pretended monarchy, do in corners and elsewhere, as they care, whisper, inculcate, preach, and persuade, and from time to time instill into the ears and heads of the poor, simple, and unlettered people, the advancement and continuance of the said bishop's feigned and pretended authority.[57]

The Act prohibited from July 1536 the extolling, setting forth, maintaining, or defending of the authority, jurisdiction, or power of the bishop of Rome, whether by writing, ciphering, printing, teaching, or preaching. Penalties dictated by the Statute of Provision and Praemunire awaited those convicted of violating the Act.[58]

The campaign against papal authority in England used parliament to put policy on record in order to alert the political nation, but Cromwell could not rely on legislation alone to carry his constitutional revolution to the nation at large. This complex task demanded both creativity and tenacity. Cromwell used the printing press to bring the written word to the literate community of the realm.[59] But the spoken word, reaching into every household, mattered more. Cromwell, determined to strengthen the voice of government, used his power as a patron to bring competent preachers to the service of policy. He also tried to ensure that the pulpit could not be used by conservative opponents of reform.[60]

Cromwell's Injunctions to the Clergy, one set in 1536, another in 1538, established criteria for the form and content of sermons. The Injunctions of

---

57 *Stat. Realm*, iii. 663 (Williams, *English Historical Documents*, 759).

58 Ibid. (Williams, *English Historical Documents*, 760).

59 Between 1525 and 1547 some 800 separate editions of religious works were printed in English, and a large proportion of these were of a strongly Protestant hue, by men such as Barnes, Coverdale, Richard Tracy, Bacon, Taverner, and Joye, as well as those by Luther, Melanchthon, and Calvin the reformers themselves: Scarisbrick, *Henry VIII*, 399. See also D. B. Knox, *The Doctrine of the Faith in the Reign of Henry VIII*, London 1961, p. iv. Elton, *Policy and Police*, 171–216 summarises Cromwell's use of printed propaganda. A valuable analysis which extends beyond these sources can be found in Edward Riegler, 'Thomas Cromwell's Printing Projects', unpublished PhD diss., UCLA 1977.

60 Much of the following material has been taken from my article 'Thomas Cromwell's patronage of preaching', 37–50.

1536 insisted that every priest with cure of souls declare at least four times a year in their sermons, 'how the bishop of Rome's usurped power and jurisdiction having no establishment nor ground by the law of God was of most just causes taken away and abolished'.[61] Two years later Cromwell set down more explicit standards for preaching. He enjoined none to preach without obtaining sufficient licence from himself, the king, the archbishop of Canterbury, or the bishop of the diocese. Duly licensed preachers had *carte blanche*. Cromwell ordered that they be warmly received to expound the word of God without resistance or contradiction. Any man who preached contrary to the Injunctions or in favour of papal authority should be reported immediately to the vicegerent.[62]

Bishops responsible for putting Cromwellian policy into effect responded in a variety of ways. Thomas Goodrich, bishop of Ely, favoured reform and vigorously brought his diocese into harmony with the Injunctions and the ideology which they reflected. The bishop changed the oath of obedience taken by those instituted to benefices in Ely. The old oath required obedience to the bishop and prohibited either by teaching or preaching advocacy of the Lutheran or other heresies. Goodrich eliminated the latter provision from the new oath and added an undertaking to renounce the pope and all his constitutions and decrees condemned or to be condemned by parliament.[63] Goodrich took a personal interest in improving the quality of preaching in Ely. He wrote to Dr John Edmunds, the master of Peterhouse at Cambridge, to inform him of the Injunctions. He asked Edmunds to preach and told him to 'command the fellows of your house to do the same in order every Sunday and solemn feast in your parish church in Cambridge, so that the parishioners thereof may have every of the said festival days the word of God'.[64]

Conservative prelates walked thin lines between Cromwellian demands and their own ideological preferences. They tempered their submissions to Cromwell's preaching directives with words of caution to their clergy. John Longland instructed his archdeacon of Bedford to preach at least eight times a year in his principal church, either personally or by deputy. He warned the archdeacon to be certain to defend the king's title and to justify for his audience the abolition of papal jurisdiction. Longland, quite explicitly, warned against the introduction of any 'doubtful matters'. Only those articles approved by convocation should be opened. Controversial issues of doctrine and practice were to be avoided.[65] Robert Sampson, bishop of Chichester, acted with similar caution. When his chancellor asked how he should order himself with respect to unfamiliar preachers, Bishop Sampson replied judiciously. First, he advised, the chancellor should ascertain whether the prospective preacher held a

---

[61] SP 6/6/78.

[62] Henry Gee and William Hardy (eds) *Documents Illustrative of English Church History*, New York 1972, 277–8; Williams, *English Historical Documents*, 812–13: either of these sources will serve. Gee and Hardy have transcribed the 1538 Injunctions from Cranmer's *Register*, fo. 215b.

[63] SP 1/94/231 (*LP* viii. 1131).

[64] BL, Egerton MS 2350, fo. 29 (*LP* viii. 933).

[65] SP 1/128/3v–4r (*LP* xiii/1. 3); Wilkins, *Concilia Magnae Britanniae*, iii. 829.

licence or special commission from the king or Cromwell. If not the man should not be allowed to preach, 'except they were persons well known both of learning and temperance'.[66] Sampson left himself as much room as possible to manoeuvre.

Cromwell on his part tried whenever possible to limit the bishops' discretionary actions. He wanted uniformity in preaching. In March 1537 he called the bishops together to hear directives on preaching, written by Thomas Starkey.[67] Authorised by Cromwell, as vicegerent in the name of the king, this discourse reveals Cromwell's attitude toward the pulpit as a crucial instrument of reform. Starkey began by asserting that man's salvation depended upon knowledge of truth. Once known, he continued, this truth ought to be opened to all faithful people through the preaching of Christ's doctrine. Those entrusted with clerical office, 'should first and above all, sincerely, truly, and plainly, according to the gift of knowledge unto them given, publish and preach the truth of God's word'.[68]

A primary concern for uniformity in doctrine dominated Starkey's presentation. He anticipated no difficulty where Scripture, of itself open and manifest, needed no interpretation. Problems would arise when doctrine lacked perfect clarity, 'because Scripture in certain places is somewhat obtuse and not easy to be understood of any man, wherein it is not meet that all men should fantasy after their own pleasure without any stay of judgment therein'. Starkey argued that as the 'sensual effects' of man are properly restrained by reason and law, so should the opinions of preachers be 'directed and tempered'. Rigid adherence to the interpretation made by 'the ancient doctors of our religion' would promote unity. And if controversy persisted, 'We think it meet that they should cleave unto the consent and laudable custom of the church of England.' Finally, of course, authority rested with the king, and Starkey left no doubt on this point:

> Wherefore to this order and rule we judge it necessary, that all curates and preachers of God's word should render themselves conformable and obedient, from the which if they wilfully at any time slip, then the same both as seditious persons and disturbers of the common quietness and unity, to be reputed, and their bodies and goods to stand in the king's pleasure.[69]

Long term education of preachers in their responsibilities toward the crown could not make up for the dearth of preachers. Edward Lee complained to Cromwell that he had dispatched his archdeacons to bring in bills from those able to preach. Not a single preacher could be found in the archdeaconry of Nottingham; few came forward from elsewhere in the archdiocese.[70] The prior of St Oswald, Robert Ferrar, felt extremely pessimistic about the state of

---

66 SP 1/116/249 (LP xiii/1. 1009).
67 For an analysis of Starkey's career and thought see Zeeveld, Tudor Policy, esp. 128–56. Cf. Elton, Reform and Renewal, 46–55; Mayer, 'Faction and ideology', 1–25; idem. Starkey, passim.
68 SP 1/100/130r–v (LP ix. 1160).
69 Ibid.
70 SP 1/126/164r–v (LP xii/2. 1093).

preaching in Yorkshire. He asked Cromwell, 'to foresee whether any harm may fall or not of this thing, that there be almost none in these parts that sincerely, plainly, and diligently preach the gospel'. Although he believed the people hungry to hear and to learn the word of God, Ferrar disconsolately noted that hardly any Yorkshire town had 'one faithful preacher that I can hear of'. Well aware that the success of reform efforts relied upon the effective use of the pulpit, Ferrar proposed to travel through Northumberland, 'there to prove if it may please the Lord to give them any light through my poor service in his word'.[71]

The shortage of preachers hindered not only the progress of Reformation. Thomas Howard, duke of Norfolk remarked, in the aftermath of the recently suppressed Pilgimage of Grace, that 'if three or four loyal preachers had continually been in these parts, instructing the unlearned people, no such follies had been attempted as hath been'. The duke suggested that the northern bishops, under compulsion if necessary, give a portion of their wealth to support preachers who would make the people more tractable.[72] Cromwell may have either winced or smiled at Norfolk's self-righteous hindsight; force of arms had quieted northern resistance, but he too recognised the need for more preachers. Patronage of preaching became a systematic and high-priority item on the agenda for ecclesiastical reform.

As early as 1534, Thomas Cranmer, acting for the government, revoked the licences of all preachers in his jurisdiction. New licences would be carefully considered, and Cranmer employed Hugh Latimer, then a Boleyn client and a leading preacher himself, to decide which of the applicants would receive authority to preach. It is not insignificant that one of England's most visible religious radicals had charge of examining for the government the suitability of individual preachers.[73] Appreciating the importance of those who would preach, Cromwell, from the earliest days of his ministry, granted substantial benefices and his full support to those who served the crown and the cause of reform by their preaching.

Eustace Chapuys was one of the opponents of the Supremacy and reform who recognised that the pulpit was being used in a new way. Dr George Browne had preached at court in January 1535. He demanded that all English bishops burn any papal bulls in their custody, replacing them with documents issued by the king. Chapuys noted the tone and source of the attack on Rome: 'This language is so abominable that it is clear it must have been prompted by the king or Cromwell, who makes this monk his right-hand man in all things unlawful.'[74] A personal friend of Cromwell, Browne probably married Henry and Anne. For his loyalty and effective preaching, he received a series of promotions which culminated in his elevation to the archbishopric of Dublin.[75]

Aptitude and enthusiasm for preaching were common elements in the careers of many men appointed by Cromwell to important ecclesiastical of-

[71] SP 1/139/218 (*LP* xiii/2. 953).
[72] SP 1/116/249 (*LP* xii/1. 1158).
[73] For Cranmer's use of his authority see Ridley, *Thomas Cranmer*, 88–92.
[74] *LP* viii. 121, 38.
[75] Knowles, *Religious Orders*, iii. 59–60.

fices. We have already noticed John Skipp, Simon Haynes, and Nicholas Heath, all of whom used their talents for preaching as direct stepping stones to advancement. John Hilsey, too, initially gained Cromwell's favour through his preaching. Eloquent in the pulpit himself, Hilsey also served as the principal organiser of the Paul's Cross sermons, a major venue in the campaign for the Supremacy. If it is understood that the potential for Cromwellian influence rapidly decreased as the distance from London increased, the vicegerent's attempt to bring Paul's Cross up to peak performance in the interest of reform furnishes a good example of the relationship between factional politics and preaching.[76]

The cross at St Paul's cathedral nominally belonged within the jurisdiction of the bishop of London. In 1535, as Cromwell began his programme to build up support for the Royal Supremacy, he instructed John Stokesley personally to arrange a series of sermons, which would set forth Henry's title as supreme head of the Church of England from England's most important pulpit. Stokesley never disobeyed this edict, nor did he endeavour to use this platform for anti-reform propaganda. He did, however, show himself reluctant either to schedule or even to attend those sermons which he felt to be hostile or threatening to his increasingly conservative approach to theology.[77]

Cromwell responded to the bishop's passive resistance by breaking Stokesley's hold on appointments. On 20 October 1535 he granted a commission to John Hilsey, which included a mandate to appoint preachers to deliver sermons at Paul's Cross.[78] By this time inducted to the bishopric of Rochester, Hilsey organised preaching activities for three years, occupying the pulpit himself on several occasions. Large crowds attended each Sunday's sermon, not always willingly. Hilsey, for example, compelled London's Carthusians to be present every week from December 1535, in the hope of reaching peaceful accommodation with them through propaganda packaged as instruction. The bishop failed in this case but not through want of effort. Between 23 January and 2 April 1536, every preacher selected under Hilsey's commission either enthusiastically advocated the Royal Supremacy, or else took great pains to stay within the bounds of conformity. Whether the voices were those of Latimer or Longland, Tunstall or Shaxton, none crossed the line which would deny Henry's right to govern the Church or Cromwell's, as vicegerent, to rule in the king's name.[79]

Cromwell supervised the Paul's Cross sermons energetically, trying to ensure a steady flow of compliant, effective preachers. With Hilsey's collaboration and occasional advice from Stokesley, he meticulously organised each step in the process. He compiled lists of prospective preachers, sent out invitations, and encouraged those selected to their best efforts. Favourable sermons did not automatically lead to Cromwellian preferment, but there are indications that preaching was a valuable path to ecclesiastical office. Cromwell wrote to Dr

[76] This story is told well by Millar MacLure, The Paul's Cross Sermons, 1534–1642, Toronto 1953, 184–9. Cf. Elton, Policy and Police, 214–16.
[77] Ibid.
[78] BL, Add. MS 48022, fos 87–8.
[79] Elton, Policy and Police, 215.

William Sandwich, dean of Canterbury College, Oxford. He had taken notice of the dean's learning in holy letters and incorrupt judgment in the same. Cromwell invited Sandwich to occupy the room of a preacher at Paul's Cross on 19 August 1537. To prepare the dean for his debut, Cromwell advised, 'that ye fail not to be there at the same day, preparing in the meantime with such pure and sincereness, truly to open the word of God'.[80] Cromwell had not met Sandwich before, but he hoped that this occasion would cause him to think true the good reports he had heard about the dean. The minister mentioned no specific reward or payment, but he told Sandwich that he 'shall not only do a right good deed, but also minister unto me thankful pleasure which I shall not fail to requite as occasion may thereunto serve'.[81]

Cromwell brought preachers into London; he also sent preachers into the outlying dioceses, following their progress with interest and encouraging them with patronage and protection. Richard Croke, humanist scholar, royal tutor, and reform activist, delivered sixty sermons at Cromwell's request. He travelled a circuit of thirty-seven churches, giving a prepared sermon in which he vigorously attacked the bishop of Rome. Croke argued that popes together with their cardinals and 'cloistered hypocrites' had created schisms. He employed Scripture and the writings of the church fathers to refute papal authority, and he believed that his preaching had a good effect. Many laymen and priests, Croke enthused, lamenting their long ignorance, asked him to stay for discussions after the conclusion of his formal sermon. 'So that if all preachers at the least in those places where they never did preach before would sincerely and effectively touch these matters, I doubt not but the people would soon be induced to be utter enemies unto the bishop of Rome and his cloisters.' Cromwell made no specific grant to Croke for his preaching. None seem needed. Croke asked only that Cromwell protect his interests with his college, so that his absence on royal business would not be turned against him.[82]

Building support for reform through the preaching office also interested Archbishop Cranmer. He frequently joined Cromwell in selecting preachers and supervising their sermons. He sent, for example, 'another copy of the sermon which Doctor Cronkehouse should preach'. A first draft had been submitted and returned for revisions. Now, Cranmer wanted Cromwell to review the changes, adding or taking away, 'as you shall think convenient'. Then Cranmer requested that Cromwell should either authorise presentation of the sermon, or else inform him of his pleasure therein.[83]

The archbishop worked hard to provide effective, loyal preachers for the dioceses of conservative prelates and their like-minded officials. In May 1537 he appealed for Cromwell's intervention on behalf of a man named Gounthorp, parson of Weeting, whom Cranmer had known at Cambridge. The archbishop recommended Gounthorp, 'not only for a great clerk, but also of such singular judgment, sobriety, and conversation of living, that in all these qualities, I have known very few like him'. Despite these qualities, according to Cranmer,

---

80 SP 1/123/174 (LP xii/2. 412).
81 Ibid.
82 SP 1/117/154v (LP xii/1. 757).
83 *Cranmer's Letters*, 389.

Gounthorp had been denied licence to preach in the diocese of Norwich. Dale, a chaplain to the bishop, opposed Gounthorp and held sway for the moment. Cranmer also knew Dale during his Cambridge days and believed him to be 'without all learning and discretion'. The archbishop accused Dale of permitting 'none to preach in his diocese that be of right judgment', and he besought Cromwell to grant Gounthorp the king's licence to preach and to protect the parson in the event that Dale promoted causes against him before the bishop of Norwich.[84] Cranmer added that he knew of two or three other substantially learned men within the see of Norwich. He hoped Cromwell would licence them also, 'for it were great pity that the diocese of Norwich should be continued in the right knowledge of God which is begun amongst them'.[85]

Preachers selected to carry reformed doctrine into the parishes often met heated opposition. Cromwell offered a sympathetic ear to their difficulties and tangible protection when necessary. Richard Qulaenus, later Cromwell's chaplain, preached in Stamford, Lincolnshire, on 22 August 1535. He took justification by faith for his theme, a red flag to several Dominicans present. As he left the pulpit the friars rose up to argue for traditional Catholic doctrine, and Qulaenus feared that the effect of his sermon had been undermined by these dissident voices. Remembering that the king had ordered preachers to reveal only the pure and sincere Gospel, Qulaenus asked for Cromwell's intervention, for without it he believed that what was built up one day would be destroyed the next.[86]

Qulaenus held more than a preaching brief from Cromwell. He also reviewed a sermon given by the abbot of Thame in St Martin's church, near Stamford. The abbot, then a suffragan bishop in the service of John Longland, charged with grievous sin men who carried the New Testament into taverns and like places to preach the word. For his part, Qulaenus thought it a good idea to preach the Gospel even in brothels. According to his account, the abbot had also attacked the campaigns against images, saints, and monasticism, and he had concluded by asserting that the Lord's Prayer should not be uttered by heretics, infidels, or imperfect men. Qulaenus, of course, refuted all the abbot's statements, while noting that the north abounded with this sort of preacher. Fortunately, he said, many substantial men had witnessed the sermon, else he would not have dared to write thus for fear of the power of the bishop of Lincoln.[87]

Cromwellian patronage and protection of men who preached frankly Protestant doctrine represented more than an annoyance to conservative prelates. It lay at the core of factional competition. Control of preachers seemed part of a broad and explicit factional assault on traditional religious practices and episcopal prerogatives. Increasingly, in fact, men who could not have obtained a bishop's licence to preach, sought and received authorisation from the king, the vicegerent, or the archbishop of Canterbury. Conservatives saw Cromwell at the centre of this aggressive factional offensive. Faced with the influx of alien

84 Ibid. 336.
85 Ibid.
86 BL, Cotton Cleopatra E v. fo. 94 (*LP* ix. 611).
87 Ibid.

preachers, many unbeneficed, committed zealously to reform, and too often supported by Cromwell, the bishops battled to defend their dignity and status within their own dioceses.

Archbishop Lee cried loud and long for Cromwell to stop sending preachers to his jurisdiction. He explained that generally he suffered no preachers 'that without discretion preach novelties'. Lately, however, when he tried to discharge those preachers who 'do rather sow seeds of dissention than do any good', he discovered that many of them presented licences issued by the king or Cromwell. Prohibited from acting in these instances, Lee voiced two concerns. First, he protested that he had lacked prior knowledge, and he asked Cromwell to 'suffer no such licence to pass, but that I shall know thereof, and what your pleasure is then'. More vexing to Archbishop Lee, however, was that men with licences from the archbishop of Canterbury were preaching in the province of York. Lee insisted that 'if they have none shall be obeyed here, but only the king's and yours'.[88]

Lee strongly resisted reform-minded preachers. At the same time, he fought rigorously against Cromwell's efforts to promote a uniform pattern of preaching. In answer to charges that a chaplain, 'being in my household at Beverly', had preached against the king's injunctions, Lee claimed never to have heard of such a preacher.[89] He argued that no bishop in England had given greater charge to his clergy, 'that no man shall preach otherwise than according to the king's injunctions'. Further, he stated, that if he had known of such a man, he would have sent him immediately up to Cromwell. 'I trust your good lordship will not think that I would maintain or nourish any such in my house, although the words in your letter be such.' Lee, nevertheless, promised a full inquiry, after peevishly remarking that Cromwell might have made the work easier by supplying more information.[90]

Goaded into action, Archbishop Lee ordered a thorough examination. Dr Downes, Dr Clifton, subdean of York, and Robert Creake, 'a good and wise gentleman', investigated all those who had preached in the city in the six months past. They asked the priests, 'whether they did perceive that any men were offended with any of their preaching, and if so, wherein, and for what words'. They discovered that Lee's former suffragan, old and semi-retired, had uttered the words in question. Lee offered to do whatever Cromwell required, but he hoped that Cromwell would allow the matter to drop. More importantly, he reported, his commissioners' investigations revealed that most of the priests examined, 'pretended ignorance what injunctions the king's highness hath given to preachers'. The archbishop promised to order wider and more effective dissemination of royal instructions and a stricter discipline in their enforcement.[91]

While Archbishop Lee, as always, directed most of his energies toward protecting himself from royal displeasure, Bishop Longland of Lincoln, far less deferential, fought with desperation to retain control of preachers in his

---

88 Ibid. iv. fo. 286v (*LP* x. 716).
89 SP 1/133/189 (*LP* xiii/1. 1247).
90 Ibid.
91 SP 1/134/93r–v (*LP* xiii/1. 1317); SP 1/133/189 (*LP* xiii/1. 1247).

diocese. Appointed to the episcopacy in 1521, Longland had both the experience and the determination to fight back against what he believed to be
unwarranted interference with his rights to decide who would be allowed to
preach in Lincoln. In 1537 the bishop demanded that Robert Wisdom, curate
of All Hallows, Oxford, 'no more to preach within my diocese under pain of
law, unless you have my licence and authority to do the same'. Marvelling not a
little that Wisdom would dare to preach without his permission, Longland
advised the curate, not without contempt, that it would be best for him to study
divinity before again aspiring to the office of a preacher.[92]

Furious at what he regarded as the arrogant behavior of a presumptuous
curate, Longland moved to ensure that Wisdom could not defy his pro-
hibitions. He wrote to the rector of Lincoln College, patron of All Hallows, to
insist that Wisdom must not preach, informing the rector that Wisdom was not
fit for the pulpit, being neither graduate, nor learned, nor a student. Rather, he
argued, Wisdom had forsaken his religion. In these circumstances Longland
charged the rector either to preach himself or to appoint some other learned
fellow of the college to occupy the pulpit. He concluded with a warning 'to
look better unto such cures as are appropriated unto your college, else I must
farther see thereunto'.[93]

Ten years earlier, Longland's remedy might have produced the desired effect.
Now, however, Wisdom, instead of meekly submitting to Longland's demands,
attempted to pressure the bishop to relent. The curate sought Cromwell's
attention and protection. At the same time he encouraged his parishioners to
make known their dissatisfaction at Longland's intervention. For Cromwell,
Wisdom presented himself and his case. The curate contended that he had
preached the gospel of God according to his duty to the town, but now he was
'forbid and commanded to silence at the suggestion of some malicious persons
which are aggrieved to lose their glory and they to give it to Christ'. Those who
opposed his preaching, Wisdom continued, were papistical maintainers of
superstition. Confidently, he asked Cromwell, 'either that I may do duty as a
curate should do, or else at your commandment to keep silence'.[94]

In the meantime, the bailiff and other prominent men of Oxford came out in
support of Wisdom against Longland. They addressed a petition to the bishop
and sent a copy to Cromwell. In their plea they praised Wisdom's parochial
work, particularly the care he devoted to the sick, at great risk to himself. Now
they hoped that the bishop might allow Wisdom to resume his teaching, 'as we
right well perceive his duty is to do'. The bishop's efforts to keep their curate
from preaching, the townsmen believed, represented a major injustice.[95] After
all, they wrote, Wisdom had demonstrated his loyalty by defending the king's
dignity during the late rebellion and by praying for Jane Seymour during her
pregnancy. The royal interest was more important than Longland's concerns

---

[92] SP 1/105/102 (*LP* xi. 136).
[93] SP 1/105/103 (*LP* xi. 137).
[94] SP 1/105/104 (*LP* xi. 138).
[95] SP 1/123/145v (*LP* xii/2. 374).

about doctrinal orthodoxy. Unless, they argued, it could be shown that his preaching violated royal commandments, Wisdom should not be silenced.[96]

Finally, the petitioners accused the bishop of attacking a man who had served their interests to their complete satisfaction:

> For we would be loath to be any longer in ignorance but would gladly at the least we might know God's commandment and the articles of our faith. It grieveth us sore that that we were not instructed in them no sooner, and more would grieve us if now he hath begun to teach then he should be thrust by ill will or malicious forging from us, and we yoked to our former blindness.[97]

No further correspondence has survived so we cannot know whether Wisdom or Longland prevailed in this instance. The curate, however, did not immediately suffer from his confrontation with the bishop. Cromwell's patronage brought him to the parish church of St Margaret's, Lothbury, which he held at least until 1539, when prosecution under provisions of the Act of the Six Articles ended Wisdom's preaching career.[98]

Cromwell's protection and advancement of Robert Wisdom sketches out a patronage relationship. The vicegerent's association with Thomas Swynnerton furnishes a fully developed picture of Cromwell's energetic use of patronage to promote factional interests and ecclesiastical reform. Thomas Swynnerton first came to court with the group of writers recruited by Cromwell to counter the defections of Fisher, More, Gardiner, and Reginald Pole.[99] Along with Starkey, Richard Moryson, Richard Taverner, and others, he worked at translating reforming tracts, when not occupied with his own original compositions. In 1534, resident in either Cromwell's or Cranmer's household, he wrote A Mustre of Scismatyke Bysshoppes of Rome, which was printed by Wynkyn de Worde for John Bedell.[100] Two years later, Swynnerton completed his literary career with a theological tract, entitled The Tropes and Figures of Scripture, 'a matter of so much necessity, that without it cannot easily be avoided the danger of heresy'. The body of the work, outspokenly Protestant in tone, defended the Royal Supremacy utilising scriptural sources and commentaries by Melanchthon, Eck, Cochlaeus, More, Barnes, and Tyndale. Swynnerton dedicated the work to Cromwell to whom he wished 'all health and increase of honour'.[101] Otherwise, the dedication is a blunt, straightforward factional manifesto in which Swynnerton recognised two categories of people within the realm. The first,

---

96 Ibid.

97 Ibid.

98 LP xi. 138 (editor's note).

99 Thomas Swynnerton, son of Robert, was from Staffordshire. John Bale, himself a radical Protestant, described him as studious in good arts and letters from his youth. He attended both Oxford and Cambridge, graduating from the latter, BA, 1515 and MA, 1519. For matriculation he used the alias John Roberts to shield himself from possible charges arising from his heretical opinions: DNB xix. 234–5.

100 STC 23552. For Swynnerton's humanist connections see McConica, English Humanists, 127, 143.

101 E 36/193/3–4. A summary of the dedication can be found in LP xi. 1422.

'with all force and power, daily promote and advance the most godly affairs of our most dread sovereign lord, the king, concerning the doctrine taught by the sweet mouth of our most merciful savior Christ Jesu'. The second group with all their strength and might covertly resisted and 'are well content and pleased, that such new fangled factions (so they call God's doctrine) never come to effect, ne have prosperous success of fortune'.[102]

In vivid language Swynnerton accused the conservative faction of subverting the pure word of God in order to serve their partisan purposes. Further, he argued, in matters of controversy, when they could not sustain their feeble arguments from Scripture, they contended that 'the letter killeth, the letter killeth'. By this miserable subterfuge, wrote Swynnerton, they stopped the mouths of the poor and unlearned: 'With this sword they subdue all dreadful doubts.' But, he continued, when it seemed as if Scripture could be used to strengthen their position:

> Lord Jesu, how then they foam and fume, yell and take on, none otherwise than furies or tormentors of Hell. Not the breadth of a hair, in this case, the devil can once move them from the literal sense. Still they cry. Thus saith the Scripture. These be the words. The words be plain. The letter killeth is now quite gone, it is forgotten, and as clear out of memory, as it had never been heard of.[103]

Swynnerton proposed to put an end to these pernicious uses of God's word. On the basis of certain Augustinian precepts to be developed in the text he would declare when it was correct to affirm the literal sense of Scripture, and when the literal sense should be denied; 'when the letter killeth (as they say) and when it killeth not'.[104]

Swynnerton's work as an author reveals the lines of patronage developed by Cromwell to furnish support for reformers. Recognising his own intellectual limitations, Swynnerton modestly set forward his ability to handle such sensitive topics. He argued, however, that necessity compelled his attention, and he confidently anticipated Cromwell's approval of his tract. Contrary to common practice, Swynnerton did not ask to be paid for his efforts, a strong indication that Cromwell had commissioned the work in advance.[105] Without private means, Swynnerton would have needed outside support for a considerable period of time. Moreover, the length and Protestant tone of the work required a comprehensive library of books prohibited to the general public. Only within the circle of either Cromwell or Cranmer could these needs have been met. Certainly, the tract had official sanction and sponsorship.

Soon after completing *The Tropes and Figures of Scripture*, Swynnerton left London on a preaching mission to Lincolnshire. Perhaps Cromwell asked him to undertake the mission; Swynnerton carried with him a licence to preach

[102] E 36/193/3r.
[103] Ibid. 3v–4r.
[104] Ibid.
[105] Ibid.

throughout the realm granted by the newly created Faculty Office.[106] Leaving London in the spring of 1536, he worked his way from parish to parish, preaching and teaching among ordinary people who sustained him with their voluntary contributions in money and kind.[107]

All went well enough until Bishop Longland learned of Swynnerton's presence. Extremely displeased, he complained to Cromwell, and his reports provide the details of Swynnerton's activities. 'Here hath been lately in these parts Sir Swynnerton', wrote Longland on 5 May 1536, 'the preacher which I showed your mastership of, and doth much discontent and offend good people for he lacketh both learning, knowledge of his doctors, and discretion.'[108] Longland had reason for concern. People often travelled long distances to hear Swynnerton. Notice of the preacher's movements advanced by word of mouth, and large crowds gathered. Sympathetic local curates and ordinary artisans hosted the events which included fiery sermons denouncing the papacy and informal meetings at which Swynnerton instructed his audiences with material drawn from his supply of vernacular Protestant writings.[109]

Longland saw heresy in these actions. He accused Swynnerton of evil living and inappropriate clerical behaviour:

He preacheth from day to day, and sometime on the workdays, and twice upon a day for the most part. And his sermons are not fruitful, but rather seditious, and preacheth those things that the king his grace did inhibit all preachers, such doubtful matters as are not yet determined. Which was commanded in all dioceses not be touched in sermons, till the determinations thereof were well known and published.[110]

Lack of authority concerned Longland most. He could not stop Swynnerton from preaching, for 'when it is told him that he ought not to speak of such things, he answereth and sayeth that he knoweth the king his mind'. Finally, the bishop blamed Swynnerton for causing idleness and poverty with his disruptive popularity. 'And here are now a late robberies committed by such idle people.' To combat these evils, Longland wanted most of all for Cromwell to revoke Swynnerton's licence to preach 'that if this priest had not licence under the king his seal, people would not admit him, nor hear him'.

Deliberately then, Longland classified Swynnerton with common criminals. Aware of the futility of accusing him of heretical preaching, Longland bracketed Swynnerton with a black friar named Threder who had been invoking the spirit world to find lost goods and buried treasure. He appealed to Cromwell 'that such unlawful things might be redressed for the common weal, which common weal, I know ye do as much tender as any man'. Longland's concern, however, was practical and political, not theoretical. The direct challenge raised by Swynnerton's preaching struck close to the hierarchical heart of

---

106 D. S. Chambers (ed.), *Faculty Office Registers, 1534–1549*, Oxford 1966, 39.
107 SP 1/103/234–5 (*LP* x. 804).
108 Ibid. 234v.
109 Ibid.
110 Ibid.

traditional ecclesiastical governance, far too close to Longland's position for him to ignore. Swynnerton went so far as to propose to preach on Holy Rood Day at Woburn, in the bishop's own church. He was prevented from his purpose only when Longland decided to occupy the pulpit himself.[111] Swynnerton's militant activism and apparent lack of discretion gave credence to Longland's charges and obliged Cromwell to authorise the arrest of both Swynnerton and Threder. The spirit world failed to warn the friar, and Longland's men captured and imprisoned him to await Cromwell's further pleasure. The order to arrest Swynnerton, however, was pure charade. By the time Longland had received permission to apprehend him, Swynnerton had escaped, 'either in London or Essex whose costs was paid for at the time of his being in my diocese by certain poor men not having sufficient for themselves'.[112] Despite official censure, Swynnerton comfortably returned to his place within the reform faction. He resumed his intellectual career, and he continued to preach. Subsequently, during Edward's reign, he held preaching posts at Ipswich and Sandwich. When Mary came to the throne, he fled to Emden, probably with John a Lasco who became pastor there. He died in exile in 1554.[113]

Swynnerton's adventures reveal Cromwell's characteristic support for loyal men who preached in favour of the Supremacy and reform. The effect of his efforts varied, according to the abilities of those selected to preach and the willingness of their audiences to hear and to respond. Each act of patronage produced a significant local impact. Carefully drawn statutes, injunctions, and directives raised encouragement of preaching to the status of national policy. Cromwell had thus furnished for the state and the reform faction a voice with the potential to reach into every household in the realm. He wasted no time in putting this voice to good use.

[111] Ibid.
[112] SP 1/103/274 (*LP* x. 850).
[113] *DNB* xix. 234–5.

6

Church and Commonwealth: the Cure of Souls

Throughout his vicegerental career, Cromwell diligently attended to the need to improve the quality of service delivered by the Church to parishes in all parts of the realm. Popular enthusiasm for reform of the Church drew support from a deep reservoir of anticlerical sentiment in England.[1] Long before Henry began to question the validity of his marriage to Catherine, widespread hostility directed toward ecclesiastical institutions and personnel had reached alarming proportions. Centuries of abused clerical privilege and poor clerical performance seriously eroded the links of obedience and respect which bound the laity to the Church. Conflicts over tithes and spiritual dues sparked resentment. Church courts, determined to uphold ecclesiastical authority, drove wedges between priests and laymen. An endemic feature of Tudor life, encouraged for a time during the divorce crisis, anticlericalism endured to furnish a backdrop against which the public policy of the Henrician Reformation unfolded.[2]

Cromwell appreciated the political advantage of an aroused anticlerical laity. He also exhibited concern for the spiritual welfare of ordinary people. Both as an architect of policy and a patron of church officials, Cromwell treated parochial reform seriously. The central position of the parish in religious life demanded no less. Cromwell blended articles, injunctions, patronage, and the creation of a new ecclesiastical office in an attempt to address parochial needs and to rally popular support for further reforms in Church and commonwealth.

---

[1] Scarisbrick (*Reformation*) and Haigh (*Reformation Revised*) construct an argument which insists that the English Reformation was the outcome of narrow factional competition for office and influence rather than a popular movement riding on waves of anticlericalism from below. Their conclusions are based on their own preferred interpretations of a carefully restricted body of evidence. Haigh sees the Reformation through northern eyes and ignores anticlerical demands issuing from more heavily populated areas closer to London. Scarisbrick clearly offers a Catholic apologetic in his book which is based on the 1982 Ford Lectures. Both ignore two centuries of post-plague unrest which had weakened the fabric of the Church, alienated many parishioners from their priests, and occasioned a crisis which can be observed in the writings of contemporary critics who nevertheless had no desire to break the bonds which placed England's ecclesiastical institutions under Roman jurisdiction.

[2] For Dickens's reply to Haigh and Scarisbrick see A. G. Dickens, 'The shape of anticlericalism and the English Reformation', in E. I. Kouri and T. Scott (eds), *Politics and Society in Reformation Europe*, London 1987, 379–410; and idem. 'The early expansion of Protestantism in England, 1520–1558', *Archivum Reformationgeschichte*, lxxviii (1987), 187–222. Despite historiographical controversies which often take on a life of their own, the volume of letters to Cromwell complaining about the poor quality of clerical performance, overwhelmingly supports the conclusion that government believed anticlericalism could be utilised to support its programme for reform, and that in its most extreme forms unreformed anticlericalism threatened to dissolve traditional social hierarchies.

The outlines of Cromwellian policy first appeared in the Articles of Religion of July 1536, and in the 1536 Injunctions to the Clergy. The former, published by Berthelet, popularly known as the Ten Articles, arose from meetings of convocation and attempted to establish a consensus on doubtful points of religion. The king, Cromwell, and members from all segments of the clerical community participated in the discussions.[3] The Articles declared that the king, concerned that his subjects know the word of God and reverently observe it, had discharged his duty as supreme head through the publication of these guidelines. Dominated by reform faction adherents and closely watched by Cromwell, the meetings of clerical leaders established the boundaries of religious dissent, the theological platform which would guide the first steps of parochial reform. Acceptance of the Royal Supremacy was *sine qua non*. Otherwise, the Ten Articles offered a pragmatic political compromise, a tentative statement which allowed, if reluctantly, that some deviations in doctrine and practice might be tolerated, so long as they did not challenge the authority of the crown. The preamble to the Ten Articles embodied Cromwell's mood:

> We have caused by the like consent and agreement of our said bishops and other learned men, the said articles to be divided into two sorts; whereof the one part containeth such as be commanded expressly by God, and be necessary to our salvation; and the other containeth such things as have been of long continuance for a decent order and honest policy, prudently instituted and used in the churches of our realm, and be kept accordingly, although they be not necessary to our salvation.[4]

As long as he conformed to the laws of the realm, any clerk could draw some measure of comfort from the Articles, whose substance guaranteed reform without making specific concessions to more radical Protestant interests. Only three of the seven sacraments appeared in the Articles, but their elucidation was orthodox, and the existence of the others was not categorically rejected. The phrasing of the Sacrament of the Altar allowed a Lutheran interpretation but acknowledged transubstantiation. Auricular confession and penance remained; prayers for the dead survived; but purgatory disappeared as it lacked scriptural authority. Salvation could be gained solely through the mercy and grace of the Father, promised freely for the Son's sake and for the merits of his blood and passion. 'But also he requireth and commandeth us, that after we be justified we must also have good works of charity and obedience toward God.'[5]

Designed to eliminate doctrinal controversy for a time, the Ten Articles made it possible for Cromwell to develop in his August 1536 Injunctions to the Clergy a policy for the reform of clerical abuses. These injunctions, issued in

---

[3] The signatories included Cromwell, both archbishops, fourteen bishops, twenty-nine abbots, eleven priors, and fifty members of the lower house of convocation: Hughes, *The Reformation*, i. 352. The official title of the Ten Articles was *Articles deuised by the Kynges highnes maiestie, to stablyshe christen quietnes and unitie amonge us, and to avoyde contentions opinions, which articles be also approved by the consent and determination of the hole clergie of this realm*.

[4] Charles Lloyd (ed.), *Formularies of Faith*, Oxford 1825, p. xvi.

[5] Ibid. p. xxxvi.

the king's name and inspired in part by the discussions on the Ten Articles, nevertheless represent Cromwell's first application of his own vicegerental authority to the practical problems of parochial reform:

> I Thomas Cromwell, knight, Lord Cromwell, keeper of the privy seal of our said sovereign lord the king, and vicegerent unto the same, for and concerning all his jurisdiction ecclesiastical within this realm . . . have to the glory of Almighty God, to the king's highness's honour, the public weal of his realm, and increase of virtue in the same, appointed and assigned these injunctions ensuing.[6]

First, Cromwell reminded the clergy that they must obey all anti-papal legislation, submit themselves to the Royal Supremacy, and preach to their flocks against the usurped power of the bishop of Rome. He further ordered clerks to explain the Ten Articles to their congregations to bring them into conformity with recent decisions of Convocation.[7] Then Cromwell set out a series of injunctions which established guidelines for parish priests to elevate the quality of parochial life. Most important in this regard were the injunctions which established the standards for parochial service. Parsons, vicars, and curates were to minister the sacraments without fail. If the incumbent did not reside, he was to provide an honest and well-learned curate

> that may teach the rude and unlearned of their cure wholesome doctrine, and reduce them to the right way that do err; and always let them see, that neither they nor their vicars, do seek more than their own profit, promotion, or advantage, than the profit of the souls that they have under their cure, or the glory of God.[8]

One injunction insisted that clerks maintain their churches in good repair; another required them to stay out of taverns and alehouses, to use their leisure to study Scripture or to occupy themselves with honest exercise, 'having always in mind that they ought to excel all other in purity of life and should be example to all others to live well and Christianly'. If the nonresident's income exceeded £40 a year, Cromwell demanded that he dispense the fortieth part of his stipend to the poor. And all beneficed priests with £100 or more were charged to give competent exhibition to at least one scholar at Oxford or Cambridge or some grammar school in order that he might serve the parish in their turn, or 'otherwise profit the commonwealth with their counsel or wisdom'. Cromwell placed great faith in education to further his goals. He believed that the clergy could best advance this didactic process by patronising students, preaching to heads of households, and by living exemplary lives. Preachers were to direct their sermons to mothers and fathers, masters and governors of youth, so that they could teach their children and servants the elements of faith, even from infancy.[9]

---

6   Gee and Hardy, *English Church History*, 269.
7   Ibid. 270.
8   Ibid. 273.
9   Ibid. 271–4.

The commonwealth delineated in Cromwell's Injunctions remained hierarchical and in many ways coercive, but the structure and power it envisioned would be directed towards the keeping of God's commandments and the fulfilling of his works of charity. A person would express the glory of God through his lay pursuits rather than through the worship of images, pilgrimages, or the observance of superfluous holy days. Sloth and idleness would be discouraged, resulting in the reduction of begging, stealing, murder, and other destructive acts.[10]

Calculated to satisfy popular concern for much-needed parochial reform, the Articles and Injunctions actually stimulated further disaffection. In the north Cromwell's public commitment to reform helped to incite resistance and rebellion in Lincolnshire and Yorkshire at the end of 1536. Though the attack on Roman jurisdiction had barely touched the substance of traditional religious doctrine and practice, fear of change abounded. Perceptions of heresy compounded by the dissolution of the lesser monasteries, connected to a host of secular grievances pushed large numbers of northern people toward insurrection. Rumours proliferated: that the parish churches would be pulled down with the monasteries; that the jewels and plate of local churches would be seized and taken to London; that licences would be needed before white bread and capon could be eaten.[11]

The lower clergy, particularly, added fuel to the embers of discontent. It was no coincidence that at Louth, Caistor, and Horncastle, the three Lincolnshire market towns which spawned the Northern Rebellion, many parish priests mixed with grumbling local residents. Cromwell had ordered the local clergy to meet special commissioners to hear how the Ten Articles and Injunctions would be applied to their cures. It has been argued that these priests, desperately afraid, constituted the crucial ingredient in the transformation of, at most, an urban riot into a full-fledged, regional mass movement.[12]

Clerical anxiety centred around the new expectations of priests established in the Injunctions. Demands that the clergy preach and teach as their central functions contrasted with the traditional ritualistic duties of the priest. It had been enough for a good priest to shepherd his flock, to perform the mass, to hear confession, to visit the sick, to baptise, marry, and bury his parishioners. The new emphasis on the sermon boded ill for many clerks too poorly educated to speak from the pulpit. The mere words contained in the Injunctions might be allowed to fade from the memory, but Cromwell's visitation could not be shrugged off. Threatened with exposure of their inadequacies and possible loss of their livings, some among the northern clergy joined the incipient revolt, and helped to translate inarticulate secular anger into a distinct language of protest against the proposed changes in religion.

Guided in part by clerical voices, in part by economic distress, in part by nameless fears, the rebels took the field and presented their petitions to the king. They insisted that the suppression of the abbeys be halted, that

---

[10] Ibid. 271.
[11] See, particularly, M. E. James, 'Obedience and dissent in Henrician England', *Past and Present*, xlviii (1970), 14–15.
[12] Ibid.

Cromwell, their archenemy, be handed over to the people, and that the 'heretical bishops', especially Cranmer, be dismissed. Indirectly attacking the Royal Supremacy, Lincolnshire rebels and Yorkshire pilgrims prescribed the amputation of reformers in order to restore the body politic to health. In a bitter letter to Archbishop Cranmer Alexander Alesius offered his own diagnosis of the rebel calls for the execution of the reform faction's leaders, the king's principal religious advisors. Alesius argued that by their actions the rebels had denied any gospel spirit or concern for purer doctrine, because any Christian theology, Catholic or Lutheran, would have taught them to die honourably in silence, rather than raise a rebellion, either on economic or religious grounds. He railed against what he characterised as priestly and monkish insanities and suggested that the truce with the papists be ended. Alesius hoped that Cromwell would take action against what he perceived to be impiety and hypocrisy, even against the opposition of the conservative bishops, who might if necessary be replaced by priests who would preach a pure gospel.[13]

In the face of this major challenge to the Supremacy and Henrician rule Cromwell remained passive, almost invisible. The king, meanwhile, with the aid of the dukes of Suffolk and Norfolk, initiated and carried through the ruthless suppression of the rebellion. Cromwell confined his efforts, seeking to determine the degree to which the outbreak threatened the Supremacy and the progress of reform. With peace restored, Cromwell began to investigate the causes of the rebellion. He drafted a series of interrogatories to be administered to captured leaders of the northern dissidents. Did these men deny the king's title or authority? Did they know of others who opposed the Supremacy? Were they in contact with foreign potentates working to abrogate English laws? Did they desire that the bishop of Rome's usurped authority be restored?[14]

Despite continuing concern, the Northern Rebellion and Pilgrimage of Grace demonstrated the futility and danger of overt resistance to royal policies touching religion. The king had proved himself supreme in a most direct manner. 'No doubt', wrote Edward Foxe to Martin Bucer, 'you have heard of these tragedies and tumults which have lately been stirred up by wicked men among us and which might have led to great evil had they not been promptly extinguished by the best of princes, who when he saw all appeased immediately turned his mind to promulgating the gospel.'[15]

The defeat of this massive protest against reform left Cromwell more firmly in control of royal government and discredited conservative factional opposition. Cromwell could turn back to the campaign for the reform of clerical abuses envisioned in his injunctions. Satisfying parochial demands for reform would not be an easy occupation. The common experience of parish life little resembled the portrait of harmonious service portrayed in the Injunctions. New standards for clerical performance reminded people of past failures. With renewed hope men critically examined their priests and began to insist on improvements which Cromwell, handicapped by limited patronage resources, could not deliver. The spiritual needs of people spread over more than 8,000

13 LP xi. 987 (SP 6/6/17).
14 SP 1/118/277–93 (LP xii/1. 1021).
15 LP xii/2. 41.

parishes depended for their fulfillment on the diverse sympathies and abilities of a host of men who served as diocesan officials, parochial functionaries, or patrons of benefices. Many parishioners, hoping to benefit immediately from the reforms promoted in the Injunctions, were bitterly disappointed. Their complaints to Cromwell reveal not only their suffering and discontent, but also their increasing refusal to tolerate longstanding clerical abuses.

In a period of rising expectations, many priests proved to be remarkably shortsighted. John Divale, parson of Wincanton, seemed to combine in himself most of the faults guaranteed to anger an already anticlerical constituency. Three men from this Somerset parish carried their grievances to Cromwell. Divale, the complaint alleged, was given to 'dicing, carding, booling, and playing at cross wasters with other unthrifty games'. A gambling cleric might annoy hard-working men in any parish, but not intolerably, except that Divale blocked the efforts of his reform-minded flock to read or hear Scripture. Realising their priest's limitations, the parishioners of Wincanton tried to get John Warde, parish priest of Castle Cray, to preach to them. Warde, an enthusiastic New Testament student, exhorted those who could read to study Scripture in English. On Good Friday, Divale responded by admonishing his audience against 'these newfangled fellows which read these new books'. He called them knaves, heretics, and Pharisees, and likened them 'to a dog that gnaweth on a marybone and never cometh to the pith'. Moreover Divale was also charged with saying that he hoped to see the bishop of Worcester, Hugh Latimer, burned with all the new books in England about him. Cromwell was petitioned to intervene to protect the parish from the parson's wrath.[16]

Although many of the complaints could have been made at any period, the influx of new religious commitments cannot be disregarded. Sir Richard Gresham, lord mayor of London, held an examination to consider charges brought against John Forde, parson of St Margaret's, Lothbury. Roger Taylor, parish churchwarden, initiated the action. Supported by other parishioners, Taylor said that he had asked Forde to begin Matins at an earlier time, because they had invited a preacher to deliver a sermon in place of the regular service. Forde retorted that he would break the hours for no man. When Taylor explained that the preacher, Thomas Rose, carried licence to preach sealed by the king, Forde replied, 'Tush for the seal; if mine ordinary come it shall be received, and if the other come I will look twice on it or I receive it.' Later, Forde invited several other witnesses to make and seal the king's writing under a bush.[17]

Animosity between Forde and his parishioners developed from the priest's unwillingness to preach. Afraid of his sophisticated flock and probably unlearned, Forde had refused to preach on a number of occasions. An adherent of the old religious customs, he also continued to ring the church bells on St Margaret's Day, and he rejected the authority of Cromwell's Injunctions, which he regarded as a thing 'to make fools afraid withall'. There is no record of any further action in this case, but with the active opposition of his vocal London

---

[16] SP 1/151/155–6 (LP xiv/1. 897).
[17] LP xiii/1. 1492.

parishioners, Forde's personal feelings about government undoubtedly took a more circumspect turn.[18]

Francis Turpyn attended services at St Bude's church in Fleet Street on 10 June 1537. There he heard a sermon preached by a Carmelite, Robert Austin, which incensed him. The white friar did not pray for the king, Turpyn charged, nor did he include the reverent style due his prince, that being supreme head under God of the Church of England. And, continued Turpyn, despite the provisions of the lately proclaimed commission, Austin, although licensed to preach by the bishop of London, refused to inveigh against the usurped power of the bishop of Rome.[19]

Thomas Wentworth also took seriously his responsibility to report violations of the Injunctions. Patron of the chantry of Edmund Daundy, Ipswich, he had heard from several credible persons that the priest, James Crawford, 'hath been ever a enemy to the word of God and never the lover nor favourer thereof'. The clerk did not fulfill the ordinances and constitutions of the chantry foundation, and he behaved poorly 'at the time of the commotions and insurrection of them in the north parts'. Wentworth dispossessed Crawford and replaced him with Thomas Becon, 'a very discreet and honest priest'.[20]

Local men everywhere seemed to be able to find copies of Cromwell's Injunctions, and they judged their priests' performance critically. Robert Ward, frustrated by resistance to the frequent commands for curates and pastors to publish the word of God and to speak out against the pope, wrote to Cromwell in October 1538. He complained that in Barking parish, Suffolk, where Richard Redmond was parson, the word of God was never preached unless a stranger came by chance. Even these infrequent visitors never set forth the king's title, nor declared Cromwell's Injunctions. According to Ward, the negligence of the local clergy left the people untaught. The clergy refused to supplement the few religious books in English. The papal name had not been erased from clerical texts in the chapels of Needham Market and Darmysdon. Ward, carried away with reforming zeal, assured Cromwell that, were it not for fear of the king's displeasure, he being married, he would set forth the Injunctions himself.[21]

Cromwell not only received and tried to resolve cases which reached him directly, he also supervised causes within the orbits of other crown officials. He ordered Thomas Cranmer to send Hugh Payne to him after his appearance before the archbishop. Payne had been curate of Hadley, Suffolk, in the jurisdiction of Canterbury. Detected for erroneous and seditious preaching, and cited to appear before the archbishop, Payne was prohibited from preaching anywhere in Cranmer's jurisdiction. But Payne disobeyed, delivering sermons both at Hadley and in London. The archbishop gave Cromwell evidence of Payne's erroneous teaching: 'He taught openly in the pulpit there, that one Paternoster said by the injunction of a priest was worth 1,000 Paternosters said of a man's voluntary mind.' Cranmer did not think Payne's judgment sufficient

---

18 Ibid.
19 SP 1/121/83–4 (*LP* xii/2. 65).
20 BL, Cotton Vespasian F xiii. fo. 1146 (*LP* xiii/2. 1063).
21 SP 1/137/149–51 (*LP* xiii/2. 571).

to allow him to instruct the people. When Payne saw the case prepared against him, he submitted himself to the archbishop's correction:

And whereas I might by justice have pronounced him perjured, and farther have proceeded against him for his erroneous preaching, I enjoined to him but certain penance and not so much as he deserved, which he did receive, and swore by the holy Evangel to accomplish the same. And therein again he was foresworn and did it not, but fled into the said county of Suffolk again and became a parish priest and preacher at Stoke Nayland, where he is (as I am informed) as well liked as he was at Hadley.[22]

Hearing this, Cranmer again cited Payne to appear before him. The curate failed to appear, 'whereupon I did excommunicate him and so now for his contumacy he standeth excommunicate'. Cranmer promised to send Payne to Cromwell as soon as he was apprehended:

But in the mean space these my letters are to desire your lordship that you will put with me your helping hand to see him punished. For although many of the Observants were wolves in sheep's skins, yet in mine opinion he ought to give place to none of them in dissimulation, hypocrisy, flattery and all other qualities of the wolfish pharisees.[23]

The reforming bishops on their own initiative tried to counter the influence of less motivated clerks. John Hilsey, bishop of Rochester, complained on several occasions about one Edward Harcocke, prior of the house of Black Friars in Norwich 'for his seditious preaching and also for keeping of a nun within the said house of friars'. Hilsey stated that Harcocke had long been opposed to the reformation of religion and to the proper ordering of himself and his house. The master-general of the order had tried to correct Harcocke, but even though he was served with commandments from Cromwell, Harcocke remained disobedient. Hilsey besought Cromwell

that the said general and provincial and the said friar Harcocke may be heard before your lordship or your commissioners whereby it may be perceived that the said Harcocke not only hath used himself craftily in his preaching against the king's highness and your lordship but also against the rules of his religion and the heads of the same and that the contents of this bill be true I and the said master general and provincial do and shall offer ourselves at all times to the trial of the same.[24]

Not all complaints to Cromwell, however, involved conflicts over religious doctrine and practices. The inhabitants of the tiny village of Wembury on the Devon shore exemplify the concrete reality of distress caused by parochial neglect. They drafted a petition against the Augustinian prior of Plympton and his priests who, they claimed, took more than fifty pounds annually from their

22 *Cranmer's Letters*, 333–4.
23 Ibid.
24 SP 1/115/140 (LP xii/1. 297).

parish. Yet, there was no priest within the parish, and 'if they have need of a priest they must go to Plympton after him which is eight miles going and coming'. As a result, many of the people of Wembury were born, reached full age, and died without benefit of sacraments, much to the displeasure of these villagers, who could be certain of seeing a priest only at the time appointed for the collection of tithes. The daily services were completely neglected. No cleric ever appeared in Wembury except on Sunday. 'Then the priest or a canon cometh from Plympton and sayeth mass, matins, and evensong before noon and so he goeth home again to the priory to dinner and cometh no more at the said parish till the next Sunday.' Many Sundays, particularly in winter, saw no priest at all. Idyllic as Wembury might seem today in its picturesque coastal setting, it had no charm for the Plympton residentiaries. Those chosen to brave the weather on the road to Wembury often fell ill, keeping them from further service to the villagers. And from their minimal labours, three priests within a year had succumbed to the fierce Devon winter.[25]

Nevertheless, it is difficult to defend the monks' poor record of service to Wembury, since nothing interfered with their vigorous collection of what they regarded as their lawful fees, such as seven pence per burial, and twenty-one shillings yearly for ministering the sacraments in the parish. Yet finally, the subject of fees was not at issue, as this incident shows:

> One John Weryn in the said parish did send his servant in the morning early for to have a priest to christen his child/ and the said child was very sick and almost dead/ and they answered and promised to send a priest in all haste that might be possible/ and so his servant was home again by seven o'clock in the morning to his master's house/ and at eight o'clock the child was achurch/ and there the godfathers and godmothers did tarry till four o'clock at afternoon/ and there came no priest/ then they went home with the child/ and before they came home the child was dead unchristened.[26]

Many similar complaints could be added to these to give greater statistical weight to the argument that anticlericalism, caused by parochial distress, constituted a major feature of religious life.[27] Cromwell's concern and his comprehensive efforts to stem the tide of anticlericalism through greater attention to parochial reform directly refute the claims of modern revisionists who contend that satisfied, orthodox congregations had unwelcome Reformation forced upon them and their priests.[28] Cromwell soon discovered that the articulation of articles and injunctions alone made little impact on deeply rooted clerical abuses. He found himself trying to resolve complaints directed to him. He also found it necessary to supervise causes within the jurisdiction of other crown officials, and he issued commissions to trustworthy people in the parishes,

[25] SP 1/100/106v (LP ix. 1147).
[26] Ibid.
[27] In addition to the material presented here, the question of anticlericalism is amply addressed in Dickens, English Reformation, esp. pp. 86–108; idem. Lollards and Protestants in the Diocese of York, Oxford 1959, passim; Elton, Policy and Police, passim; Heath, English Parish Clergy, 70–92, and passim; Margaret Bowker, The Henrician Reformation, Cambridge 1981, passim.
[28] See n. 1 and below.

asking them to report on the performance of their local clerks. One such commission went in February 1537 to William Phelepott of Newark-upon-Trent. Phelepott responded by keeping close watch on the vicar and curate for a period of six weeks before delivering his findings to Cromwell. During this time, he had heard no sermon extolling the true word of God, or setting forth the king's title of Supreme Head of the Church of England. 'Neither preached anything at all, but only the accustomable bidding of the beads, wherefore according to my bounden duty and true allegiance unto my most dread sovereign lord the king's grace, thus to your honourable lordship I do make certificate.'[29]

Cromwell exerted steady pressure on the parochial clergy. In the effort to reduce drastically residual papal influence following the formal schism, the minister demanded that the name of the bishop of Rome be put out of all books in the realm. Many priests, perhaps encouraged by their religious beliefs and their distance from authority, either ignored this command or performed it in a less than permanent manner as by covering the papal name with wax. In the course of time many of these incidents were revealed to Cromwell. For example, on entering a church William Wood of Stamford found books, missals, and other writings with the pope's name unerased. He confiscated many of these and made his report to Cromwell. Wood expected no reward for his diligence, though he did ask Cromwell to make his pleasure known quickly, 'as your poor beadman lieth here upon his great cost and charge and is but of small substance'.[30]

Episcopal dignitaries were often as confused as Wood in dealing with specific cases of clerical disobedience. Archbishop Cranmer sent some depositions to Cromwell concerning Henry Totehill 'for naughty communication which he should speak concerning the bishop of Rome and Thomas Beckett'. He did not attempt to carry the investigation any further himself. Rather, he sent Totehill and his principal accuser to be questioned by Cromwell. Cranmer admitted that 'I have taken upon me your office in punishing of such transgressors as break the king's injunctions.' In one such case he imprisoned two priests for 'permitting the bishop of Rome's name in their books'. Yet, even this small matter, which involved fines of £4 to be distributed to the poor, was felt to be of sufficient importance for referral to Cromwell.[31]

John Hilsey, bishop of Rochester, became similarly perplexed while on a preaching tour of his diocese. At the parish church of Paul's Cray, he also found that certain books were still uncorrected. Cromwell probably ordered that every case of this type be referred for his personal adjudication, because Hilsey had no idea what action to take. The bishop ordered the priest to appear at a forthcoming visitation and applied to Cromwell for instructions. When the priest appeared at Dartford, Hilsey, apparently at Cromwell's behest, intended simply to correct the abuse. However, the priest had with him another clerk to help him answer the charges. Impatient with the attempt to defend such minor

[29] SP 1/117/143 (LP xii/1. 741).
[30] SP 1/113/236 (LP xi. 1496).
[31] SP 1/142/33 (LP xiv/1. 47 (1, 2)).

charges, Hilsey advised the companion 'not to take so much upon you. You know what will be laid against him'. Notwithstanding these words, the second priest repeated that he would make answer for his friend. Hilsey, then, 'for to avoid him and to put him to some honest silence', more strongly warned, 'perchance there may be laid unto him little less than treason, in which it shall not become you to be a proctor'.[32]

Hilsey adjourned the hearing, and for more quietness said that he would come to the parish to hear the matter further. When he arrived with a commission, Hilsey found that his efforts towards quiet had produced havoc. The silenced second priest now accused the parish priest of a felony, citing Hilsey's admonition as supporting a charge of treason. Charges and countercharges flew. Each side called in witnesses; appeals came to Hilsey from all directions. Confounded, perplexed, and by now desperate, the bishop begged Cromwell to untangle the mess, 'knowing that this matter passeth my determination, your lordship herein knoweth what is to be done'.[33]

Cromwell obviously wanted more information from the parishes, particularly from those in troublesome areas. He recognised that the quality of service delivered by the parochial clergy would, at best, improve slowly, and that any change would require the appointment and supervision of diocesan officials responsive to a governmental policy of ecclesiastical reform. Here then was the crux of the problem. For although Cromwell had some indirect influence over diocesan patronage through his early episcopal appointees, his direct patronage resources did not include any nominations to established diocesan offices. For the most part bishops selected their own administrators. And Cromwell could not expect to command the unalloyed loyalty of men initially patronised by and dependent for their careers upon his political opponents on the episcopal bench.

Cromwell found a way through this political impasse in the mass of statutes originally passed to make final the separation from Rome. One of these (25 Henry VIII c. 20),[34] provided regulations for the appointment of bishops in the absence of the pope. Deans and chapters were to elect the king's nominee on receipt of the royal *congé d'élire*, and if after twelve days they failed to do so the king might appoint by letters patent. The act provided that the bishop-elect swear an oath to the king and that the archbishop perform the rites of consecration.[35] Cromwell routinely used this procedure throughout his ministry to fill vacant sees. However his political acumen allowed him to perceive in a technical piece of legislation an innovative means of improving the cure of souls. The agent of Cromwell's vision appeared in the garb of the suffragan bishop.

Traditionally, the office of suffragan occupied a low order of importance within the diocesan administrative hierarchy. The appointment was made by commission for a limited period and renewed as necessary. There was no fixed tenure, and the suffragan, usually a friar, could be dismissed at the will of the

---

[32] BL, Cotton Cleopatra E vi. fo. 256r–v (*LP* xiii/1. 987).
[33] Ibid.
[34] *Stat. Realm*, iii. 462–4.
[35] Ibid.

diocesan. The commission generally emanated from the bishop, but it could proceed from the vicar-general in the prelate's absence. Provided either with a titular see *in partibus infidelium*, or with the equally barren dignity of an inaccessible Irish see, suffragans were easily dispensable. They performed in the bishop's stead those duties which required episcopal orders: confirmations, consecrations of chapels and churchyards, reconciliations of consecrated sites polluted by bloodshed, benedictions of heads of religious houses, the blessing of numerous objects for sacred use.[36] A minor officer, the suffragan was decidedly less important than the bishop's other deputies, and the quality of the men who served the position underlined its low status. They were general utility men, did what they were told, and had no independent jurisdiction.[37]

Cromwell reorganised the office of suffragan bishop, took its patronage into his own hands, and upgraded the calibre of nominees for the position. He appointed thirteen suffragans between March 1536 and February 1539. No formal changes were made in their duties, but Cromwell did alter their titles, granting them dignities within the diocese of their consecration. The process for electing a suffragan bishop closely followed the episcopal model. Upon receipt of the king's letters the bishop selected two candidates. Cromwell made the final choice, and after official appointment by letters patent, the archbishop of Canterbury consecrated the recipient.

Cromwell's innovative plans for the suffragans depended on his effective use of patronage to fill vacancies with highly qualified men. Islands of royal policy in seas of local interest, usually important reformers in their own right, the men chosen by Cromwell were marked for further advancement within the ecclesiastical hierarchy. Most of the new suffragans had begun their careers as monks and long resided within the dioceses they were to serve. They moved from their monastic houses to the bishop's household, there to perform their duties in the king's name and interest.

John Salisbury, descended from an ancient family in Denbighshire, moved from the Benedictine order into his suffragan office. A Cambridge graduate and monk of Bury St Edmund's, Salisbury, suspected of holding heretical opinions, had been imprisoned for a time by order of Cardinal Wolsey and then confined to his abbey for about five years. He emerged in the early 1530s as prior of the small monastery of St Faith at Horsham in Norfolk.[38] In March 1536, Cromwell chose Salisbury to serve as bishop of Thetford, suffragan to the see of Norwich.[39] Recognised by the crown, Salisbury, hitherto ignored, became the recipient of patronage. In 1537 he was collated to the archdeaconry at Anglesey, and in 1538 he received a prebend in the cathedral church of Norwich.[40] The next year he was promoted to the deanery, worth more than £100.[41]

---

36 For the best discussion of the medieval suffragan see A. H. Thompson, *The English Clergy and Their Organization in the Later Middle Ages*, Oxford 1947, 48–9.

37 Bowker, *Secular Clergy*, 22–5.

38 *Alum. Cant.*, iv. 7.

39 *LP* x. 237 (g. 5).

40 *Alum. Cant.*, iv. 7.

41 Salisbury received the deanery of Norwich from the crown: *LP* xiv/2. 113 (g. 24). Valuation of benefice from *VE* iii. 489.

Salisbury subsequently lost the deanery and his other preferments, deprived for being married when Mary Tudor ascended the throne. Protected for a time by the duke of Norfolk, he regained his benefices under Elizabeth, and in 1570 became bishop of Sodor and Man, a position he held until his death in 1573.[42]

Henry Holbeach became bishop of Bristol, suffragan to the see of Worcester, in March 1538.[43] Like Salisbury, Holbeach began his career as a Cambridge graduate and a monastic residentiary. His first promotion established him as prior of the Benedictine house in Cambridge known as Buckingham College.[44] Holbeach found a powerful early patron in Archbishop Cranmer. When he heard that the priory of Worcester would soon be vacant, Cranmer offered to Cromwell the names of two men he believed qualified to govern the house:

> And if the priorship of Worcester shall not be vacant, yet I pray you be good master unto these ii men when you shall find places meet for they; for I know no religious men in England of that be of better learning, judgment, conversation in all qualities meet for an head and master of an house.[45]

We hear little more of the other nominee, Richard Gordon, but Holbeach received the priory in March 1536 by royal mandate.[46] At Worcester Holbeach formed a close relationship with Bishop Hugh Latimer, a factional connection which resulted in his promotion to the suffragan bishopric. Holbeach never looked back. In 1542 he became the first dean of Worcester under the charter of foundation. In 1544, then the king's almoner, Holbeach was elected bishop of Rochester, holding that see until his translation to Lincoln in 1547. Throughout his career he worked among other reformers, promoting parochial improvements and compiling the liturgical revisions which helped to define Anglicanism.[47] His will, dated 2 August 1551, reveals the depth of his Protestant commitment:

> I bequeath my soul to Almighty God our heavenly father by whose only mercy through the merits and death of our saviour Jesus Christ I have a sure confidence to be saved for I confess that there is none other name under heaven given unto man whereby he may be saved but only name of Jesus Christ our saviour.[48]

The new suffragans did not function simply as unofficial agents of governmental policy. They performed valuable diocesan services, and their assistance was often prized, even by less reform-minded bishops. Edward Lee, archbishop of York, who constantly complained of his heavy administrative burdens, eagerly looked forward to the appointment of a suffragan for York. Throughout 1537 he petitioned Cromwell to honour his request for the new suffragan.

42 *Ath. Cant.*, i. 105–6.
43 *LP* xiii/1. 240 (g. 2).
44 *Ath. Cant.*, i. 105–6.
45 SP 1/95/93 (*LP* ix. 97).
46 *Ath. Cant.*, i. 105–6.
47 Ibid.
48 PROB 11/34/28.

Three months of silence followed, whereupon Lee renewed his suit: 'And as I am informed your lordship liketh well the prior of Gisborough whom I have named for one, I entirely pray for your good lordship to help me that I may have the said bill assigned.'[49]

Despite Lee's apparent willingness to approve Cromwell's nominee in order to obtain a greatly needed suffragan, 1538 arrived; winter passed into spring, and the matter remained unsettled. Robert Sylvester, the aforementioned prior of Gisborough, also watched the changing seasons with growing impatience. From his doomed religious house in the midst of a decaying monastic establishment, Sylvester tried a direct approach. He reminded Cromwell that Lee had offered him the position as his suffragan if the king's approval could be obtained. 'Wherefore if it seem good unto your lordship, that I may do service unto the said Archbishop in that ministration and that I may be appointed thereunto by your good lordship's preferment, I will gladly accept it of your hands.' Sylvester promised that if he secured the office of suffragan he would do his best to perform his duties to the utmost of his will and wit, to the honour of God, and the edification of those under his cure.[50] But if Sylvester hoped to don the episcopal vestments in time to rival the splendour of a Yorkshire summer, he was to be disappointed. The arrival of autumn saw Archbishop Lee still pleading with Cromwell for help:

> I am sorry to encumber your good lordship so often with my suit for a suffragan. The bill hath been in Master Wriothesley's hands by your commandment ever since Easter and as I hear your lordship hath put in the bill the prior of Gisborough I pray you entirely be so good lord unto me to get the bill signed. I have great need of one.[51]

Sylvester did eventually become bishop of Hull, suffragan to the province of York, but snow had covered the ground before he could take up his dignity and duties.[52]

Though Cromwell presented highly qualified men as suffragans, men who held other livings and who had other responsibilities, he seems to have been genuinely interested in providing for the cure of souls. With one exception the suffragans resided in their dioceses, attempting to implement government policy, and to improve the quality of religious life. At the same time Cromwell was able to provide an attractive dignity and valuable training ground for men of talent who would eventually move up in the ecclesiastical hierarchy.

John Byrde was the nonresident exception. For him the presentation to the bishopric of Penreth within the see of Llandaff but in the jurisdiction of the archbishop of Canterbury, was simply a reward. Byrde, a native of Coventry, became a Carmelite friar and, as a member of that order, studied at both universities, receiving a DD degree from Oxford in 1513.[53] In 1516 he was

---

49 SP 1/133/189 (*LP* xiii/1. 1247).
50 SP 1/132/159 (*LP* xiii/1. 1045).
51 SP 1/137/193 (*LP* xiii/2. 599).
52 *LP* xiii/2. 497 (g.28).
53 *Ath. Oxon.*, i. 238.

elected provincial of his order, held office for three years, stepped down for three years, and was again elected in 1522.[54] Byrde became a strenuous supporter of reform, often called upon to preach the Royal Supremacy. He was sent to confer with Bilney in prison, and was also one of the persons dispatched to persuade Catherine of Aragon to forbear the use of the title of queen.[55]

Following his elevation to Penreth,[56] Byrde remained at court as an agent for the king and Cromwell. At the beginning of 1539, he went on an embassy with Nicholas Wotton with instructions from Cromwell to get the picture of Anne of Cleves which induced Henry to take her for his queen.[57] On his return in July, Byrde was elected bishop of Bangor.[58] He survived Cromwell's fall, subscribing to the decree in favour of the divorce from Anne of Cleves despite his work for the marriage. By letters patent dated 4 August 1541, he was translated to the newly created see of Chester.[59] Married, Byrde was deprived in March 1554, but he again saved himself, this time by recanting all heretical opinions and by putting away his wife. Soon afterward Edmund Bonner, bishop of London, took him as his suffragan and instituted him to the vicarage of Great Dunmow, Essex. Byrde, with one eye and a low reputation for chastity, died about the close of 1558, owing the crown over £1,000.[60]

As with most benefices, suitors for the suffragan bishoprics outnumbered the available sees, and letters began to reach Cromwell from friends and allies of the hopeful. William More's presentation to Colchester as suffragan to bishop Thomas Goodrich of Ely in September 1536,[61] was facilitated by a letter to Cromwell from the lord chancellor. Audley described More as his steward, and proposed a plan whereby More would be able to pay off his first fruits at the rate of 100 marks down and 100 marks yearly in addition to the tenths. All would be guaranteed by a surety under More's own convent seal unless Cromwell wished Audley to refrain from meddling in the matter of the first fruits.[62]

More, educated partly at Cambridge and partly at Oxford, later became a master in chancery. Rector of Bradwell-juxta-mare, and West Tilbury, both in Essex, More was an active pluralist. In 1537 be became abbot of Walden, and in 1538 he received the prebend of Gevendale in the cathedral church of York.[63] Audley remained an active patron on his behalf. In 1539 he learned that Cromwell intended him to have the next presentation to the archdeaconry of Leicester in exchange for £80 to be paid to the bishop of Hereford. Asking Cromwell to help him to expedite the incumbent's resignation, Audley also asked Cromwell to write to the bishop of Lincoln for the election of More. If More was elected, Audley's servant would discharge the £80 at London, and

54 DNB iii. 538.
55 Ibid.
56 LP xii/2. 81 (g. 19).
57 Ath. Cant., i. 190.
58 Ibid. 191.
59 Ibid.
60 Ibid.
61 LP xi. 209 (g. 19).
62 SP 1/196/179 (LP xi. 465).
63 Ath. Cant., i. 77.

Audley promised further to give Cromwell £20 for his help.[64] More received the archdeaconry, which he held until his death in late 1540.[65]

Conflict over patronage often created hardship, especially for those men who had given long service to the Church only to be displaced by Cromwell's first wave of episcopal appointees. When be began electing suffragans, Cromwell remembered the loyalty and competence of his former servants. One of the temporarily dislocated was John Hodgekyn. A scholar in orders, Hodgekyn studied for thirteen years at Cambridge and three years in Paris, proceeding DD in 1525/6. He returned to England, resumed his duties as a Dominican friar, and became provincial of the Black Friars in 1527.[66] Somewhat later Hodgekyn was deposed from the provincialship to make way for the rapidly ascending John Hilsey, leaving Hodgekyn caught between an impotent monastic establishment and a temporarily unresponsive state ecclesiastical establishment.

Writing to Cromwell from Sudbury, Hodgekyn lamented his fate which left him in a condition of 'poverty without comfort and succor of any friend'. He had made suit on numerous occasions, but as yet had not been informed of Cromwell's plans for him:

> So that without your goodness and help your said orator shall never be able to do service in the administration of the word of God neither to the common utility of Christ's Church having no manner of living to sustain him nor friend to speak to your mastership for him but as I fear rather against him and so would it prove and should so find if your high discretion did not ponder and weigh his innocency and how that a man in favour of the world hath many friends but once depressed or cast down then none or few. Considering therefore that your said orator hath now a long time abiden and tarried the suit of his friends and to know your honourable pleasure it might please your most abundant goodness and gentle heart to look with your eye of pity and let not your poor orator thus decay with might yet a long time God willing do some service and all ways might be ready to do you such service and pleasure as ye would command him whom ye shall all ways to the king's majesty a faithful and true subject and ever ready to do in the most lowly manner such service as he shall be commanded.[67]

In case Cromwell was not familiar with his qualifications and loyalty to crown interests, Hodgekyn advised him that the lord chancellor would supply supporting 'information of this my small petition when your pleasure shall be to commune with him to whom I have spend my mind'.[68]

The reasons for Hodgekyn's original removal from the provincialship of the Dominican order are not clear. His successor was John Hilsey, who advanced from that office to the bishopric of Rochester. Cromwell felt that the two offices were incompatible, and would not allow Hilsey to remain provincial.

[64] BL, Cotton Cleopatra E iv. fo. 201 (LP xiv/2. 36).
[65] Ath. Cant., i. 77.
[66] Ibid. 206–7.
[67] SP 1/104/250r–v (LP x. 1235).
[68] Ibid.

Having held the office previously, Hodgekyn must have been the most qualified of the remaining candidates, though Richard Ingworth had been Hilsey's deputy. Ingworth, also a Dominican friar,[69] relied on powerful and well placed friends in his attempt to gain the provincialship. His neighbour, Sir John Russell, petitioned Cromwell on his behalf in the event that Hilsey would not be allowed to serve in both posts: 'Sir the prior of Langley hath taken great pain in exercising the said office and hath spent as much as he is able to make therein.' Russell had heard that Cromwell was also considering bestowing the office on the prior of Oxford. 'And if it so be I beseech you to be good master to him that you would give him the general's office which is worth but vj l by the year.' In any case, Russell stated that Cromwell would find Ingworth an honest man, able to perform his responsibilities justly and truly.[70]

Ingworth was also helped in his efforts at promotion by Thomas Bedyll, already an established royal servant. Bedyll wrote to Cromwell, praising Ingworth's efforts in the king's affairs, 'riding to and fro with and for the provincial of the Black Friars now elected bishop of Rochester and hath been his deputy in many parts of his visitation'. Bedyll suggested that Ingworth be rewarded with the provincialship now vacated by Hilsey. In the meantime Bedyll hoped that Cromwell would allow Ingworth to continue to serve as deputy, a *de facto* guarantee of eventual advancement. 'Which shall be to the comfort of him and others which have been ready and diligent to do the king's grace service in the reformation of old abuses deeply rooted in the minds of many, which be now brought to good conformity.'[71]

Hodgekyn's suit was successful, and this appointment marked his re-entry into the ecclesiastical hierarchy. From this point he advanced rapidly. In December 1537 he was nominated, with Robert Struddel, by John Stokesley, bishop of London, for the suffragan bishopric of Bedford and was selected by the crown.[72] In later years he was vicar of Malden, Essex, rector of Laingdon, prebendary of St Paul's, and rector of St Peter's, Cornhill.[73] In 1554 Hodgekyn was deprived of all his preferments because he was married but received restitution under Elizabeth and served in these offices until his death in 1560.[74] Ingworth was not forgotten, for in December 1537 he became suffragan bishop of Dover, serving the archdiocese of Canterbury.[75]

Cromwell's parochial reforms and his use of patronage had considerable immediate effect. According to an anonymous contemporary source, a number of abuses, usurpations, and superstitions had been reformed or abolished. The exactions of bishops and archdeacons for probate of testaments had been moderated by statute. Mortuaries levied by the curates had been abolished. Commercial land exploitation and negotiation had been taken away from priests and other spiritual persons. Beneficed persons *cum cura* were compelled

---

69 Ingworth attended Cambridge (BD, 1522–3; DD, 1525–6): *Alum. Cant.*, ii. 449.
70 SP 1/97/165 (*LP* ix. 598).
71 SP 1/96/175 (*LP* ix. 373).
72 *LP* xii/2. 486 (g.5).
73 *Ath. Cant.*, i. 206–7.
74 Ibid.
75 *LP* xii/2. 467 (g. 13).

to reside, and dispensations for pluralities were reduced. This article reveals the efficacy of the Cromwellian measures separating the Church of England from Rome. The ecclesiastical courts had been reformed and all processes were to be determined within the realm. Bishops were elected and consecrated in England. Payment of annates to Rome was discontinued. Payment of Peter's pence was stopped. Dispensations would now be granted by the archbishop of Canterbury with royal consent. The bishoprics created in Rome upon sees in Turkey and Barbary would no longer be admitted in England, but suffragan bishops were appointed for places within the nation.[76]

This partisan exposition and vindication of parochial reform is perhaps optimistic and exaggerated, but reports, even from outlying districts, suggest that Cromwell's policies for the improvement of the cure of souls had an immediate if limited impact on religious life. Archbishop Cranmer, who shared Cromwell's concerns, systematically sought information about the effects of government measures on parochial cures. It was Cranmer who recruited John Marshall of Little Carlton, Nottinghamshire, to report on the state of the people in his county and in neighbouring Lincolnshire.[77] Cranmer enlisted Marshall to survey an area which had been deeply involved in rebellion against Cromwell's ecclesiastical reforms: Henrician government continued to worry about the maintenance of domestic peace as further demands for reform issued from London.

Marshall's letters, written in February, April, and June 1539, furnished reassuring words. All was well in February. The peace remained undisturbed as the most recent measures against the pope filtered through the diocesan hierarchy to each parish. Ordinary people seemed to accept if not to welcome Cromwellian reforms. According to Marshall the English paternoster gained popularity with the dissemination of a uniform translation. Little sympathy remained for the abbeys. Dissolution of the greater monastic houses proceeded unopposed. People looked to the advantages of suppression in terms of good farms and other benefits. Institution of parish registers upset some because they feared that better records would lead to higher taxes. The poor would not as yet labour on abrogated holy days, but Marshall noted that the better sort had accepted the change. The most serious local issue was the state of highways made impassable by every rainstorm. Life in general seemed to have returned to normal. No signs of rebellion appeared among the laity.[78]

Marshall's second letter touched on persistent problems in religious observance. Churches in Nottinghamshire were not well furnished with clerkly sermons according to royal injunctions. Old practices thus continued in the face of reform policy. The people, for example, had not accepted the king's liberty to eat white meats in Lent. Overall, however, Marshall thought that men would quietly consent to the king's ecclesiastical policy, so long as there was peace and men were not called to arms in a religious cause. Men of substance, particularly, hoped and trusted that the peace would be maintained.[79]

---

[76] SP 1/143/197–206 (*LP* xiv/1. 402).
[77] See Elton, *Policy and Police*, 329.
[78] Ibid.
[79] *LP* xiv/1. 839.

Two months later Marshall wrote most confidently to Cromwell that he had uncovered no lewd or superstitious fashions among the king's people. 'And nothing is said here of your good lordship but well.'[80] Minor complaints persisted against such priests as those who kept cows in the churchyard or those who were too proud in their apparel. Otherwise, the people seemed well content with their local clergy, who out of fear for the injunctions had become gentler in their behaviour and more chaste.[81]

Cromwell must have been encouraged by Marshall's letters which arrived during the crisis created by the Act of the Six Articles, but the conservative reaction of 1539 reminded everyone that Cromwell's parochial policies had yet to set deep roots. His statutes, proclamations, and injunctions had barely been developed. The patronage bestowed on thirteen men, strong faction members, in making them into suffragan bishops, promised at most a long-term approach to parochial reform. The immediate value of Cromwell's work for improvement in the cure of souls was in the support it provided for the advancement of the Royal Supremacy and in the heightened conviction that whatever doctrinal settlement prevailed, the parish would continue to receive attention and resources from Henrician officials. Concerns for the enhancement of the cure of souls would be addressed, and members of the reform faction would be at the heart of the process.

[80] SP 1/152/59 (LP xiv/1. 1094).
[81] Ibid.

7

The Protestant Faction

Early in 1537 Cromwell presided over an important doctrinal debate which brought into the open the factional strife which had been building up in England during the years of his ministry. The account of this conference derives from the tract, *Of the Authority of the Word of God against the Bishop of London*, written by the Scottish reformer Alexander Alesius.[1] Born in 1500, Alesius went from Scotland to Germany in 1532 after spending time in prison for his forceful advocacy of the Lutheran cause. He reached Wittenberg in 1533, where he met Luther and Melanchthon and declared his agreement with the Augsburg Confession. Within the Lutheran circle Alesius addressed himself to the question of the free circulation of vernacular Scripture. Opposition validated his intellectual credentials. Johannes Cochlaeus, secretary to Duke Gregory of Saxony, wrote a refutation of Alesius's pamphlet.[2]

In August 1535 Alesius left Germany for England. Carrying letters and gifts from Melanchthon to the king and Archbishop Cranmer, he went directly to Lambeth, where he and Cranmer met and became friends. When Cromwell succeeded Bishop Fisher as chancellor of Cambridge University, Alesius was appointed to lecture in divinity. Although he later claimed to have enjoyed the experience, Alesius did not win the hearts of theological conservatives in Cambridge who acted in concert to deny him economic support. Poverty oppressed him, and necessity forced him to resort to Cromwell for sustenance. Alesius hoped for a regular stipend granted under royal letters-patent to relieve his distress, but he suspected that an annuity was out of the question. He suggested as an alternative that Cromwell might be able to furnish him with a prebend.[3]

Cromwell rejected both proposals, and Alesius felt constrained to abandon Cambridge for London. He briefly studied medicine and initiated a successful practice. On the day the conference convened, he happened to encounter Cromwell, who invited him to hear the proceedings at Parliament House.[4] Certainly biased, Alesius was nevertheless an eyewitness to the sessions called to discuss the theological issues dividing reformers and conservatives. The meeting opened with Cromwell ascending to the highest place to accept, as vicegerent, obeisance from the bishops. After thanking his audience for their attendance, Cromwell noted that the king studied day and night to set a quietness in the Church. Henry wanted to establish a path for the unlearned

[1]   STC 292.
[2]   DNB i. 254–5.
[3]   LP xi. 988 (SP 1/110/204–5).
[4]   DNB i. 256.

people who in their consciences doubted what they might believe. He ordered the conferees to set aside malice and obstinacy, to debate in a friendly fashion in order to obtain a godly and perfect unity.[5]

While Cromwell stated in the king's name that any religious changes would come from convocation and parliament, he said on his own authority as vicegerent that no alterations would be suffered that defaced Scripture. Neither glosses nor papistical laws, nor the mere authority of doctors, nor the councils of the Church, nor the continuance of time and custom would be admitted as the basis of doctrine, except where they had a foundation in Scripture.[6]

The discussion on the number of sacraments which followed quickly became heated and partisan. According to Alesius, the bishop of London began with a Catholic defence of the sacraments and was rebuked by Cromwell for his maintenance of 'unwritten verities'. The archbishop of York and the bishops of Lincoln, Bath and Wells, Chichester, and Norwich concurred with Stokesley in support of the seven sacraments, while the bishops of Salisbury, Ely, Hereford, and Worcester agreed with the archbishop of Canterbury, who, citing Scripture, argued that only the ceremonies of baptism and the Lord's Supper deserved to be called sacraments.

Cromwell sided with the reformers, using his vicegerental authority to make final determinations and clearly establishing his factional and doctrinal commitments. As a further demonstration of his political ascendancy, Cromwell called Alesius from the audience to present his views to the assembled bishops, introducing him as 'the king's scholar'. Alesius quoted Scripture and St Augustine to prove that only the sacraments of baptism and the Lord's Supper could claim divine origin. Edward Foxe, bishop of Hereford, supported Alesius and praised the Germans for setting the Gospel before the world, so that 'Truth', the daughter of time, could triumph. Stokesley replied for the conservatives and continued to maintain the authority of councils and the respected doctors of the Church to what Alesius called the polite amusement of the enlightened:

> Now when the right noble Lord Cromwell, the archbishop, with other bishops who did defend the pure doctrine of the gospel, heard this, they smiled a little one upon another, forasmuch as they saw him flee, even in the very beginning of the disputation unto his old rusty sophistry and unwritten verities.[7]

When Stokesley finished, Alesius would have continued the debate, but Cromwell bade him be content and adjourned the session. He returned the next day, but Cromwell, warned of the conservatives' hostility, excluded him from further participation.

The significance of this controversy does not reside with Alesius, whose self-centred account provides the text, although Cromwell's patronage of a doctrinally radical foreigner is not without interest. Rather, the conference

---

5 *LP* xii/1. 790. For a good account of this debate see A. G. Dickens, *Thomas Cromwell and the English Reformation*, London 1959, 141–5.
6 Ibid.
7 Ibid.

offers valuable portraits of Cromwell and the bishops caught acting out their roles during a crucial scene in the factional drama of the English Reformation. First we see Cromwell playing the lead as the king's deputy and spokesman, reading lines that he himself had written. He moderated the debate, a layman among clerics, capable of grasping the intricacies of the theological disputation. But he was not a neutral chairman. He captained the reform faction, supported advocacy of a doctrinal settlement largely based on Lutheran interpretations of Scripture, and invited Alesius to stake a religious position as far to the left as any man dared to articulate in Henrician England. The conservatives, upstaged and forced to play bit parts, spoke the required lines and quietly retired to the wings to wait and to prepare for another season.

For a brief span of time during 1537 and 1538, Cromwell found himself relatively free of political pressures generated by conservative factionalism. Outright rebellion had been suppressed and Cromwell returned unscathed and unchallenged to his position as Henry's chief minister. The king seemed satisfied with Cromwell's management of affairs. In his domestic life the death of Jane Seymour was compensated by the birth of Prince Edward. The conservative faction dared not raise opposition to Cromwellian religious policy lest they be regarded as supporting dissident voices from the north. Within this small space of unruffled political calm, Cromwell concentrated on bringing to the realm the ideological programme for the reform of the English Church and commonwealth. Cromwell employed his authority, explicitly, to advance Protestant factional interests. His Injunctions of 1538 and his determined effort to protect overzealous reformers and doctrinaire radicals, furnish evidence of the depth of his ideological affirmation and recognise the factional nature of a political system which survived Cromwell's fall and execution in 1540.

Cromwell's emerging Protestant sentiments, more evident as fears about the Supremacy diminished, can be discerned most directly through an exposition of his Injunctions of 1538. Drawn up in the autumn of 1538, the Injunctions initially appeared in a letter to Cranmer of 30 September, and the archbishop, who must have exercised an intellectual influence on Cromwell's programme, ordered them to be published throughout his province. Whether the product of collaboration or not, the Injunctions encapsulate Cromwell's personal vision of the English commonwealth. Exhibiting much more confidence in his authority, Cromwell asserted in the preamble to the 1538 Injunctions his right to act in the king's stead as 'vicegerent to the king's said highness for all his jurisdictions ecclesiastical within this realm'.[8] He stated his intention to issue injunctions 'for the true honour of almighty God, increase of virtue, and the discharge of the king's majesty'. This time, however, the vicegerent became much more specific in his demand that the Injunctions 'be kept, observed, and fulfilled upon pains hereafter declared'. Apparently dissatisfied with the clergy's past performance, Cromwell, first, reminded them to observe truly all the injunctions previously disseminated under his authority. He pointedly warned those who continued to resist or ignore his authority to comply immediately or to face 'further punishment to be straitly extended towards you by the king's

8   Gee and Hardy, *English Church History*, 275.

highness's arbitrament or his vicegerent aforesaid'. The range of penalties included deprivation, sequestration of fruits, or other such coercive measures as might be convenient to either the king or his chief minister.[9]

Neither content nor able to rely upon the physical resources of his government to guarantee acceptance of his religious policy, Cromwell in the Injunctions encouraged the nation to adopt a reformed, yet conformable doctrinal orientation which would commit them both to the government's conception of the Royal Supremacy and to the Reformation which the implementation of the Supremacy encompassed. He intensified the social and educational bases of reform, moving from the earlier requirements that parishioners learn by rote simple prayers and articles of the faith to an injunction which established Scripture as the fuel to power the parochial engines of reform. Cromwell ordered the clergy to place a Bible of the largest volume in English in some convenient place within their churches by the feast of Easter 1539, 'whereas your parishioners may most commodiously resort to the same and read it'. The costs of the book were to be shared by the parson and his flock.[10]

Provision of an English Bible was no empty gesture. Convinced of the importance of Scripture to the health of the commonwealth, Cromwell exhorted the clergy

> that ye shall discourage no man privily or apertly from the reading or hearing of the said Bible, but shall expressly provoke, stir, and exhort every person to read the same, as that which is the very lively word of God, that every Christian man is bound to embrace, believe, or follow if he look to be saved.[11]

This injunction was the culmination of Cromwell's protracted campaign to bring a vernacular Bible to the English people. John Foxe, the martyrologist, told the story of Cromwell memorising the whole of the Latin New Testament of Erasmus in his travels between England and Rome. Whether true or not, and the episode has been discounted as a method employed by him to learn Latin, Cromwell from all reports had good command of scriptural text. His personal experience heightened his determination to make Scripture available to the nation at large. Cromwell had composed an injunction in 1536 for the provision of an English Bible which closely paralleled the injunction drafted in 1538. Three copies of the article have survived, but when the fall of Anne Boleyn threatened the entire reform movement, Cromwell deleted the injunction. He did not abandon it.[12]

Cromwell's political involvement with the Bible predated his ministry. As early as 1527, Miles Coverdale, then an Augustinian friar, wrote to Cromwell about the progress of his study of Scripture. Referring to a conversation they had had at the house of Sir Thomas More upon Easter eve, he complained

9 Ibid.
10 Ibid. 276. Dickens account still holds up well. See both *English Reformation*, 129–38, and *Thomas Cromwell*, 109–23; also A. J. Slavin, *The Precarious Balance*, New York 1973, 147–52.
11 Gee and Hardy, *English Church History*, 276.
12 Dickens, *English Reformation*, 131.

again about his inability to get essential books. Coverdale did not claim to have been working on an English biblical translation at this time, but, as A. G. Dickens has noticed with interest, Coverdale and Cromwell were discussing preparatory studies and eventual goals years before the latter's ministry began.[13]

A figure in stature second only to William Tyndale, whose Bible of 1526 could not be used openly, Coverdale was hard at work on an English Bible by 1534. He received indirect encouragement from Cranmer and Cromwell, who influenced the Convocation of Canterbury to petition the king, 'that holy Scripture shall be translated into the vulgar tongue by certain upright and learned men, to be meted out and delivered to the people for their instruction'. In 1535 Coverdale, probably at Zurich, published his Bible with an unauthorised dedication to Henry VIII.

This early Cromwellian attempt to deliver vernacular Scripture to the English people received enthusiastic support from English Protestants. James Nycolson, who was a Southwark printer, wrote to Cromwell in 1535, asking him to be a good master, 'not only to me: but also unto the truth', by forwarding to the king a dedicatory letter which he had composed. Noting that Cromwell had ever and only put forth his foot for the preferment of God's word, Nycolson asked him to 'set to your helping hands that the whole Bible may come forth'. Sending excerpts of the Coverdale Bible, Nycolson hoped that 'the pure word of God' contained in Scripture might go forth from his press under the king's privilege, 'which if your mastership may obtain the whole realm of England shall have occasion to have your act in more high remembrance than the name of Austin that men say brought the faith first unto England'. Nycolson assumed that Cromwell would lend a sympathetic ear to his suit, and he included as a gift a copy of Melanchthon's *Commonplaces*, 'newly overseen and dedicated to the king's highness'.[14]

Nycolson looked to Cromwell for support for his plan to publish the Coverdale Bible in England, but it is difficult to portray the printer merely as an aggressive businessman, eagerly groping for coins beneath the robes of the Royal Supremacy. The inherent economic difficulties of biblical publication quickly dampened passions for profit, leaving to the residual heat of Protestant zeal the task of bringing forth an English Bible. Large sums of money were required to cover the costs of printing, with no guarantee before 1538 that sales would be sufficient to recompense backers. Even then the threat of policy reversals or the overthrow of Cromwell by the conservative faction lingered. Moreover, a competitor to the Coverdale Bible entered the lists. A translation by John Rogers, known as the Matthew Bible, wore the favour of powerful men including Archbishop Cranmer.

Cranmer, a consistent advocate of an English Bible, set out to find a satisfactory translation. It was August 1537 before he made known his selection:

This shall be to signify unto the same that you shall receive by the bringer hereof a Bible in English both of a new translation and of a new print

---

13 Ibid. 129.
14 SP 1/96/36 (*LP* ix. 226).

dedicated unto the king's majesty as farther appeareth by a pistle unto his grace in the beginning of the book, which in mine opinion is very well done, and therefore I pray your lordship to read the same.[15]

Rogers, a colleague and close friend of both Tyndale and Coverdale, was known to be working intimately with German Lutherans. He consciously constructed his New Testament after Tyndale's model, and his Old Testament followed Coverdale, Lefevre d'Etaples, and Olivetan of Noyen who was Calvin's relative and early mentor. The preface and glosses contained in the Matthew Bible relied heavily on Luther, and the more than 2,100 notes drew from works by Lefevre, Olivetan, Bucer, and Tyndale.

It is notable that Cromwell not only showed the Matthew Bible which he received from Cranmer to the king, 'but also hath obtained of his grace that the same shall be allowed by his authority to be bought and read within this realm'. Cranmer thanked Cromwell and assured the vicegerent that 'for the contentation of my mind you have showed me more pleasure herein, than if you had given me a thousand pound'. The archbishop applauded the service performed on behalf of God and the king, and he promised Cromwell, that besides God's reward, 'you shall obtain perpetual memory for the same within this realm'.[16]

Cromwell licensed both the Coverdale Bible, printed by James Nycolson, and the Matthew Bible, published by Richard Grafton, a London grocer and merchant adventurer of Antwerp. Hearing that he had been granted the king's licence to set forth the Bible, Grafton sent six copies as a gift, 'given for those most godly pains, for which the heavenly father is bound even of his justice to reward you with the everlasting kingdom of God'. He thanked Cromwell for moving the king on his behalf, concurring with Cranmer that the deed made him happier than an outright grant of money.[17]

Money, however, was not far from Grafton's thoughts. He expressed his concern to Cromwell that certain people refused to believe that the king had licensed publication of the Bible:

Wherefore if your lordship's pleasure were such that we might have it licensed under your privy seal it should be a defence at this present and in time to come for all enemies and adversaries of the same. And forasmuch as this request is for the maintenance of the Lord's word, which is to maintain the Lord himself I fear not that your lordship will be earnest therein. And I am assured that my lord of Canterbury, Worcester and Salisbury, will give your lordship such thanks as in them lieth. And sure ye may be that the heavenly Lord will reward you for the establishing of his glorious truth.[18]

Cromwell felt that an additional licence under his privy seal was unnecessary, and he denied Grafton's request. Under the pressures of high printing costs and competition from trade rivals Grafton kept after Cromwell. The printer

[15] *Cranmer's Letters*, 344–5.
[16] Ibid. 346–7.
[17] BL, Cotton Cleopatra E v. fo. 349 (*LP* xii/2. 593).
[18] Ibid.

complained that he and his backers had turned out 1,500 Bibles at a cost of £500, but they were beset by others who, printing their editions in a lesser letter, intended to sell their 'little books' at a lower price. Claiming to be primarily concerned that unrestrained publication of Bibles would result in errors, Grafton asked Cromwell for monopoly rights for at least three years, so that he could sell out his stock and recover his costs. He suggested that Cromwell compel every curate to have a Bible and every abbey to have six, set in different places for convent residents to read. Sales could be increased still further by applying extra pressure on papistical bishops to purchase Bibles; a small commission would suffice for Canterbury, Worcester, and Salisbury. Besides solving his financial problems, Grafton believed that the implementation of his plan would terminate the schism between the new and the old religious doctrines and practices. Everyone now would follow one God, one book, and one learning.[19]

Grafton achieved his goal of becoming the sole publisher of the English Bible when, early in 1538, Cromwell took steps to end the confused state of affairs inhibiting the smooth dissemination of a vernacular Scripture. With his partner, Edward Whitchurch, Grafton received authorisation to print a new and authoritative English Bible. Cromwell entrusted Coverdale with the revision. After encountering much hardship because Cromwell decided to have the Bible printed in Paris, Whitchurch and Grafton sent two samples to Cromwell:

> one in parchment, wherein we intend to print one for the king's grace, and another for your lordship; and the second, in paper whereof all the rest should be made, trusting that it shall be not only to the glory of God, but a singular pleasure, also, to your good lordship the causer thereof, and a general edifying of the king's subjects, according to your lordship's most godly request.[20]

The *Great Bible* appeared for general use in April 1539, with Cromwell carefully monitoring its distribution. Although the printers wanted to market it at 13s 4d, Cromwell preferred a price of ten shillings. To achieve this economy, Cromwell obtained a patent which prohibited any biblical publication without his express permission. This finally gave to Grafton and Whitchurch a measure of the protection they had sought, but Cromwell refused to grant them a complete monopoly. He authorised a translation by Richard Taverner in 1539, and in April 1540, he allowed Berthelet to print an inexpensive edition of the *Great Bible* intended for the personal use of interested subjects.

Cromwell's forceful advocacy of the Bible could have encouraged readers to define Scripture to suit themselves, creating a situation calculated to threaten religious uniformity, a major pillar of Tudor rule. Delicately balanced between his ambitions for a commonwealth based upon a scripturally educated laity and a social system which could not stand the strain of popular scriptural interpretation, Cromwell resisted the temptation to move too quickly. He cautioned the clergy to avoid all contention and altercation which might attend biblical

---

[19] Ibid. fo. 325 (*LP* xii/2. app. 35).
[20] *CSP Span.*, iv/1. 575–6.

study, and he warned them to use 'an honest sobriety in the inquisition of the true sense of the same'. Explanation of obscure places was to be left to men of higher judgment in Scripture.[21]

In the 1538 Injunctions Cromwell carefully designed new exercises of conformity to the Church of England to replace discarded rituals associated with Rome. He instructed clerks to recite openly one particle or sentence of the paternoster or creed to their parishioners every Sunday and holy day, 'twice or thrice together, or oftener, if need require'. The intent was that they learn the paternoster and creed by heart and understand the contents fully, so they could in turn teach their children and servants the same, 'as they are bound in conscience to do'. When this task had been completed, the same procedure was to be applied to the learning of the Ten Commandments.[22]

Typically thorough, Cromwell ordered the clergy to examine in confession every person who came before them, 'whether they can recite the articles of our faith, and the Paternoster in English'. If they could not perform perfectly, 'ye shall declare to the same that every Christian person ought to know the same before they should receive the blessed sacrament of the altar'. The clerk with these new disciplinary powers was to admonish those who could not recite to learn the same more perfectly by the next year following,

> or else, like as they ought not to presume to come to God's board without perfect knowledge of the same, and if they do, it is to the great peril of their souls; so ye shall declare unto them that ye look for other injunctions from the king's highness by that time, to stay and repel all such from God's board as shall be found ignorant in the premises, whereof ye do thus admonish them, to the intent they should both eschew the peril of their souls, and also the worldly rebuke that they might incur hereafter by the same.[23]

Cromwell wanted to draw the English people away from papistical religious mores, which, he believed, both inhibited the final separation from Rome and kept the laity mired in superstition. He ordered that at least one sermon every quarter of the year be preached in every cure, 'wherein ye shall purely and sincerely declare the very gospel of Christ'. Cromwell insisted that works of charity, mercy, and faith be encouraged, as prescribed and commanded in Scripture; but people must not repose their trust in other works devised by men's fantasies,

> as in wandering to pilgrimages, offering of money, candles, or tapers to images or relics, or kissing or licking the same, saying over a number of beads, not understood or minded on, or in such-like superstition; for the doing whereof, ye not only have no promise of reward in Scripture, but contrariwise, great threats and maledictions of God, as things tending to idolatry and superstition, which all other offences of God Almighty doth most detest and abhor, for that the same diminisheth most His honour and glory.[24]

[21] Gee and Hardy, *English Church History*, 276.
[22] Ibid.
[23] Ibid. 276–7.
[24] Ibid. 277.

Cromwell authorised the removal of all 'feigned images' and an end to pilgrimages and offerings thereunto 'for avoiding of that most detestable sin of idolatry'. No candle or taper was to illuminate any statue or picture; 'only the light that commonly goeth across the church by the rood-loft, the light before the sacrament of the altar, and the light above the sepulchre' would be suffered. Cromwell advised parochial clerks to teach their congregations that images performed no function other than to serve as 'books of unlearned men, that can no letters'. If used except as remembrances, images became idols to the detriment of the worshipper's soul, and therefore 'the king's highness graciously tendering the weal of his subject's souls, hath in part already, and more will hereafter, travail for the abolishing of such images as might be an occasion of so great an offence to God, and so great danger to the souls of his loving subjects'.[25]

To buttress the physical removal or destruction of images a Cromwellian injunction required clerks who had set forth images, relics, pilgrimages, 'or any such superstitions in the past' to recant publicly, 'showing them (as truth is) that ye did the same upon no ground of Scripture, but as one being led and seduced by a common error and abuse crept into the church through the sufferance and avarice of such as felt profit by the same'.[26]

Three injunctions, dealing with minor changes in ritual, backed Cromwell's policy concerning images. The crown claimed the right to determine the sequence and manner of fasting days, completely eliminated the commemoration of Thomas Becket, and enjoined the parochial clergy from interfering with the alterations. Knelling of Aves after services and at certain other times, a practice begun by the papacy, was prohibited, and the pardon for saying Aves, formerly granted in the ringing of the bells, was also abrogated. The last injunction in this series terminated the common processional practice of singing to the saints, recommending in their stead the performance of other suffrages.[27]

Cromwell's decisive action against images affirmed the ideological position he had taken in the Injunctions. On 28 October 1538 he had Bishop Latimer, armed with the king's commission, repair to the monastery of Hales to view and examine a certain supposed relic known as the 'Blood of Hales'. Latimer spent the morning sifting the 'Blood' and found that, when the round, silver-encased glass barrel was opened, the substance turned out to be a coloured, unctuous gum, 'and though it seemed somewhat like blood while it is in the glass, yet when any parcel of the same is taken out it turneth to a yellowness and is cleaving like glue'.[28] After displaying the relic to the assembled multitude, he enclosed it in red wax, affixed the seals of the commission members, and locked it in a coffer to await knowledge of the king's future pleasure.[29]

Monasteries harboured most of the images and relics, and Cromwell's

25 Ibid. 277–8.
26 Ibid. 279.
27 Ibid. 280.
28 SP 1/138/49 (LP xiii/2. 709).
29 *Sermons and Remains of Hugh Latimer*, ed. George E. Corrie, Cambridge 1845, 407–8 (LP xiii/2. 710).

campaign against the veneration of images closely parallelled the general attack on monastic life. From 1538 tales about images became a regular feature of the reports from monastic visitors. They provided Cromwell both with ammunition to use to defend his religious programme and an index against which to measure its progress. Elis Price, touring the diocese of St Asaph at Cromwell's command to detect and expel 'certain abusions, superstitions, and hypocrisies used within the said diocese', discovered an image of Darvel Gatheren, which the people worshipped in expectation that the image 'hath power to fetch him or them that so offers out of hell when they be damned'. Respecting the popularity of Darvel Gatheren, Price sought further instructions from Cromwell concerning the disposition of the image 'in whom the people have so great confidence, hope, and trust, that they come daily a pilgrimage unto him, some with kyne, other with oxen or horses, and the rest, insomuch that there was five or six hundred pilgrims to a man's estimation that offered to the said image'.[30]

Richard Ingworth, suffragan bishop of Dover, also travelled throughout North Wales, serving Cromwell in monastic visitations. While thus engaged, he found so many images that to write of them all 'would take a sheet of paper'. Ingworth did send Cromwell what he called 'the holiest relic in North Wales', worth over twenty pounds annually to the black friars of Bangor. No man could kiss the image, 'but he must kneel so soon as he sees it, though it were in the foulest place in all the country, and he must kiss every stone, for in each is great pardon'.[31] John London tore down the image of Our Lady at Caversham near Reading, and Richard Pollard with Thomas Wriothesley and John Williams 'swept away all the rotten bones that be called relics' contained in the monasteries of Hyde and St Mary.[32]

These examples of iconoclasm and the intensive patronage of the English Bible mark tentative steps taken to translate policy into practice. Having set out his ideological designs, Cromwell in his injunctions grounded his reform programme in parochial soil. He planned to increase government influence among the common people in part by making the parish the administrative centre of both the reformed Church and the state. His injunction in this regard placed responsibility for recording all births, deaths, and marriages in the hands of the local clergy.[33] Although many conservatives claimed that parish registers presaged new taxes and exactions, Cromwell explained in a circular letter issued in December 1538 that he had introduced the registers to avoid strife, processes, and contentions arising from questions of age, lineal descent, titles of inheritance, and for sundry other causes.

Whether or not the parochial clergy welcomed the burden of their obligation to keep the register, they could all applaud the injunction commanding every man to pay his tithes. Men had become accustomed to withholding payment of tithes if they were disenchanted with their priests. Cromwell recalled the law which bound parishioners to pay tithes without restraint or

---

[30] Wright, *Three Chapters*, 190–1.
[31] Ibid. 212.
[32] Ibid. 221–5.
[33] Gee and Hardy, *English Church History*, 279.

diminution. Rather than redubbing one wrong with another, Cromwell suggested 'that such lack and default as they can justly find in their parsons and curates, to call for reformation thereof at their ordinaries' and other superiors' hands who upon complaints and due proof thereof shall reform the same accordingly'.[34]

After publishing the Injunctions Cromwell, as with his other official reforms, viewed their dissemination as a major endeavour. An article of the 1538 Injunctions commanded the clergy to read these and the former Injunctions at least four times a year, openly and deliberately to their parishioners 'to the intent that both you by the same may be the better admonished of your duty, and your said parishioners the more incited to insure the same for their part'.[35] Cromwell instructed nonresidentiaries to appoint curates who would promptly execute the Injunctions and otherwise do their duty to the profit of their cures with examples of good living as well as through declaration of the word of God. 'Or else', the vicegerent threatened, 'their lack and defaults shall be imputed unto you, who shall straitly answer for the same if they do otherwise.'[36]

Finally, Cromwell used the Injunctions to tighten further official surveillance and authority over preaching. He ordered the clergy not to admit any man to preach in their dioceses, except those who held sufficient licence from the king, the archbishop of Canterbury, the bishop of the diocese, or himself. As in 1536, Cromwell insisted that licensed preachers be gladly received to declare the word of God without resistance or contradiction. Further, Cromwell demanded that any man who preached contrary to the word of God, or against the Injunctions, or in favour of papal authority should be immediately detected and presented to the king, his council, himself, or the local justice of the peace.[37]

Upon receipt of the Injunctions members of Cambridge University, understanding Cromwell's intentions for the reform of the Church of England, thanked Henry for his support of a policy which had produced the two great gifts – peace and a purified religion. Feeling that the king had turned his mind late to the reformation of religion, they were, nevertheless, satisfied, considering how much had been accomplished in the short space of time. They flattered the king's love for truth and applauded his subjects' ardent piety. 'Like an excellent artificer he has done a work, the beauty of which will preserve the memory of his past labours.' To reward his efforts, the writers claimed, God had finally sent them Prince Edward, a child worthy of his father.[38]

The Injunctions of 1538 directly demonstrate Cromwell's determination to encourage ecclesiastical reforms central to the Protestant experience. He stimulated a climate in which consciousness of the accelerating pace of religious change grew and in which Reformation, parallel to the continental experience, could be seen as the ultimate goal of his ministry. Writing policy in London, however, was much easier than bringing changes in doctrine and practice to

---

34 Ibid. 280.
35 Ibid. 279–80.
36 Ibid. 278.
37 Ibid. 279.
38 BL, Cotton Cleopatra E vi. fo. 242 (*LP* xiii/2. 593).

individual ecclesiastical jurisdictions. When faction members and adherents attempted to reform their cures, they often ran up against powerful local interests and doctrinaire conservatives opposed to religious change and those who promoted it. These conflicts kept Cromwell active on behalf of men who needed his support and protection.

On Easter Day 1539 John Goodall, vice-bailiff of Salisbury, and Nicholas Shaxton's chief agent in the city, tactlessly reopened a long-standing controversy between the bishop and the mayor concerning municipal jurisdiction. Goodall, definitely in Cromwell's service by late 1538, and probably earlier, owed his position at Salisbury to his master's patronage. With Shaxton's approval he accelerated a policy of insisting upon the bishop's rights in the city as a weapon to overcome conservative resistance in religious matters. The hole into which Goodall was to fall had been widened and deepened by Shaxton's Scottish chaplain, John Macdowell. In February 1537 he preached a sermon so distasteful to the city officials that they angrily demanded his removal. Forced to defend himself, Macdowell charged Cromwell to view injustice and put it right. The chaplain complained about the hostility with which his sermon against the bishop of Rome had been received. Moreover, according to Macdowell, these same people had plucked down the king's dispensation *pro lacticiniis* from the city gate, and the mayor refused to make any inquiry. Yet, when another man had posted on the same gate a schedule of charges against a Minorite named Wattes, who had preached seditiously, Macdowell charged, the author was cast into close prison and forbidden visits for some time, even from his wife. He complained that while a man who had written against a wretched friar had been tortured, no attempt had been made to find the man who had torn down the king's commission and letters.[39]

Bishop Shaxton, once allegedly accused by Cromwell of having a stomach more meet for an emperor than for a bishop, helped to keep the controversy simmering, failing to notice that his servant, Goodall, had fallen into the pot. The vice-bailiff of Salisbury had observed some people kneeling before and kissing an image of Christ which stood on an altar located on the north side of the cathedral choir. Unknown to Goodall the altar itself contained the sacrament. He ordered the image taken away, citing the king's commandment which prohibited the kissing of images or creeping to the cross except on specified days. 'And the priest being not our priest nor ready to take it away, and the people fast pressing to kiss the image, the said John Goodall commanded his servant to take it down . . . and to set it by at the altar's end.'[40]

The conservative city officials seized upon this incident, interpreting Goodall's actions to be to the dishonour of the sacrament and against the king's proclamation that all laudable ceremonies should be maintained unless specifically proscribed by royal commandment. Moreover, they accused Goodall of having an heretical opinion of the sacrament itself and of wilfully ignoring the king's proclamation in that behalf. Shaxton claimed that his servant 'hath done more diligence at all occasions to set forth the king's

[39] *LP* xii/1. 746 (SP 1/117/153).
[40] SP 1/150/140r (*LP* xiv/1. 777).

injunctions and things contained in his proclamations than they all'. The bishop admitted that Goodall's fervent mind at times oustripped his discretion, and Shaxton stated that this had occurred when Goodall should have been most circumspect. 'But as for any heretical opinion that he hath of the blessed Sacrament: I dare swear for him, but he doth utterly detest Sacramentaries and ever hath done since I knew him.'[41]

Goodall wrote to Cromwell on his own behalf for protection against the mayor and his brethren. Alluding to his past service for the extirpation of popishness, he defended his motives and contended that his action, which, they claimed, blasphemed the blessed sacrament, aimed only at correcting the abuse of the image. 'And if it be well taken (as I trust your lordship will) it is true obedience to the king's injunctions and proclamations.'[42]

Led by the mayor of Salisbury and one Master Burrowe, a justice of the peace, Shaxton's opponents imprisoned Goodall and his servant. Though Shaxton said that he wrote to constrain everything gently, 'They gave me thanks for my charitable writing, but followed no thing my counsel. They think surely that they shall now have all their desires which they have so long longed for.'[43] Goodall was released from prison soon after Cromwell heard of his plight. Within a short period of time the vice-bailiff informed Cromwell that although he had sustained diverse displeasure for declaring the manifest enormity of the clergy within the close of Sarum, something had been obtained thereby. The residentiaries now not only preached, but they also read at their dinners a chapter of the Old and New Testaments. But, Goodall warned, from Salisbury westward the injunctions had little effect. He suggested that Cromwell send surveyors to inquire by a verdict of twelve men whether the injunctions were observed.[44] The bishop and the mayor did not resolve their jurisdictional struggle during the life of Cromwell's ministry. The incident shows, however, that although Cromwell might have been exasperated with Shaxton's imperious pretentions and Goodall's unbridled zest for reform, the vicegerent protected factional interests and personnel by quickly and effectively shielding with his own authority both of his exuberant subordinates.

Even Cromwell's power, however, had finite boundaries. His attempts to protect radical Protestants in Calais had repercussions in London and helped to bring the reform faction to grief. Cromwell's serious troubles came to the fore in 1537, but the factional struggle had a long history. Calais, a continental enclave, was governed by Sir Arthur Plantagenet, Lord Lisle, who ruled as Lord Deputy with assistance from a council appointed by the king. The town presented complex problems of administration, and Cromwell, throughout his ministry, faced a host of tangled political, social, and ecclesiastical issues. Lisle jealously guarded his privileges and perquisites, and nothing Cromwell ever did in Calais came easily. Religious matters were particularly difficult. Ecclesiastical governance had been in the hands of the archbishop of Canterbury since 1379, although a commissary generally exercised routine administration. Over the

41 Ibid.
42 SP 1/150/142 (LP xiv/1. 778).
43 SP 1/150/140r (LP xiv/1. 777).
44 LP xiv/1. 894.

years, a variety of abuses had become institutionalised. Twenty-five parish churches furnished nonresident livings for English clerical pluralists. Numerous monastic houses produced little evidence of charity or piety.[45]

Both Cromwell and Cranmer accorded Calais a substantial amount of time and attention. In 1536 the vicegerent secured an act of parliament with supporting injunctions which commanded every resident of Calais to speak English, to have an English name, to be provided with an English priest, and to receive preaching and catechism in English. Implementation of these objectives in a locality characterised by its religious divisions exacerbated factional conflict.[46] Cranmer tried to strengthen the government's reform efforts in the Pale. Immediately after Cromwell's elevation to the vicegerency, the archbishop asked the minister to support his request for the king's letters 'in the favour to ii such chaplains of mine, as I intend to send thither with all speed to preach the word of God'.[47]

Cranmer held Calais in low regard, and he asserted in a letter to Cromwell that no place in the king's dominions more needed good instruction of God's word. He argued that the present residents were blind and ignorant, that the common people lacked knowledge of doctrine and Scripture, and that the presence of aliens and strangers inhibited his attempts at reform:

> I think that it will no less be a charitable and godly deed than a singular commodity for this realm, to have in these parts at the least two learned persons planted and settled there by the king's authority in some honest living, whose sincerity in conversation of living and teaching shall shortly (no doubt) clearly extinct and extirpate all manner of hypocricy, false faith, and blindness of God and his word, wherein now the inhabitants there be altogether wrapt, to the no little slander (I fear me) of this realm, and prejudice of the good and laudable acts lately conceived by the king's grace and his high court of Parliament.[48]

Cranmer hoped that his plea would move Cromwell to grant the soon to be vacant parsonage of St Peter's beside Calais to Thomas Garret, 'whose learning and conversation is known to be right good and honest', or else another with similar qualities.[49]

Cromwell refrained from engaging formally in the early struggles between Cranmer and the conservatives responsible for civil administration in Calais, but in the summer of 1537 he launched an attack in the name of religious

---

[45] The above information has been drawn from A. J. Slavin, 'Cromwell, Cranmer and Lord Lisle: a study in the politics of reform', *Albion*, ix (1977), 316–36. See also M. St Clare Byrne, *The Lisle Letters*, 6 vols, Chicago 1981, v. passim. Byrne does not add much of analytical value to the episode of the Calais Sacramentaries. Her work, however, is indispensable both for the documents she has painstakingly collected and for the full portrayal of Calais life which adds texture to the investigation of religious factionalism.
[46] Ibid. See also A. J. Slavin, *Thomas Cromwell on Church and Commonwealth*, New York 1969, 185.
[47] *Cranmer's Letters*, 298.
[48] Ibid. 310–11.
[49] Ibid.

uniformity against the forces of Catholic loyalism. He wrote to Lisle, demanding that two priests, William Minsterly and William Richardson, be sent to London as prisoners in assured custody. Cromwell said that the king marvelled 'to hear of the papistical faction that is maintained in that town, and by you chiefly that be of his grace's council'. Reacting against what he felt to be the contempt shown his authority, he threatened to replace Lisle and the council if more abuses came to light. 'And if you should think any extremity in this writing, you must thank yourselves that have so procured it. For neither of yourselves have you regarded these matters nor answered to many my letters written for like purposes and upon like occasions.'[50] Cromwell's uncharacteristic display of anger quickly faded, suggesting that the strong language of his letter to the Council of Calais was intended to serve as a political warning. One week later, the vicegerent explained to Lisle that he had addressed the council sharply to caution those who leaned much to their superstitions, old rites, and observations to 'be induced to bring their hearts inward to the conformity of the truth'. Reminding Lisle that he remained his perfect and sincere friend, Cromwell hoped that the king's deputy would join in the campaign 'to alter such evil instructed and inclined hearts to their old ceremonies and observations and exhort them to know and follow the truth declared unto them and to set all obstinacy and hardness of heart apart not thinking themselves wiser in such things than the most learned and best of the realm'.[51]

The conservative Council of Calais bitterly resented what they felt to be Cromwell's improper influence in their lawful administration of Calais. Doctrinal differences and deep divisions about the substance and pace of ecclesiastical reform gave purpose to the general fight for power between the council in Calais and the reform faction, with the king acting as referee. While Lisle moved to exploit his connections with London-based conservatives, such as the duke of Norfolk and Sir Anthony Browne, Cromwell and Cranmer began to infiltrate reform-minded men into Calais. The garrison harboured many forms of Protestantism, and Cromwell hoped to furnish increased strength and direction for this growing popular movement.

John Butler, a zealous reformer, went to Calais as Cranmer's commissary to enforce conformity to Reformation statutes and injunctions. Thomas Palmer, Cromwell's man, was placed in charge of the Carmelite abbey at Sandingfield. Cromwell and Cranmer both used their patronage to place two of Cranmer's chaplains, Dr Hoore and Dr Champion, in Calais for the express purpose of converting the Pale to the religion of England. The Calais conservatives countered by attempting to portray Cromwellian reform as essentially the same as the religion practised by the heretical splinter group of Sacramentaries, universally persecuted for their denial of the doctrine and practice of the Eucharist.

Cranmer asked Butler for a report, which Richard Champion delivered on his return to his benefice in Kent. Champion concurred with Butler, claiming that the rumours of Calais over-run with heretics were untrue. None denied

50 Merriman, *Life and Letters*, ii. 64–5.
51 Ibid. 65–6.

Christ, as had been charged, and, Champion alleged, the common people of Calais were comparable with those in any town in England.[52] Soon afterward Butler added to Champion's assessment. He complained that there were several 'false papists' being held in Calais who were as yet unpunished. The commissary asked Cranmer to take the matter to Cromwell, and Butler hoped that Cromwell could be persuaded to provide some good curates to help to bring the people to the truth.[53]

Cromwell's first concern was to quiet the charges of heresy emanating from the Council of Calais. He knew quite well the danger of allowing himself to be tarred with charges of supporting either Sacramentary doctrine or those who espoused it. Cromwell, then, risked slowing the reform offensive to keep from slipping on perilous ground. And so he wrote that he was unhappy to hear 'that the town of Calais should be in misorder by certain Sacramentaries alleged to be in the same'. He feigned surprise that Lisle, 'having good knowledge and experience of my good will and continual desire to the repression of errors', should not report on the 'lewd persons amongst you'. He reminded Lisle how much he esteemed Calais and how concerned he felt about the danger which might arise from diversity of opinion, 'specially in matters so high and weighty'.[54]

Cromwell then dropped his air of injured innocence and attempted to force the conservatives' hand. Asserting that the king wanted a full investigation of Sacramentary activity in Calais, Cromwell ordered Lisle and the council to assemble themselves 'and make due and circumspect inquisition of this and all other such matters as do or may in anywise interrupt the quiet and unity that should be amongst you'. Cromwell warned Lisle to separate 'the perfect truth' from 'men's corrupt affections of favour, malice, or displeasure'. He assured Lisle that his personal political power continued undiminished, despite the attempts by the Council of Calais to undermine his authority through hints that he had supported the Sacramentaries. The vicegerent promised 'the reformation of things if it so require', but he advised also that the conservative faction 'be men of that sort that shall beseem you towards the maintenance of truth and honesty and the repression of the contrary as appertaineth'.[55]

Forced to substantiate their hitherto vague charges or to abandon the political contest with Cromwell, the Council of Calais struck boldly. With Lord Lisle present, they directed a formal order against Adam Damplip who served as a preacher in Calais under the delegated authority of the archbishop of Canterbury, dispensed by his commissary. Damplip, whose real name was George Bowker or Bucker, had been chaplain to Bishop John Fisher of Rochester. After a brief exile in Rome where he enjoyed Reginald Pole's friendship, Damplip became committed to Protestantism and left Padua to wander through Italy and Germany. In 1538 he felt that he could safely return to England, but gales in the Channel delayed his crossing from Calais. While awaiting fair weather, he received permission to read Scripture to the people, and the subsequent offer

---

[52] SP 1/131/196 (LP xiii/1. 833).
[53] SP 1/132/39 (LP xiii/1. 934).
[54] Merriman, Life and Letters, ii. 139–40.
[55] Ibid.

of the chapter house of the White Friars as a permanent pulpit changed his mind about further travel. Much to the chagrin of John Dove, the Carmelite prior, and other conservatives, Damplip stormed against official immorality and a plethora of superstitious practices. He publicly attacked images and relics, and his ridicule of the supposed miraculous holy wafers of the Resurrection Shrine was the final straw which made him the central figure in the struggle for political and religious control of Calais, a battle with much wider implications for Cromwell and the reform faction.[56]

The council charged Damplip with contentious preaching on the subject of the Sacrament of the Altar, 'somewhat to the abuse of diverse persons that hath not well understood nor taken the same by reason whereof the opinions of diverse and sundry persons have been showed the one to the other inquisitions, disputations amongst them to the contrary opinion'.[57] John Butler was called before the council and officially warned that he would be held accountable for any 'tumult or inconvenience' that might arise from Damplip's preaching:

That in anywise the said Sir Adam should not declare, open, nor read anything otherwise than as may stand with the king's pleasure and his council. And if he do the contrary here before you Mr. Commissary I do discharge myself before all my fellows of the Council and them also, and charge you, Mr. Commissary with the same because it is you that hath licensed him to read chapters and preach.[58]

At about the same time, Lisle wrote to Cromwell, again complaining about the large number of soldiers and common people who declared against the Sacrament of the Altar, 'saying it was not in a knave priest to make God and that the mass was not made by God but by the envisioning of man, and that a mouse would as soon eat the body of God as another cake'. Then Lisle accused a young English priest of speaking in a sermon of the Sacrament in a way much at variance with royal policy, causing great offence among many people, 'so they care not for the mass and wish they never heard mass in their lives'.[59]

In his answer to Lisle's letter on 16 July Cromwell perceived that in Calais 'there is some infection of certain persons denying the holy sacrament of Christ's blessed body and blood of such opinions as commonly called Sacramentaries'. His prescription called for Lisle to examine suspects thoroughly and cause them to be punished if they maintained any errors against the 'true doctrine'. This gesture toward orthodoxy, however, was rather empty, because Cromwell gave no authorisation regarding Damplip. He noticed that there were issues dividing John Dove and Damplip, and he ordered an examination to determine the accurate claims of both sides. But he also demanded that all the information be sent to London 'to the intent that I may signify the same to

---

[56] Slavin, *Thomas Cromwell*, 193–4 and note; *Lisle Letters*, v. 7–10 (nos 1178, 1188–91), 151–83.
[57] BL, Royal MS 7c, xvi. fo. 257 (*LP* xiii/1. 1219).
[58] Ibid.
[59] SP 3/9/44 (*LP* xiii/1. 1291).

the king's majesty and thereupon know his further pleasure for a direction to be taken in the same'.[60]

Lisle commanded the preacher and the prior to set down their opinions in writing.[61] In the meantime, the Council of Calais tried to trap Cromwell in nets of dangerous religious sentiments. They asked the vicegerent to advertise to them whether or not the Sacrament of the Altar should be honoured according to the *King's Book*:

Sir we desire you herein not as a counsellor to give us your counsel but as our especial friend not being a known what you wrote you nor we to be a known what answer you make us but that we might know how to follow the king's pleasure herein to the intent we would not run in his grace's indignation.[62]

Sensing the fierce intensity of the upheaval around him, Damplip decided to come in out of the rain. In July 1538 he crossed the Channel bearing a letter from Butler to Archbishop Cranmer which explained the reasons for his flight. The commissary wrote 'that certain which favour nothing the truth would gladly hinder him (if it were in their power) that he should neither teach nor preach the word of God'. Butler castigated the council for their malice and again denied that Calais was infected with Sacramentaries. He asked Cromwell to be Damplip's patron during his stay in England and hoped that the preacher would soon return to Calais, 'with your grace's favourable letters and my lord privy seal's if it be possible they may be obtained of his lordship to be curate of our Lady's church in Calais'.[63]

Cranmer dispatched Damplip to Cromwell and, full of fight, also requested the minister's letters authorising Butler to pull down images contained within the priory of the Black Friars at Calais:

And whereas my said Commissary hath written unto me concerning this bearer Adam Damplip desiring to have certain requests accomplished, as farther shall appear unto your lordship by his letter herein enclosed. I right heartily desire you my lord so to tender the said requests, that this said bearer may return again thither, and there to proceed with quietness as he hath begun. Assuring your lordship that he is of right good knowledge and judgment as far as I perceive by him. And therefore if it would please your lordship to direct your favourable letters unto the Council there in his behalf you should do a right meritorious deed. And surely I will myself write to like effect, but I know your letters shall be much more esteemed and accepted than mine.[64]

With both sides girding themselves for the showdown, Damplip lost his taste for battle. Called before Cranmer to answer to heresy charges for allegedly denying the Real Presence, the preacher disappeared. Reports found him first

---

60 Merriman, *Life and Letters*, ii. 148–9.
61 SP 1/134/176 (*LP* xiii/1. 1387).
62 SP 1/134/177 (*LP* xiii/1. 1388).
63 SP 1/134/227 (*LP* xiii/1. 1436).
64 *Cranmer's Letters*, 372–3.

in the entourage of Nicholas Shaxton, then in the West Country as a school-master.[65] Cranmer notified Cromwell of Damplip's flight and of a written defence he had left behind. According to the archbishop, Damplip utterly denied that he ever taught or preached 'that the very body and blood of Christ was not present in the Sacrament of the Altar, and confesseth the same to be there really'. Rather, the preacher contended that the controversy between Dove and himself arose because he had confuted the opinion of transubstantia-tion, and therein, Cranmer stated, 'I think he taught but the truth'.[66] The archbishop, regretting Damplip's desertion, tried to divorce the charges against him from the cause of Protestant reform:

> Howbeit there came ii friars against him to testify that he had denied the presence of the body and blood to be in the sacrament which when he perceived straight ways he withdrew himself, and since that time no man can tell where he is become, for which I am very sorry, because that I think he is rather fled, suspecting the rigour of the law, than the defence of his own cause.[67]

Cranmer hoped to balance the loss of Damplip in Calais by removing John Dove from his office as prior of the Carmelites there. Arguing that further reform in the city was impossible unless Dove could be restrained, the arch-bishop asked Cromwell to prohibit the prior from returning to the Pale, either by suppressing his house, 'or else that an honest and learned man may be appointed in his room'.[68] But by this time political momentum had shifted to the conservative camp, and Cromwell could only compel Dove on his return to Calais to reaffirm his loyalty to crown policy.

Encouraged by success against Damplip, Lisle and the council turned their attention to John Butler, Cranmer's commissary. Lisle accused him of creating great unrest in Calais by maintaining a private congregation in the town and by destroying images without sufficient authorisation. Assuming that Damplip had confessed his heresy by his flight, the council judged that Butler, who licensed Damplip to preach, therefore supported his heretical behaviour. Although Butler attempted to refute these charges by ascribing their origins to papists on the council, his defence failed, and his censure became an effective instrument of Lisle's campaign against the reformers of Calais. Throughout 1538 and 1539, Lisle sent a steady stream of correspondence across the Channel, accusing Cromwell and the reform faction of fomenting misgovernment in Calais.[69]

The pressure of the conservative challenge, reinforced by the passage of the Act of the Six Articles in May 1539, goaded Cromwell to an active defence of the Calais Protestants. He acknowledged in a letter of 27 May 1539 receipt of

---

[65] Damplip lived quietly until 1543 when he was detected and executed on charges of heresy. See Lisle Letters, v. 165.
[66] This is the earliest statement made by Cranmer on the subject of transubstantiation, a point ignored by the archbishop's biographers, and one which suggests that the religious heterodoxy of the 1530s served a full menu of doctrinal alternatives.
[67] Cranmer's Letters, 375–6.
[68] Ibid.
[69] Byrne, as noted above, and Slavin, Thomas Cromwell, 187.

Lisle's correspondence and related depositions, and he stated that, although the king had not had time to read them,

> I have thought convenient not only to give you mine advice for the ordering and quieting of things till in those matters you shall know further of his majesty's pleasure, but also to declare some part of mine opinion touching the effects of the said depositions and concerning the quieting of the bruits and rumours which have risen and be spread abroad by your advertisements and earnest proceedings in these matters and examinations.[70]

Cromwell agreed with Lisle that sedition must be punished for 'there might be men who would rather desire to put men in trouble and despair, than to reform what is amiss'. But, he emphasised, punishment must be discreet and charitable:

> And therefore, mine opinion is that you shall by all means devise how with much charity and mild handling of things to quench this slanderous bent as much as you may, ever exhorting men discreetly and without rigour or extreme dealing to know and serve God truly and their prince and sovereign lord with all humility and obedience.[71]

Cromwell peremptorily dismissed the substance of Lisle's depositions. 'It is sore to note any man for a Sacramentary', Cromwell lectured, 'unless he that shall be the author of the infamy know well what a Sacramentary is.' Moreover, he warned Lisle that it was 'more sore' to charge an officer with so heinous a crime, referring to Butler, 'except it might be duly and evidently proved against him'. Even with these qualifications, Cromwell allowed that with some in the city the accusations brought by Lisle appeared to have more weight. 'And yet', Cromwell maintained, 'the final number that be accused of that offence might have been punished without an infamy to the whole town.'[72]

Cromwell's personal defence of men charged as Sacramentaries pushed the vicegerent deeply into dangerous territory. Lisle had by now sent the bulk of his evidence against Adam Damplip's preaching, which, he contended, had contributed substantially to the split in Calais's religious community. Cromwell wrote to Lisle on 8 June 1539 stating that he found the articles against Damplip 'very pestilent', but he expressed surprise 'that the same were not presented heretofore against him, when he was accused of the matter of transubstantion'. Cromwell was forced to concede that 'if it be true that he taught them, then taught he most detestable and cankered heresy'.[73] Damplip had been safely away from Calais for a year, and apparently immune from punishment, but Cromwell, trapped finally by Lisle, found it necessary to withdraw his support for Butler. Brought from Calais to London, the commissary received correction for his encouragement of Damplip's preaching.[74]

---

[70] Merriman, *Life and Letters*, ii. 222–4.
[71] Ibid.
[72] Ibid.
[73] Ibid. 226–8.
[74] Slavin, *Thomas Cromwell*, 187. Byrne's handling of the Calais episode in general, and

Cromwell covered his losses, but he did not retire from the struggle with the Calais conservatives. Lisle's manipulation of evidence concerning Damplip and Butler gave Cromwell an opening which he used to admonish the council for dividing Calais into bitterly opposed religious factions:

> As I wrote before that I thought it necessary that such slanders chancing to rise amongst you, the same should be rather discreetly and charitable appeased, and the offenders quietly punished, than so handled as should give courage to the king's majesty's enemies to note much division amongst us and percase cause them the rather to advance sundry evil practices. Even so I must advise you again, being the same counsel that I would in like case follow myself, not seeking but offenders may as well be punished without too great a tumult, as if the faults of a few in respect of the multitude there were bruited through the whole world.[75]

Cromwell again required Lisle to moderate his vengeful campaign against the Calais Protestants. Using a medical metaphor, he insisted that Calais must be reformed to preserve the health of the community against the infection of religious discord:

> And . . . touching the occasioners of the bruits which have been spread of these matters. I meant none other than to ascribe the same chiefly to those which were the first setters forth of any erroneous opinions. And yet to be plain with you as with my friends, many times many diseases that be of their own nature disposed to very evil effects, if it chance them to be espied by a good physician, his learning, wisdom, knowledge and good disposition may in such wise provide remedy, as the patient shall with little pain attain perfect health. Whereas, if the physician should, upon respect wink till the infection were more deeply settled, percase all his cunning to be practised upon the sick man should daily rack him with his medicines. And surely we be no less but more in fault which labour not to avoid evil from our neighbours where we see the same imminent, than if we should be ourselves the very authors and workers of the same evil towards them.[76]

The vicegerent informed Lisle that the king had now taken charge of the examination into the discord at Calais. Referring to Lisle's attempt to trap him by withholding evidence, Cromwell turned the deputy's own words into a less than subtle threat:

> The evil (as you write therein truly) will labour to pervert the good. And even so, those that be well disposed will both lament the folly of evil and do what they can to make them better. He that either fears not God nor esteems

---

Butler's part in it, in particular, is at best maddeningly dispersed and unsatisfactory. She has not been able to integrate the letters with a broad, analytical narrative (*Lisle Letters*, v. 160-7), and she has neglected Slavin's work on the connections between Calais and Cromwell's fall, claiming, 'as far as I am aware this has not previously been recognized': p. 351.

[75] Merriman, *Life and Letters*, ii. 226.
[76] Ibid. 227.

the king's majesty's injunctions, precepts, ordinances and commandments, is no meet herb to grow in his majesty's most catholic and virtuous garden. If you know, therefore, any more of that sort to be opened than you have already revealed by such examinations as you lately sent unto me, I doubt not but without respect you will give the king's majesty advertisement of them.

Suggesting, thus, that Lisle produce evidence of heresy and sedition if he had it, rather 'than thus to put all men generally and openly in fear of the loss of their livings', Cromwell concluded by promising that the king, seeing the experience of many inconveniences, 'will very shortly so play a part of a most noble king and arbiter amongst us, as all parties shall be brought to a godly order, with relief of the honest and the punishment of the malefactor accordingly'.[77]

Although he was able to salvage a measure of dignity, Cromwell saw his programme for protecting and advancing the Protestant interest in Calais end in failure. By the close of 1539 most of the Calais reformers patronised by Cromwell and Cranmer were in exile, in hiding, or in prison. Lisle and the Council of Calais had wrested from Cromwell candid statements of his religious sympathies which were to leave him vulnerable to the political coup directed by the conservative faction in England. Lisle, however, could not for long savour his victory. During the struggle, Cromwell discovered that Lisle's chaplain had made a secret trip to Ghent to talk to Cardinal Pole, and this was close enough to treason to bring the deputy down. Ironically, Lisle and Cromwell later shared quarters for a time in the Tower of London.

Calais was but one example of a case where Cromwell's vision of a Protestant commonwealth met effective resistance. Government-sponsored violation of traditional practices and the introduction of new doctrine caught many men between royal policy and conservative conviction. While direct complaints regarding the actions of radical priests rarely reached Cromwell, reports from diocesan officials alerted him to serious clashes between priests carrying out his reforms and parishes which opposed any changes in their religious lives. John Worthiall, chancellor to the bishop of Chichester, found that the parishioners of Graffham within his jurisdiction much resented their parson, Master William Roll. The priest refused to supply the consecrated bread or holy water, a service traditionally performed by Graffham's clerical incumbent. He had also allowed his hair to grow, covering his formerly tonsured crown. 'Whereof hath and daily doth gender and rise a great rumour and grudge amongst the people of these parts and more is feared to ensue except there be some discreet direction taken therein.' Upset but wary, Worthiall told Cromwell that he dared not meddle, 'your pleasure and commandment not first known'.[78]

Variations in the form of the mass fostered tension. Thomas Brabyn, a marshall of the King's Hall, Cambridge, violently denounced Mr Hewyt, a chaplain and trainbearer for the bishop of Ely, for the performance of a service which, he felt, offended both lay and learned. On Easter Sunday Hewyt first

[77] Ibid. 228.
[78] SP 1/102/25 (LP x. 277).

148

refused to sanctify the breads designated for the mass. Then, with the host laid upon the altar the vicar intoned the consecration in English without celebration and began to minister the sacrament to his parishioners in both kinds. Several in the congregation refused to participate, leaving to take the sacramental offering at a different church, whereupon Hewyt ascended to the pulpit in defence of his actions. Although he admitted to fear of worldly punishment, the priest drew strength, he asserted, from the Holy Ghost in setting forth the verity of the gospel which bound all Christians to receive communion under both kinds, notwithstanding devilish holy councils. Brabyn asked Cromwell to expel Hewyt from his benefice, so that the people might all be of one mind and not daily vexed with diverse determinations. The marshal hoped that Cromwell would favour his report, because he also had information that the vicar of Caxton within seven miles of Cambridge had celebrated mass with ale instead of wine in full view of his flock on Easter Day.[79]

Even Cromwell's agents experienced difficulties in attempting to translate policy into procedure. Sir William Waldegrave, a commissioner of the peace for Suffolk, shattered local religious mores by establishing a vernacular church service. Much anger ensured, and Cromwell thought it prudent to check Waldegrave's enthusiasm. He ordered the reformed service suspended. Waldegrave obeyed, but he regretted the retreat, cited the hurt done to many in the congregation, and reminded Cromwell that there was much work to be done on behalf of the king's injunctions. Afraid to act without direct commandment from Cromwell, Waldegrave complained that his enemies had been encouraged by their victory. 'Wherefore I fear the weed will overgrow the corn, for they say all things shall be as it hath been, and then all things shall be naught again.'[80]

Waldegrave's plight typified many of the localised struggles waged to determine the impact and direction of ecclesiastical reform. Cromwell could only estimate the effective penetration of his policies, because with the exception of a few letters about clearly heretical practices touching the Sacrament of the Altar, Cromwell did not receive many complaints from opponents of reform. Conservatives understood that their religious views had political consequences, and they tried to channel their discontent to sympathetic ears. Thomas Bell, sheriff of Gloucestershire, addressed his charges against several of Bishop Latimer's preachers to John Stokesley, bishop of London, rather than to Cromwell who, Bell believed, would not take action against the zealous minions of the bishop of Worcester. The sheriff concentrated his attack upon James Asche, parson of Stanton, for allegedly speaking slanderous words against the king, and also upon Thomas Benet for preaching in the city of Gloucester that 'if the purgatory priests do pray with their tongues till their tongues be worn to stumps, yet their prayers shall not help ne prevail the souls departed'. Bell also charged Benet with speaking out against masses for the dead, shocking and alienating many among his audience.[81]

---

[79] SP 1/118/90 (LP xii/1. 876).
[80] SP 1/140/225–6 (LP xiii/2. 1179).
[81] SP 1/104/157 (LP x. 1099).

Bell assigned responsibility for the growing religious and political conflict in Gloucestershire to Latimer's misuse of patronage. One appointee, he stated, a black friar known as 'two year old', had earlier been banished from the diocese 'for his abominable living, and daily use of drunkenness'. Buttressed by allies among the local gentry, Bell accused Latimer of indiscretion in patronising preachers who 'do not edify the people nor be regarded of them because they be so slenderly learned and defamed persons obscurely preaching always'.[82]

Bell's charges were not without substance. Latimer, with full support from Cromwell, did work to furnish benefices in his diocese for reformers. In October 1537 the bishop agreed to grant a living to Cromwell's friend, Anthony Barker, whom he knew to be a man of good conversation and education. But, confident of Cromwell's favour, Latimer imposed two conditions. The first asked that Barker be personally responsible for the pension for the outgoing incumbent.

> The other that your lordship would persuade Master Barker to tarry upon it, keep house in it, preach at it and about it, to the reformation of that blind end of my diocese. For else what are we the better for either his great literature or good conversation if my diocese shall not taste and have experience thereof. And their houses (I thow) be toward ruin and decay and their whole town far out of frame for lack of residence when the head is far off the body is the worse.[83]

An ideologue himself, Latimer laboured unstintingly to surround himself with like-minded subordinates. Often brought to Worcester from other parts of the realm, these men usurped the influence of local conservative religious interests which had become entrenched during the absentee episcopal tenure of the Italian Cardinal Ghinucci. And so the charges raised by Thomas Bell, although probably exaggerated for political effect, were based on accurate assumptions about the importance of patronage. The sheriff hoped that Stokesley shared his opinions and would seek an alliance with the duke of Norfolk to create a counterweight to the reform faction.[84] Bell's proposal, however, was premature, and the appearance of his letter to Stokesley among Cromwell's papers plainly attests to the failure of this attempt at political intrigue.

Overt opposition to Cromwellian ecclesiastical policy began only after acceptance of the Royal Supremacy had been assured. Until that time, marked by the defeat of the northern rebels, conservatives made every effort to acquiesce publicly in the rejection of papal authority. When the revolutionary potential of the Supremacy became manifest, conservatives began to drift toward opposition. Cromwell made the organisation of effective resistance more difficult by isolating the two most capable conservative leaders. Until late in 1538 both Gardiner and Tunstall were kept from voicing their displeasure with Cromwell's ecclesiastical policies. Gardiner's exile was complete. He spent three years from 26 September 1535 in France, forced to watch helplessly as

[82] Ibid.
[83] SP 1/125/209r–v (LP xii/2. 909).
[84] SP 1/104/157.

Cromwell consolidated his dominance of English politics and religion. Much happened during the bishop's absence. Rumours suggested that Gardiner's ambassadorial assignment served Cromwell's domestic purposes, for if he were at home, 'many things would have been brought to pass otherwise'. After the first year Gardiner repeatedly asked to be recalled, but although Henry and Cromwell kept his hopes alive, promising a replacement on several occasions, necessity always intervened, and the bishop would be told that it would be unwise to change ambassadors in 'this troublous time'.[85]

The exile of Cuthbert Tunstall differed substantially from that of the bishop of Winchester. Cromwell felt safe enough as long as the bishop of Durham kept the length of England between himself and London and outwardly conformed to the king's pleasure and to that of his vicegerent. Although Tunstall never wavered in his personal preference for Catholic doctrine, openly challenging those Cromwellian measures which directly threatened the conservative faction, his belief in the need to submit to Henrician rule and his identification of royal and national interests led him to administer unenthusiastically policies which he did not favour.

Nevertheless, it was Tunstall's administrative abilities that kept him alive, in England, and in office. He served as president of the Council of the North from 1530 to 1536 and from 1537 to 1538. The participants in the Pilgrimage of Grace received no encouragement from him, and he willingly assented to the curtailment of the liberties of the palatinate. At the end of his twenty-nine year episcopate, Tunstall left his diocese with undiminished revenues, some special privileges, and with its old boundaries.[86]

Tunstall was a careful man, a cautious politician. He proceeded carefully, as a conductor measures his orchestra, listening with a sensitive ear for the least note of discord. In 1531 he had opposed the king's assumption of the title of supreme head of the English Church. Tunstall issued his protest at a convocation held at York. He argued that while the title contained no intrinsic danger, yet because it could encourage heretics to question the jurisdiction of their ordinaries, more precise definition was required. The words should be ordered, he suggested, to remove the implication that Christ had conferred spiritual jurisdiction upon the king.[87]

This protest and the king's reply, which rejected Tunstall's qualifying language, had been copied into the episcopal register by Christopher Chaytor, the registrar. But in December 1539, Chaytor deposed that

vj or vij years past this examinant then being servant to doctor Henmarsh chancellor to the bishop of Duresme, and writing in the register . . . of Duresme at the commandment of the said Chancellor did write in the register book of Duresme a protestation made by the said bishop touching the bishop of Rome's Authority, and divorce between the king's highness

85 Muller, *Stephen Gardiner*, 66.
86 *The Registers of Cuthbert Tunstall, Bishop of Durham, 1530–59, and James Pilkington, Bishop of Durham, 1561–76*, ed. Gladys Hinde, Durham 1952, p. xxx.
87 Ibid. p. xxviii.

151

and the lady dowager which protestation was after cut out of the same book by the said doctor Henmarsh.[88]

The king had ordered Tunstall's residences searched for incriminating evidence in May 1534. Presumably the mutilation of the register occurred about this time at the bishop's command. Although copies of the whole protestation survive in other sources, the portions of this document not cut out of the register have all dangerous words erased and the once bold challenge was made to appear a strong expression of submissive loyalty.[89]

Also from this time, the format of the register changed. Twenty-four of the fifty-seven folios of Tunstall's register deal with the first five years of his episcopate (1530–5). The entries for these years are detailed and carefully written by the registrar. The later leaves, however, are no longer neat, the entries are in many hands, sometimes illegible, and often incomplete, although Chaytor remained registrar throughout the bishop's tenure.[90] Tunstall's activities, thus, are masked, no evidence from the register would come forth to weigh against his reluctant discharge of royal policies.

Tunstall took care to disguise his resistance to Cromwellian ecclesiastical measures; but resist he did. An examination of the bishop's ordination lists reveals in part how he laboured to frustrate the extension of Cromwell's patronage into the diocese of Durham. It should first be noted that in those sees far from London and the universities, the smaller benefices went to local clerks who had been ordained within the diocese. More valuable livings, of course, attracted the attention of prominent clerical pluralists, usually closely tied to Cromwell and the reform faction. Thomas Legh, for example, a principal monastic visitor, was appointed master of Sherburn hospital, and it is significant that he thanked the king and Cromwell for the preferment, even though it was in the gift of the bishop.[91]

To counter Cromwell's potential for influencing the appointment of reform-minded clerks to Durham livings, Tunstall ignored vacancies and restricted the number of ordinands. No priest at all seemed preferable to a Cromwellian nominee. Tunstall's register contains forty-three ordination lists: twenty-one were held between 1531 and 1535, six occurred in 1542, another six between 1543 and June 1547, and ten between 1555 and 1559. The interval between 1535 and 1542, during which no ordinations were scheduled, can be explained in a number of ways: it was difficult to find suitable titles for ordinands after the dissolution of the monasteries; many of the dispossessed religious were gradually absorbed into the ranks of the parochial clergy; the bishop was preoccupied with national business.[92]

There is, however, another possibility. The periods in which no ordinations took place, 1535–42 and 1547–55, were years of revolutionary religious policy. Following these periods, great numbers of ordinations had to be organised to

[88] Ibid. p. xv. Cf. SP 1/155/192r–v.
[89] *Registers of Cuthbert Tunstall*, p. xxix.
[90] Ibid. pp. xv–xvi.
[91] Ibid. p. xxii.
[92] Ibid. p. xvii.

take up the slack. The earlier qualifications no longer seem to apply. There were now plenty of titles, and the bishop had ample time to preside over their dispensation. Clearly then, Tunstall's orchestration of ordinations served the political aim of keeping Cromwell from extending reformation ideology to the conservative north. That his challenge to Cromwell at his most powerful succeeded, boded ill for the future of factional reform.

Covertly, the conservative prelates gathered to plan their opposition to Cromwell's ecclesiastical policies. Evidence of this conspiracy derives from the deposition given by Richard Sampson, bishop of Chichester, while a prisoner in the Tower in June 1540. Sampson faced charges of treason and in answering questions presented by Sir William Petre, one of Cromwell's chief aides, he exposed many facets of the core of resistance to the expansion of religious reform. Sampson's preoccupations were personal. Anxiously he tried to shift responsibility for his plight to Cuthbert Tunstall. Although he understood that the bishop of Durham had refuted the allegation, Sampson insisted that 'He hath comforted me to lean and stick to the old usages and traditions of the church.' The bishop marvelled at Tunstall's denial, because, he asserted, the matter had been raised on so many occasions, 'especially as I have said in the time of the late bishop of London, when we were busied with the Germans and also with the book'. Sampson asked his interrogators to bring to Tunstall's mind the remembrance of their several meetings at Lambeth and an old book in Greek which contained diverse usages and traditions of the old Church. Sampson alleged that while travelling in a barge, Tunstall instructed him in their validity. Stokesley, too, would bring books, 'and so they conferred together'.[93]

Questioned specifically about Tunstall's recent activities, Sampson replied that 'The comfort that hath given me was now lately not to fear to help things forward for the king's highness was very good lord in them.' Tunstall advised him to leave the controversy over ceremonies to the king's pleasure; sound advice in 1540. Sampson asserted, however, that at other times, when they spoke of old usages and traditions, 'He was clear in that opinion that they were not to be broken without a great cause and that some of them in no wise were to be broken.' He perceived that Bishop Gardiner concurred with Tunstall's determination. 'And my lord of Winchester told me that they were all one opinion very few except that many old traditions needs must be kept as they had the example of praying for souls and baptism of infants and yet others which I remember not.'[94]

Sampson told Cromwell that Tunstall had showed him books which set forth the old usages, and that the late bishop Stokesley had pleaded earnestly on their behalf. And he trusted that Tunstall would not say otherwise, 'but that he and my late lord of London were fully bent to maintain as many of the old usages and traditions as they might'.[95] In his own defence he delineated a portrait of himself as a politically unsophisticated victim of Tunstall, Stokesley, and Gardiner; a simple man exposed to the high-pressure tactics of complex

---

[93] BL, Cotton Cleopatra E v. fo. 308v (*LP* xv. 758).
[94] Ibid.
[95] Ibid.

colleagues who sought to seduce him from the arms of the king, and now would leave him to bear alone the bitter fruit of their passions.

Sampson, certainly an able politician, despite his disclaimers, had always been a somewhat reluctant ecclesiastic. Legal and administrative talents furthered his rise in the church hierarchy. He had been a chaplain in Cardinal Wolsey's household and there he met Cromwell. He also developed useful connections with the Boleyns, joining Thomas Boleyn on an embassy to Spain in 1522. During the years preceding the divorce, Sampson worked on legal questions and helped to collect the opinions of the universities on the legality of Henry's marriage to Catherine.[96] He published an oration in 1535 favouring the Royal Supremacy, and Cromwell, following a familiar pattern, patronised him without investigating his conscience too closely.[97]

Sampson became bishop of Chichester, succeeding Robert Sherbourne in June 1536, and received permission to hold the episcopate *in commendam* with the deanery of St Paul's. As he also held the deanery of the Chapel Royal[98] and the deanery of St Stephen's, Westminster, Sampson rarely visited his diocese. Occupied on the king's business in London, Sampson's religious expectations for Chichester counted quietness as the most valuable achievement of successful episcopal rule. He steadfastly avoided disquiet through literal interpretation and administration of the king's commandments. And he refused to recognise the implications of Cromwellian legislation or injunctions for the advancement of reform.

In August 1538, for example, Sampson wrote to Mr Welles, possibly his vicar general, to thank him for enterprising not to sing openly any church service in English. 'I am so much the more glad, praying you, for the common quietness to forbear any such novelties, till it shall please the king's majesty to declare his pleasure.' Alluding to tradition, which Cromwell refused to accept as a test for the establishment of ecclesiastical practices, Sampson noted that ministers of the Church in all places sang and said their offices or prayers in Greek or Latin, while people prayed apart in the vulgar tongue. He only wished that the ministers were learned enough in Latin so that they could understand what they were saying. Regretting that he was unable to visit his diocese more often, the bishop also thanked Welles for 'a space of such quietness that I was very glad of'. Yet he worried about the spectre of contention raised by the penetration of Protestant doctrine for of late he had perceived 'our ghostly enemy travaileth as he hath been at all times wont to do with his seed of dissention, wherefore we have so much the more need to be vigilant to pray for grace that we may withstand him'.[99]

Sampson counteracted the poltergeist in a most practical way through the use of his patronage. He informed Welles that he had appointed an 'honest man' to a living in Rye, a clerk who would purely preach the word of God,

---

[96] *DNB* xvii. 720.

[97] Ibid. Sampson received the rectory of Hackney on 31 March 1534 and the office of treasurer of Salisbury on 16 March 1535. His career is a model of the steady advancement common to crown servants in these years.

[98] E 404/99/70. Sampson seems to have received fifty marks from the king every Good Friday.

[99] BL, Cotton Cleopatra E v. fo. 296r (*LP* xiii/2. 147).

while using himself with such discretion 'that he shall be a means of much quietness there, with the help of almighty God'. The bishop insisted that Welles supervise the clergy and warn him instantly of any clamour for change or any person grieved by traditional religious practices. Sampson sent a copy of a religious concord he had devised to protect Welles from local resentment, and he promised to resolve 'especial points that are now causes of any discord'. He further advised Welles not to rely for direction on the *Bishops' Book*, because the king had not fully approved it. But until his grace should determine otherwise, the book should not be rejected.[100] Having thus provided for his diocesan servant, the bishop, probably with great relief, turned back to his work as a crown administrator.

Sampson's attempt to quiet dissent by suppressing religious innovation failed, and in 1538 a reform faction in Chichester began a campaign to discredit him. Aware that his opponents had gained access to Cromwell, Sampson launched his defence, hampered though it was by ignorance of the allegations against him. Attending to the crucial task of shoring up his political relationship with Cromwell, the bishop claimed that he had never offended in thought, word, or deed. Sampson begged to be informed if there had been any sinister report against him. 'And if your lordship think that I have offended you, I pray you as charity requireth, admonish me thereof, that I may know my fault to amend it, or to recompence, to my power.'[101]

Searching his mind for particular instances which might have reached Cromwell's ears, Sampson recalled that he had preached in Chichester Cathedral on Assumption Day. But he thought that Cromwell would have been content with his sermon, and he felt that he could make answer for anything he might have said. If some other preacher within his diocese had transgressed, Sampson promised 'if I may know his ill preaching, I should endeavour me to reform him, or else to bring forth his fault, that it may be corrected in example of other'.[102]

Sampson blamed present difficulties on the amount of time required by duties in London which detracted from his performance as diocesan supervisor. He promised more rigour in future in setting forth all doctrine determined by the king: 'I trust in almighty God, that neither his highness, nor your lordship shall need to have any travail, for that poor diocese, for I doubt not God willing, to settle them in such a sort, that if every bishop, will so do for his part, the king's people shall be right shortly in a quietness.' Stating the obvious, Sampson admitted that he was not friendly to religious 'novelties', except when required by the demands of political expediency. Yet, he argued, he had long opposed such superstitious practices as the worship of images. As for allegations that he favoured the bishop of Rome, Sampson most vehemently denied these charges. 'He is not in England, or Germany, but in that matter I durst adventure my life with him, that I am no more papist than he is.'[103]

Sampson reinforced his protestation of loyalty to the king by sending

[100] Ibid. fos 296v–297r.
[101] Ibid. fo. 306r (*LP* xiii/2. 278 (1)).
[102] Ibid. fo. 306v.
[103] Ibid. fo. 307r.

Cromwell a copy of some instructions he had conveyed to the Chichester clergy. The bishop alerted his subordinates to the responsibilities of their ministries and explained that every good Christian man and woman ought to obey the king's ordinances because he was God's minister and because he was their king. In concluding his defence the bishop asked to be heard before any credence was attached to other specific allegations which he felt would come from Rye and Lewes, and he reaffirmed his loyalty to Cromwell:

> My lord, after the king my sovereign lord, he is not in England, whose counsel or advice, that I will so follow, as only yours. And I assure you, I neither speak this for fear, nor flattery, but to show you the truth of my mind, as I suppose your lordship knoweth to have found and known it, and so shall know it.[104]

This time Cromwell accepted Sampson's effort at reconciliation, and soon afterward the bishop signified his pleasure at receiving the minister's recent letters. He said that while he was confident of his innocence he felt relieved to have purged himself of his own doubts and worries. Apologising again for abuses which he attributed to his necessary absence from Chichester, Sampson thanked Cromwell for his injunctions, 'for now they shall be, God willing, obeyed and well accomplished'.[105] Once restored to Cromwell's good graces, Sampson of course had no intention of working for Cromwell's 1538 Injunctions. Rather, as his later presence in the Tower testifies, the bishop and other members of the conservative faction began an even more vigorous crusade against Cromwellian ecclesiastical policy, an initiative which relentlessly pushed the vicegerent along the path to the scaffold.

[104] Ibid. fo. 307v.
[105] SP 1/136/146r–v (LP xiii/2. 339).

Conclusion: Cromwell's Fall and the Triumph of Faction

Bishop Gardiner's return from France on 28 September strengthened and gave direction to the conservative movement against Cromwell's authority. Although out of favour for some months, early in 1539 Gardiner began to seize with increasing success upon every opportunity to thwart and embarrass Cromwell. In January he defied the vicegerent's control of patronage by ejecting John Palmes, the owner of the parsonage of Bentworth. Palmes took the matter to Cromwell. He argued that the king's letters-patent by which he had been granted the benefice discharged him from the bonds of celibacy imposed by the bishop of Rome. As the letters did not forbid marriage, 'especially to them that hath neither taken the holy orders neither avowed the contrary of which number I am one as by my letters-patent may appear', Palmes for urgent and necessary reasons took upon himself the estate and divine ordinance of marriage, 'wherefore I am now called into my lord of Winchester's court by a citation *ex-officio*'.[1]

Palmes expressed little hope of favour at the hands of the bishop's court, perceiving rather 'their speedy readiness toward my undoing'. He asked for Cromwell's determination whether 'a wife and a benefice may not stand together as the ordinances of God and as the king's highness hath dispensed with me in that behalf'. Should the vicegerent's judgment go against him, he asked that a day and time be appointed for his voidance of the benefice, and that he be allowed to keep the things granted by the king's letters, 'for though they have both temporal lands and tithes spiritual, yet may no wedded man take one crumb that falleth from their board'.[2]

Despite Cromwell's support for Palmes, the episcopal court ruled to eject him from his rectory. Palmes sent a bitter account of the proceedings, appealing to Cromwell, as the apostle Paul 'sharply persecuted and vexed, the heads of the Jews their cruel intent and purpose espied, appealed to Caesar'. He claimed that although he had been the only man in that part of Hampshire to preach against the usurped power of the bishop of Rome, yet, 'for their inequity and covetousness shall be heavily laid upon my neck . . . as shall seem rebuke and shame of the truth'.[3]

Palmes vilified the hypocrisy of the 'foreign laws' under which he had been charged. He knew that the parson of Burfield, who was in holy orders, had kept

[1] SP 1/142/135 (*LP* xiv/1. 120).
[2] Ibid.
[3] SP 1/142/223 (*LP* xiv/1. 206).

a concubine for twenty years and had children by her, 'by dispensation as it is said, and no man sayeth black is his ye'. Citing other abuses which commonly occurred in the Church, Palmes complained that he alone had been singled out for punishment before the bishop of Winchester to his own great charge and undoing:

> So great a triumph it is accounted to suppress and tread under the foot a poor blind man neither offending God neither his prince in this case. God that helped the children of Israel at the Red Sea against the Egyptians and by Samuel in Ramoth against the Philistines, aid and succor me by whom he liketh that I be not compelled to eat the unwholesome droppings of the stinking Antichrist.

Palmes begged that if his marriage and benefice were not compatible then Cromwell should take the living and rid him of bondage and subjugation to the bishop of Winchester.[4]

Not only could Cromwell not save Palmes, he was further humiliated by Gardiner's selection of a replacement, one Wigg, a seditious person, preacher, and sometime friar who had earlier been imprisoned for suspicious preaching by John Kyngsmyll, sheriff of Hampshire.[5] Nor had Gardiner finished with Palmes. Notwithstanding Cromwell's letter on his behalf, John Cook, Gardiner's registrar, discharged Palmes from the deanship of Alton, claiming that he was not a parson. Palmes stated that he did not think that bishops ought to 'admit, create, and institute any priest minister of Christ and disposer of the secrets of God where the king and governour is a Christian without his special commission and commandment'. He also accused Gardiner of keeping court within his realm and dominion against God's ordinance, which reserved this power to kings. Palmes then concluded by returning to the subject of his marriage and his calling:

> I marvel why it is so odious in our bishops' ears and noisome to their eyes that a beadman should preach and set forth Christ saying that it appeareth in the story tripartite that in the antique church wedded men besides the apostles were called to that office but of this I will not be ambitious if it shall please your lordship to admit me to a lecture of Scripture in the church of Bentworth or else where that I be not compelled to hide my talent in the ground by their violence.[6]

The Palmes episode might seem at most a minor crack in Cromwell's shield, but as we can now see, added to the conservative faction's successes in Calais, Gardiner's triumph spoke volumes. Cromwell's principal rival had returned from ambassadorial exile and re-entered the lists of high politics with authority. Encouraged by their victories over the reform faction, conservatives confidently prepared to fight for political ascendancy. Their device prominently

---

4 Ibid.
5 LP xiv/1. 775.
6 BL, Cotton Titus B i. fo. 80 (LP xiv/1. 890); Elton, *Policy and Police*, 42–3.

displayed The Act of the Six Articles. The Six Articles seem to have resulted from a combination of interests and political forces which brought together the king's anxiety about religious uniformity with the revival of factional conservatism.[7] For some months Henry had displayed concern about the doctrinal innovations paraded before him. Private masses, married priests, merely symbolic Communion services offended the king's orthodox temperament. What might come next? New heresies, including Anabaptism, appeared to be spreading like a rash across the continent. Would the contagion reach England?

The king pronounced an emphatic 'No'! Henry wanted uniformity, and he was prepared to go to considerable lengths to end doctrinal experimentation. The destruction of John Lambert, charged as a Sacramentary, in November 1538, quickly followed by a royal proclamation which denied a place in the realm to Anabaptists, signalled an end to the control of religious ideology by the reform faction. Moreover, Henry knew about the events in Calais and could not have welcomed reports of religious radicalism or the charges of heresy directed against his vicegerent. Thus the conservative faction found a receptive ear for their recommendations for an official return to orthodoxy. With the duke of Norfolk in their train, the conservative bishops, led by Stephen Gardiner[8] convinced the king to resolve upon 'a device for the unity of religion'. The duke presented six articles for the consideration of the full parliament. These articles touched the most sensitive areas of doctrine and practice: transubstantiation, clerical celibacy, vows of chastity, private masses, and auricular confession; all received Catholic interpretation and affirmation. Repudiation would be fatal. Debate ensued, but the issue had already been resolved in the king's mind. His personal intervention guaranteed the act and marked an end to this phase of religious heterodoxy. Although Gardiner had no direct involvement in the formal presentation and passage of the articles, his biographer, noting that the duke of Norfolk was no theologian, conceded that his ally, the bishop of Winchester, was the author of 'this ferocious act'. They were dubbed 'Gardiner's Gospel', and he was prominent among the conservative bishops pressing for their passage through the House of Lords. Gardiner also served on one of the two committees charged with suggesting the penalty clauses of the act, and his recommendations generally won favour.[9]

The reform faction correctly regarded this reactionary religious settlement as a disastrous defeat. Latimer and Shaxton resigned their sees, the former possibly

[7] Henry played an active part in both inspiring and implementing a return to orthodoxy in matters of doctrine. See Glyn Redworth, 'A study in the formulation of policy: the genesis and evolution of the Act of the Six Articles', *Journal of Ecclesiastical History*, xxxvii (1986), 42–67. Redworth has corrected earlier analyses which ignore the king as a major force in the shaping of policy, and he has given greater depth to our understanding of the Six Acts as a process rather than an event. If we place Redworth's argument and evidence within the context of a determined factional conflict and continue to recognise the ideological component of such factional struggles, we shall have gained a solid sense of the depth and complexity of an important episode in the history of English Reformation politics.

[8] In trying to emphasise Henry's part in the process of evolution of the Six Acts, Redworth has almost eliminated Gardiner from the political machinations which attended its passage from inspiration to legislation: ibid. 44–5.

[9] Muller, *Stephen Gardiner*, 80–1 remains convincing on the question of Gardiner's political role in the passage of the Act of the Six Articles.

at Cromwell's protective urging. The letter from the once imperious bishop of Salisbury well illustrates the mood which dominated England's Protestant vanguard:

> Nicholas Shaxton wisheth to the lord Cromwell the lord privy seal, that he may prosperously proceed in all things, and please God and his prince. And because we offend our God daily many ways (my good lord), . . . so in like sort if we offend our prince in any things as we do indeed offend him also many ways: our refuge after God is to him: . . . as your good lordship is, and I pray God, that ye may so be ever more and more, as ye seek the pleasure of God, as doubt not ye do, and intend to do. And therefore I most humbly beseech your good lordship . . . if my offence be such that ye may not speak for me hand me even up now and if it be a pardonable fault, and may stand with your honour to speak for me to the gentle prince that can well judge between stubborn malice and simple ignorance: I beseech your lordship once again to speak for me. My suit in two words is, to be at liberty, and that by your mediation the king's highness will give me a pension to live by according to his good pleasure and my poor calling.[10]

Passage of the Act of the Six Articles had an immediate political effect. Cromwell's domination of religion, challenged by Calais conservatives, now began to dissolve, as the vicegerent lost control of Paul's Cross. In the summer of 1539 preaching, especially at St Paul's, became a dangerous occupation. Hilsey urged Cromwell to greater activity in planning the sermons at the Cross. No one would accept the preaching office except Hilsey himself and one of his chaplains. The bishop returned the book he used for the ordering of the sermons and suggested that Cromwell forward it to Stokesley whom he now perceived best placed to make provision for the continuation of preaching.[11] The reform faction had suffered a serious setback. Hilsey had tried to ignore the signs until he found that he could no longer recruit preachers. All sermons were reported to Stokesley who had regained control of the programme. Anxiety reigned. According to Hilsey,

> whereas a chaplain of mine preached a Sunday last at the Cross, now he is cited to appear afore the bishop of London a Sunday next. But I trust he hath neither preached against God's laws nor the king's, and a Sunday next for lack of one to preach I must preach there myself, with more fear than ever I did in my life.[12]

Cromwell barely withstood this factional challenge. He did not lose the reins of government, but he never regained his hold on Paul's Cross. Reform had lost its momentum and Cromwell appeared vulnerable.

The Act of the Six Articles threatened Cromwell's political future. He was forced to submit himself to Henry's strong lead in matters of doctrine, and his relationship with Gardiner became one of open confrontation. Cromwell's

---

[10] BL, Cotton Cleopatra E iv. fo. 65 (*LP* xiv/2. 488).
[11] SP 1/152/207 (*LP* xiv/1. 1297).
[12] Ibid.

exercise of episcopal patronage is a measure of the moderate posture he resolved to adopt in the face of the conservative assault. John Salcot succeeded Shaxton in the bishopric of Salisbury. Regarded by later Protestant writers as a false, dissembling bishop, a time-server, and a papist, Salcot's major qualification for translation seems to have been the absence of any affiliation with the conservative faction. Formerly a Benedictine, he graduated from Cambridge University and began a career in the monastic establishment. His brother William, an architect, scene painter, and decorative artist, served as chaplain to Wolsey, and Salcot also came to enjoy the cardinal's favour. He met Cromwell in 1525, forming a connection which in 1534 led to his consecration in the Welsh see of Bangor. Salcot's translation to Salisbury at this crucial moment in 1539 recognised his political loyalties and lack of disabling religious convictions. Almost invisible, Salcot pursued his undistinguished career until his death in 1557.[13]

John Bell, who replaced Latimer at Worcester, brought more substantial credentials to his diocesan dignity, although again, Gardiner's political presence influenced Cromwell's selection. Bell attended both Oxford and Cambridge Universities and took an LLB degree from the latter university in 1504. He started his career as a secular priest beneficed principally in his native Worcestershire. By 1518 he was vicar general and chancellor in the diocese of Worcester. In the late 1520s he became a royal chaplain and moved to London where he was in constant attendance on the king. He was frequently employed in the business of the king's divorce, serving as Henry's counsel before the legates at Blackfriar's Hall in 1529 and again at Dunstable before Cranmer and the bishop of Lincoln in 1532. He also argued for the validity of the divorce at Oxford University.[14]

Bell seems to have been a secondary figure among the reformers. In 1537 he participated in the composition of the *Bishop's Book* and was called upon in the course of its preparation to define the true meaning of various church ordinances. He served on the committee of six bishops charged in 1540 to examine the ceremonies to be retained by the Church. A year later he promised Cranmer that he would support 'an act for the advancement of true religion and the abolishment of the contrary', but he reneged when the strength of the opposition acted upon his will. In 1542, when Convocation undertook a revised translation of the New Testament, the first and second epistles to the Thessalonians were assigned to Bell. For undetermined reasons the bishop resigned on 17 November 1543, retiring to become a simple priest in Clerkenwell parish. He died in 1556.[15]

John Stokesley, who had been promoted with the divorce in mind but later balked on wider issues, died in 1539. Cromwell replaced him with Edmund Bonner, a strong personal adherent with, at the time, no coherent religious ideals. Bonner received his education at Oxford University, where he was admitted DCL in 1525. Wolsey's household again provided a springboard for

---

[13] *DNB* iii. 931–2. Salcot was prior of St John's, Colchester in 1517 and later became abbot of St Benet's, Hulme in Norfolk.
[14] Ibid. ii. 165–6.
[15] Ibid.

clerical ambitions. A chaplain to the cardinal, Bonner performed secretarial duties, conveying important messages to the king and his then secretary, Stephen Gardiner. After Wolsey's fall Bonner stayed to help Cromwell try to rescue their patron. It was probably this political crisis which fostered a bitter enmity between Bonner and Gardiner which lasted until Cromwell's death.[16]

Cromwell used Bonner almost exclusively on ambassadorial assignments. He was at the papal court from 1532 to 1535, and after a brief respite in England, which he spent writing defences of the Royal Supremacy, was dispatched to Hamburg to cultivate an understanding between the king and the Protestants of Denmark and northern Germany. Cromwell supported Bonner's secular embassies with clerical promotions, including the archdeaconry of Leicester in 1535 and a prebend in St Paul's in 1537. In 1538 he first sent Bonner with Simon Haynes to attempt to dissuade the emperor from attending a general council called by the pope. Later in the same year Bonner replaced Gardiner at the French court.[17]

While in France, Bonner learned that he had been selected to succeed the late bishop, Edward Foxe, at Hereford, but he did not return to England to take up the bishopric. Cromwell undertook supervision of the financial administration of the diocese. Grateful for his promotion and his patron's help, Bonner sent gifts from France and gave Cromwell several advowsons.[18] He was still abroad, helping in the printing of the *Great Bible*, when Bishop Stokesley died. Bonner was elected to the bishopric of London on 20 October 1539, and six months later he was consecrated at St Paul's.[19]

Forced by his episcopal status to subscribe to a religious ideology, Bonner, with Cromwell's execution fresh in his mind, chose to follow Gardiner rather than Cranmer. He participated in a commission to try heretics and supervised enough martyrdoms to earn a prominent, permanent, pejorative place in the major Protestant martyrologies. One of Somerset's first acts was to imprison him first in the Fleet and then in 1549 in the Marshalsea after depriving him of his bishopric. Released and restored to episcopal dignity in 1553, Bonner emerged to resume his career as one of England's most unpopular prelates. He revived the trappings of Catholic orthodoxy, including processions and images, and he actively undertook the religious persecutions which accompanied Mary's reconciliation with the papacy. When Elizabeth became queen, she looked coldly upon him, even refusing him her hand to kiss on meeting the other bishops at Highgate. Bonner declined to take the oath of supremacy in 1559 and returned to the Marshalsea where he died ten years later.[20]

Cromwell continued the pattern of moderation in his other episcopal nominations. He promoted John Byrde to Bangor, Nicholas Heath to Rochester, and John Skipp to Hereford, hoping that their personal loyalty and doctrinal temperance would satisfy the king and undermine the opposition. Until the early

---

16 Ibid. 819.
17 Ibid.
18 G. M. V. Alexander, 'The Life and Career of Edmund Bonner Bishop of London until his Deprivation in 1549', unpublished PhD diss., London 1960, 69.
19 *DNB* ii. 820.
20 Ibid. 820–2.

months of 1540 Cromwell seemed to be recovering, but then events both at home and abroad ended his hopes. The Lutheran alliance, painstakingly constructed by Cromwell and sealed with the king's reluctant marriage to Anne of Cleves collapsed, to the delight of Norfolk, who, advocating reconciliation, had made a special embassy to France in February.

That same month Robert Barnes reminded the unhappy royal newlywed of his chief minister's Protestant sympathies. Since returning from Germany, Barnes had played a useful role on embassies to continental Protestant courts in 1534, 1535, 1536, and 1539. At home in June 1538 he was appointed by the king to a commission which endeavoured to establish doctrinal accord between English and German Protestant leaders. Later that year he was chosen to act with Cranmer, Stokesley, and others on a commission to proceed against Anabaptists. Barnes enjoyed Cromwell's patronage as late as December 1539, receiving the prebend of Llanboidy in the diocese of St David's.[21]

Within two months, however, elated perhaps by the farcical union of Tudor and Cleves, Barnes seriously wounded his patron by preaching a violent sermon at Paul's Cross against Gardiner, at the exact moment that Cromwell was meeting Gardiner in a final exhaustive effort to come to terms with him. After conferring with Gardiner at the king's command Barnes was ordered to preach a sermon of recantation. He did this so badly that he earned for himself first a room in the Tower, then a place at the stake. Cromwell studiously avoided any sign of sympathy, but control of ecclesiastical affairs continued to slip from his grasp. Gardiner, Tunstall, and Clerk came to the council, and a parliamentary committee appointed to define doctrine was heavily loaded with conservatives. Cromwell had no voice in these matters.

Ironically, the king chose this moment to bestow upon Cromwell the earldom of Essex and the office of Great Chamberlain. Henry still valued his minister. In the brief Indian summer of his ministry Cromwell toyed with the idea of decisively and permanently eliminating his enemies. Thus Sampson went to the Tower, arrested on Cromwell's sole authority. Dr Nicholas Wilson, another of Gardiner's lieutenants, was also seized, and rumours circulated that five more conservative bishops soon would join them. Cromwell, however, did not act with sufficient speed if, indeed, he intended to act at all. A month passed, and while Cromwell busied himself with parliamentary routine, Gardiner struck. Dangling another Norfolk niece, Katherine Howard, under Henry's lustful gaze, the duke and the bishop convinced the king that Cromwell was guilty of treason and heresy. On 10 June 1540 Cromwell was arrested, stripped of his honours, and taken off to the Tower. Nothing remained for the fallen minister but to act out the rituals of Tudor justice and execution.[22]

Cromwell, at his most powerful in March 1538, had allowed himself to reveal his heartfelt sense of vocation. He and Nicholas Shaxton had engaged in a long dispute over a minor matter, and the bishop, typically, widened the issue by

[21] Muller, 'Stephen Gardiner', 83–4.
[22] Elton, 'Thomas Cromwell's decline and fall', in Elton, *Studies*, i. 187–230. Originally published in 1951, this analysis remains the best study of the issues and events surrounding Cromwell's fall.

accusing Cromwell of letting down the cause of reform. In his reply to a man he considered a friend Cromwell answered the charge by stating

> I know who works all that is wrought by me and who, as he is the whole doer, I intend not to offer him this wrong: he to labour and I to take the thanks. Yet, as I do not cease to give thanks that it has pleased his goodness to use me as an instrument and to work somewhat by me, so, I trust, I am as ready to serve him in my calling, to my little power, as you a priest . . . My prayer is that God give me no longer life than I shall be glad to use mine office in edifications and not in destructions.[23]

Cromwell's sense of himself, a layman engaged in God's work, provides a focus around which we can draw together the legacy of factional struggle between 1528 and 1540 which defined the opening stages of the English Reformation and pointed the way towards a future of continuing conflict. The first years combined an emerging reformist ideology with traditional concerns of grand faction. Hatred of Cardinal Wolsey and ambition for office shaded clear tones of ideological commitment as Henry's matrimonial hopes released the long suppressed energy of new political forces. As Anne Boleyn gained ascendancy, she herself became both the focus and facilitator for the reformers who saw in her rise an opportunity to transfigure the newborn Church of England. With Cromwell as her factional partner, Anne brought to her cause numerous men dedicated to continental patterns of religious reform. Responding to the religious orientation of the Boleyn faction conservatives organised themselves around the twinned issues of support for Catherine of Aragon and the maintenance of traditional religion. And so two factions informed by religious ideology had coalesced, and they would persist. Each believed that as they competed for power, they were engaged in God's work.

Cromwell's death in 1540, then, closed the book on a chapter in the history of the reform faction. Much had changed in the first dozen years of its existence. The Church of England had been established and its Protestant character, grounded in Scripture, even after the Six Articles, remained viable. Much would depend on post-Cromwellian ecclesiastical politics, and Cranmer had a valuable legacy at hand in Cromwellian reform initiatives. More importantly, the reform faction itself survived, personnel substantially intact, despite the loss of Barnes, Garret, and Jerome, despite the temporary but forceful wave of persecutions under the harsh penalties of the Six Articles. The Royal Supremacy and estrangement from Rome could not be reversed. An English Bible in the hands of avid readers ensured a steadily increasing number of Protestant adherents.

The execution of Cromwell thus produced a brief hiatus in the battle over the reform of the English Church and commonwealth. As proved true with the deaths of Fisher and More, or that of Anne Boleyn, the passing of leaders changed the outward character of reformation politics, but not its inner nature. Reformers and conservatives, clinging tightly to ideological positions, continued to use religion as the voice of factional politics in their ongoing struggle for control of the spiritual destiny of the Tudor state.

---

[23] Merriman, *Life and Letters*, ii. 129.

Bibliography

Manuscript Sources

BL, Additional MS
BL, Cotton Cleopatra E iv, v, vi
BL, Cotton Titus B i
BL, Cotton Vespasian F iii, xiii, xiv
BL, Egerton MS
BL, Harleian MS
BL, Royal MS
E 36/193
E 334/1
E 404/99
SP 1
SP 2
SP 3
SP 6
PROB 11

Printed Sources

Alumni Cantabrigienses, ed. J. Venn and J. A. Venn, 4 vols, Cambridge 1922–7
Athenae Cantabrigienses, ed. C. H. Cooper and T. Cooper, 3 vols, Cambridge 1858–1913
Athenae Oxonienses, ed. J. Foster, 4 vols, Oxford 1891–2
Calendar of State Papers. Spanish, ed. G. A. Bergenroth et al., 13 vols, 2 supplements, London 1862–
Chambers, D. S. (ed.), *Faculty Office Registers, 1534–1549*, Oxford 1966
Dictionary of National Biography, ed. L. Stephen and S. Lee, 22 vols, London 1908–9
The Divorce Tracts of Henry VIII, ed. Edward Sturtz and Virginia Murphy, Angers 1988
Emden, A. B., *A Biographical Register of the University of Oxford, 1501 to 1540*, Oxford 1974
Gee, Henry, and William Hardy (eds), *Documents Illustrative of English Church History*, New York 1972
Harwood, I., *Alumni Etonenses, 1433–1797*, Birmingham 1797
The Letters of Henry VIII, ed. M. St Clare Byrne, London 1936
Letters and Papers, Foreign and Domestic, of the Reign of Henry VIII, ed. J. S. Brewer, J. Gairdner and R. H. Brodie, 21 vols, London 1862–1932
The Lisle Letters, ed. M. St Clare Byrne, 6 vols, Chicago 1981

Lloyd, Charles (ed.), *Formularies of Faith*, Oxford 1825

Miscellaneous Writings and Letters of Thomas Cranmer, ed. John Cox, Cambridge 1846

Le Neve, John, *Fasti Anglicanae*, ed. T. D. Hardy, 3 vols, Oxford 1854; revised edn, 12 vols, London 1962–7

Ollard, S. L., *Fasti Wyndesorienses*, Windsor 1950

Original Letters Illustrative of English History, ed. Henry Ellis, 11 vols in three series, London 1824–46

Piele, J., *Biographical Register of Christ's Church*, Cambridge 1910

The Registers of Cuthbert Tunstall, Bishop of Durham, 1530–59, and James Pilkington, Bishop of Durham, 1561–76, ed. Gladys Hinde, Durham 1952

Registrum Caroli Bothe, Episcopi Herefordensis, 1516–35, ed. A. T. Bannister, London 1921

Sermons and Remains of Hugh Latimer, ed. George E. Corrie, Cambridge 1845

A Short-Title Catalogue of Books Printed in England and Ireland and of English Books Printed Abroad, ed. A. W. Pollard and G. R. Redgrave, London 1969

State Papers during the Reign of Henry VIII, 11 vols, London 1830–52

Statutes of the Realm, ed. A. Luders et al., 11 vols, London 1810–28

Strype, John, *Ecclesiastical Memorials*, 7 vols, London 1816

Tudor Royal Proclamations, ed. Paul L. Hughes and James F. Larkin, 3 vols, New Haven 1964–9

Valor Ecclesiasticus, ed. J. Caley and J. Hunter, 6 vols, London 1810–24

Venn, J., *Biographical History of Gonville and Caius College*, Cambridge 1898

Wilkins, David (ed.), *Concilia Magnae Britanniae et Hiberniae*, 4 vols, London 1737

Williams, C. H. (ed.), *English Historical Documents, 1485–1558*, London 1967

Wright, Thomas, *Three Chapters of Letters Relating to the Suppression of the Monasteries*, London 1843

Secondary Sources

Adams, Simon, 'Faction, clientage, and party: English politics, 1550–1603', *History Today*, xxxii (1982)

Bell, Gary, *A Handlist of British Diplomatic Representatives, 1509–1688*, London 1990

Block Joseph, 'Thomas Cromwell's patronage of preaching', *The Sixteenth Century Journal*, viii (1977)

Bowker, Margaret, *The Henrician Reformation*, Cambridge 1981

—— *The Secular Clergy in the Diocese of Lincoln, 1495–1520*, Cambridge 1968

Brigden, Susan, *London and the Reformation*, Oxford 1989

—— 'Thomas Cromwell and the "brethren" ', in Claire Cross, David Loades and J. J. Scarisbrick (eds), *Law and Government under the Tudors*, Cambridge 1988

Caspari, Fritz, *Humanism and the Social Order in Tudor England*, Chicago 1954

Cavendish, George, *The Life and Death of Cardinal Wolsey*, ed. Richard Sylvester, London 1959

Chester, Allan G., *Hugh Latimer, Apostle to the English*, Philadelphia 1954

Clark, Peter, *English Provincial Society from the Reformation to the Revolution: religion, politics and society in Kent, 1500–1640*, Hassocks 1977

Dickens, A. G. 'The early expansion of Protestantism in England, 1520–1558', *Archivum Reformationgeschichte*, lxxviii (1987)

——— *The English Reformation*, London 1964

——— *Lollards and Protestants in the Diocese of York*, Oxford 1959

——— 'The shape of anticlericalism and the English Reformation', in E. I. Kouri and T. Scott (eds), *Politics and Society in Reformation Europe*, London 1987

——— *Thomas Cromwell and the English Reformation*, London 1959

Dowling, Maria, 'Anne Boleyn and reform', *Journal of Ecclesiastical History*, xxxv (1984)

——— *Humanism in the Age of Henry VIII*, Beckenham, Kent 1986

Elton, G. R., *Policy and Police*, Cambridge 1972

——— *Reform and Reformation: England, 1509–1558*, London 1977

——— *Reform and Renewal: Thomas Cromwell and the commonweal*, Cambridge 1973

——— 'Sir Thomas More and the opposition to Henry VIII', in *Studies in Tudor and Stuart Politics and Government*, i, Cambridge 1974

——— *Star Chamber Stories*, 2nd edn, London 1974

——— *Studies in Tudor and Stuart Politics and Government*, 3 vols, Cambridge 1974–83

——— 'Thomas Cromwell's decline and fall', in *Studies in Tudor and Stuart Politics and Government*, i, Cambridge 1974

Fox, Alistair, 'Facts and fallacies: interpreting English humanism', in Alistair Fox and J. A. Guy (eds), *Reassessing the Henrician Age*, Oxford 1986

——— 'Sir Thomas Elyot and the humanist dilemma', in Fox and Guy, *Reassessing the Henrician Age*

——— *Thomas More: history and providence*, New Haven 1982

Friedmann, Paul, *Anne Boleyn: a chapter of English history, 1527–1536*, 2 vols, London 1884

Gunn, S. J., *Charles Brandon, duke of Suffolk, c. 1484–1545*, Oxford 1988

Guy, J. A., 'The Privy Council: revolution or evolution?', in Christopher Coleman and David Starkey (eds), *Revolution Reassessed*, Oxford 1986

——— *The Public Career of Sir Thomas More*, New Haven 1980

——— *Tudor England*, Oxford 1988

Haigh, Christopher (ed.), *The English Reformation Revised*, Cambridge 1987

——— *Reformation and Resistance in Tudor Lancashire*, Cambridge 1975

Heath, Peter, *The English Parish Clergy on the Eve of the Reformation*, London 1969

Hughes, Philip, *The Reformation in England*, 3 vols, London 1950–4

Ives, E. W., *Anne Boleyn*, Oxford 1986

——— 'Faction at the court of Henry VIII: the fall of Anne Boleyn', *History*, lvii (1972)

——— *Faction in Tudor England*, London 1979

James, M. E., 'Obedience and dissent in Henrician England', *Past and Present* (xlviii), 1970

Jones, Whitney R. D., *The Tudor commonwealth, 1529–1559*, London 1970

Kelly, H. A., *The Matrimonial Trials of Henry VIII*, Stanford, CA 1976

Knowles, David, 'The matter of Wilton', *Bulletin of the Institute of Historical Research*, xxxi (1958)

—— *The Religious Orders in England*, III: *The Tudor Age*, Cambridge 1961

Knox, D. B., *The Doctrine of the Faith in the Reign of Henry VIII*, London 1961

Lehmberg, Stanford E., *The Reformation Parliament, 1529–36*, Cambridge 1970

—— 'Sir Thomas Audley: a soul as black as marble?', in A. J. Slavin (ed.), *Tudor Men and Institutions*, Baton Rouge 1972

—— *Sir Thomas Elyot, Tudor Humanist*, Austin, Texas 1960

MacCulloch, Diarmaid, *Suffolk and the Tudors: politics and religion in an English county, 1500–1600*, Oxford 1986

MacLure, Millar, *The Paul's Cross Sermons, 1534–1642*, Toronto 1953

Marius, Richard, *Thomas More*, New York 1985

Mattingly, Garret, *Catherine of Aragon*, Boston 1941

Mayer, Thomas, 'Faction and ideology: Thomas Starkey's Dialogue', *Historical Journal*, xxviii (1985)

—— *Thomas Starkey and the Commonweal*, Cambridge 1989

McConica, J. K., *English Humanists and Reformation Politics*, Oxford 1965

Merriman, R. B., *Life and Letters of Thomas Cromwell*, 2 vols, orig. pub. Oxford 1902; Oxford 1968

Miller, Helen, *Henry VIII and the English Nobility*, Oxford 1986

Muller, James A., *Stephen Gardiner and the Tudor Reaction*, London 1926

Nicholson, Graham, 'The Act of Appeals and the English Reformation', in Cross, Loades, and Scarisbrick, *Law and Government under the Tudors*

Paget, Hugh, 'The youth of Anne Boleyn', *Bulletin of the Institute of Historical Research*, liv (1981)

Parmiter, Geoffrey de C., *The King's Great Matter*, London 1967

Parsons, W. L. E., 'Some notes on the Boleyn family', *Norfolk and Norwich Archaeological Society*, xxv (1935)

Pollard, A. F., *Henry VIII*, orig. pub. London 1902; New York 1966

Porter, H. C., *Reformation and Reaction in Tudor Cambridge*, orig. pub. Cambridge 1958; Hamden, Connecticut 1972

Redworth, Glyn, *In Defence of the Church Catholic: the life of Stephen Gardiner*, Oxford 1990

—— 'A study in the formulation of policy: the genesis and evolution of the Act of the Six Articles', *Journal of Ecclesiastical History*, xxxvii (1986)

Ridley, Jasper, *Thomas Cranmer*, orig. pub. Oxford 1962; Oxford 1966

Rupp, E. G., *Studies in the Making of the English Protestant Tradition*, Cambridge 1966

Scarisbrick, J. J., *Henry VIII*, London 1968

—— *The Reformation and the English People*, Oxford 1984

Sergeant, Philip, *The Life of Anne Boleyn*, New York 1924

Slavin, A. J., 'Cromwell, Cranmer and Lord Lisle: a study in the politics of reform', *Albion*, ix (1977)

—— *The Precarious Balance*, New York 1973

—— *Thomas Cromwell on Church and Commonwealth*, New York 1969

Starkey, David, 'Court and government', in Coleman and Starkey, *Revolution Reassessed*

—— 'From feud to faction: English politics c. 1450–1550', *History Today*, xxxii (1982)

—— *The Reign of Henry VIII*, London 1985

—— 'Representation through intimacy', in Ione Lewis (ed.), *Symbols and Sentiments*, London 1977

Thompson, A. H., *The English Clergy and Their Organization in the Later Middle Ages*, Oxford, 1947

The Victoria History of the County of Norfolk, ii, ed. William Page, London 1906

Virgoe, Roger, 'The recovery of the Howards in East Anglia, 1485–1529', in E. W. Ives, R. J. Knecht, J. J. Scarisbrick (eds), *Wealth and Power in Tudor England*, London 1978

Warnicke, Retha M., 'Anne Boleyn's childhood and adolescence', *Historical Journal*, xxviii (1985)

—— *The Rise and Fall of Anne Boleyn: family politics at the court of Henry VIII*, Cambridge 1989

—— 'Sexual heresy at the court of Henry VIII', *Historical Journal*, xxx (1987)

Williams, Glanmor, *Welsh Reformation Essays*, Cardiff 1967

Zeeveld, W. G., *Foundations of Tudor Policy*, Cambridge, Mass. 1948

Upublished Dissertations

Alexander, G. M. V., 'The Life and Career of Edmund Bonner Bishop of London until his Deprivation in 1549', unpublished PhD diss., London 1960

Block, Joseph, 'Church and Commonwealth: ecclesiastical patronage during Thomas Cromwell's ministry, 1535–1540', unpublished PhD diss., UCLA 1973

Brigden, Susan, 'The Early Reformation in London, 1522–1547: the conflict in the parishes', unpublished PhD diss., Cambridge 1972

Dowling, Maria, 'Scholarship, Politics and the Court of Henry VIII', unpublished PhD diss., London 1981

Nicholson, Graham, 'The Nature and Function of Historical Argument in the Henrician Reformation', unpublished PhD diss., Cambridge 1977

Riegler, Edward, 'Thomas Cromwell's Printing Projects', unpublished PhD diss., UCLA 1977

Starkey, David, 'The King's Privy Chamber, 1485–1547', unpublished PhD diss., Cambridge 1973

Index

Casual references to major figures are usually not noted, nor are references to modern writers

DATE DUE

DEC 24 '94			
DEC 12 1995			
DEC 31 '97			